TUNISIA
SINCE INDEPENDENCE

TUNISIA SINCE INDEPENDENCE

The Dynamics of One-Party Government

CLEMENT HENRY MOORE

UNIVERSITY OF CALIFORNIA PRESS

Berkeley and Los Angeles   1965

University of California Press
Berkeley and Los Angeles, California

Cambridge University Press
London, England

To ELIZABETH R. RODGER

FOREWORD

When I first visited the United States in 1954, there were few American students of North Africa who were equipped to threaten the monopoly of the field exercised by Italian, Spanish, and especially French scholars. Those few were, in any case, isolated individuals without a following. Nevertheless, one could find a few books dealing with North Africa, written by journalists or well-intentioned men or women who, for the most part, espoused independence for the countries of the Maghreb and were concerned more to support a cause than to engage in academic research. Nowadays these books are of much more interest to readers wishing to study American opinion about North Africa than to those desirous of learning about the area itself.

Things have changed in the ensuing years. Since Morocco and Tunisia became independent in 1956, followed by Algeria six years later, numerous scholarships for the study of the Maghreb have been established by American agencies, and courses on North Africa are now offered in several universities, either by political science departments or by area studies centers.

Thus North African studies are on the march in the United States. Still young but already vigorous, they have a promising future and should develop rapidly, if one may judge by their promising beginnings.

They may encounter serious obstacles, however, if current practices are not modified. Nowadays American scholars generally spend little time in the countries they study, because the funds and the time at their disposal are limited. Preoccupied with their own research, they buckle right down to work without taking the time to look about them and slowly immerse themselves in their new environment. Accordingly, if they are not extremely careful, they risk seeing only one aspect of the Maghreb and neglecting the rest for lack of time. Yet we all know the dangers of isolating one aspect of human activity at the expense of others: Removed from its context, a series of facts may possess little significance, no matter how painstakingly it may have been studied.

Those in responsible positions ought therefore to arrange for American students to spend several years in North Africa, because adequate time is a prerequisite for the intimate understanding of any society.

Otherwise, we shall be confronted with fragmentary and overly theoretical studies written by very talented students who may have been well prepared for their assignments but who will not have had the time necessary for losing themselves in the society they are studying.

I am led to reflect in this way because of my interest in and sympathy for the pioneers of North African studies in the United States and because of my hope that they and their students may be enabled to derive the maximum advantage from their activities.

The first significant work of the group I have mentioned was Douglas E. Ashford's important thesis, *Political Change in Morocco* (Princeton, 1961). Next came Manfred Halpern's book, *The Politics of Social Change in the Middle East and North Africa* (Princeton, 1963); Charles F. Gallagher's *The United States and North Africa* (Harvard, 1963); I. William Zartman's *Problems of New Power: Morocco* (New York, 1964); and Charles A. Micaud's *Tunisia: The Politics of Modernization* (New York, 1964), written in collaboration with L. Carl Brown and Clement H. Moore. These represent the first wave; other books are in preparation or in process of publication, as is the one that I have the pleasure of introducing in the present instance.

Tunisia interests American students for several reasons. For one thing, President Bourguiba's personality is pleasing to many Americans. Among newly independent countries, Tunisia is reassuring in its cohesion and stability. Although poorly endowed with natural resources, the country has made notable efforts in the economic and social spheres, and thus attracts sympathy, whatever the results of its undertakings. Also, because of its modest size, Tunisia lends itself to careful study within a relatively limited period of time.

A specialist in political science, Mr. Moore has chosen to study the political regime of Tunisia since independence. This is a subject of great interest, since it concerns a highly original system in which democracy and authoritarianism are both present in proportions that must be ascertained precisely and in which personal and historic factors are more influential than ideological positions.

Mr. Moore's great merit, in my opinion, is his ability to free himself of American or more generally Western categories of thought in order to examine a highly original society from a fresh perspective. I do not know exactly how many months he spent in Tunisia, but I am certain that he took the time to wander, to chat with Destour militants in Sahel village cafés, as well as to interview high government dignitaries on specific subjects. He absorbed the Tunisian atmosphere, all the while diligently pursuing his investigation, and the result is a book that is

rich not only in precise data but in all that one learns, almost un-
awares, simply by participating in the life of any people.

But of course this is not a book about atmosphere alone. Because
Mr. Moore never forgets that a thesis is not a novel, his work provides
new and useful information on the phenomenon of the Neo-Destour,
now called the Destour Socialist Party.

The past is sketched only in broad lines, since L. Carl Brown has
studied this topic in detail (in "Tunisia under the French Protectorate:
A History of Ideological Change," Harvard University doctoral dissertation, 1962). Nevertheless, Mr. Moore makes several very shrewd
observations, as, for example, in his comparison of the villagers of the
Sahel with the Third Estate of the French Revolution. Just as was the
case in the 1930's, so today the real strength of Tunisia lies in the Sahel,
and not in the Tunis bourgeoisie, which is intelligent but skeptical,
depleted and lacking in resilience, as Georges Duhamel made so clear
—not without a touch of malice—in his *Prince Jafar*.

Mr. Moore's account of the high purposefulness with which the Neo-
Destour prepared during the year of struggle for its present responsibility is very good. I also like his subtle analysis of "Bourguibism," an
important element in any portrait of Bourguiba, who, because he
represents the cornerstone of the Tunisian system, naturally stands at
the center of the book. We may be grateful to the author for having
studied Bourguiba's relations with those of his collaborators who, having on occasion deviated, have known or still know their moments of
disgrace. It is in this context that one perceives how "instinctive" and
opportunistic this man is. Here political analysis verges upon psychological analysis, as Mr. Moore understands so well.

Political analysis regains its rights in the study of the Party itself,
without which Bourguiba, despite all his gifts, could not have constructed his "presidential monarchy," as the author calls it. In this domain, too, Mr. Moore has had to draw on all the subtlety at his command, for the Neo-Destour, well organized administratively though it
may be, appears to lack a doctrine—or did so at any rate before the
emergence of Tunisian socialism. It is an instrument for impressing
the wishes of the regime upon the population, but also one for transmitting the aspirations and grievances of the masses to the leadership.

I would wager that Mr. Moore has experienced moments of doubt
whether the democracy to which the Tunisian regime lays claim really
exists in the monolithic and authoritarian organization of the Neo-
Destour or in a political system in which the National Assembly may
be regarded as a rubber stamp rather than as an organ of control or as a

source of legislation. But he points out, doubtless with relief, that within the branches and parallel organizations of the Party, the voices raised from below are generally heard and often heeded, so that he is not entirely pessimistic about the future of the Tunisian regime.

I do not know whether political theoreticians will find this book of absorbing interest, since it concerns a phenomenon that is difficult to fit into the framework of a duly categorized system. But I think that the author has indeed understood his many-faceted subject and has presented it effectively. In my opinion, his is a considerable achievement, and I am pleased to have received this opportunity to say so.

ROGER LE TOURNEAU

Aix

ACKNOWLEDGMENTS

THIS MONOGRAPH is based primarily upon a large number of interviews accorded me by Tunisians from all walks of life over a two-year period in their country. I should like to express my gratitude to those including President Bourguiba who generously gave of their time and hospitality to answer my questions. Without their patience and cooperation my research would not have been possible.

I consulted many scholars during the course of my work. In Tunis, Henri de Montety provided a wealth of information, including unpublished manuscripts as well as insights during his long career as a civil servant in Tunisia and as a scholar generally sympathetic to the new ruling elite. Moncef Dellagi, a Tunisian student who was writing his doctoral dissertation on the history of the Neo-Destour Party, was also very helpful. He showed me parts of his thesis and brought to my attention material that otherwise would have been unavailable. Professor Maurice Robin and Professor Douglas E. Ashford read parts of my first draft in Tunis. Père Demeerseman very kindly lent me useful documents from his personal collection and afforded me the library facilities of the Institut de Belles Lettres Arabes. I am especially indebted to Professor Charles A. Micaud, who, in the course of many discussions, encouraged my research and helped me to clarify my ideas. Of great assistance, too, was Professor L. Carl Brown, whose ideas about Tunisia's ideological development so greatly influenced my own. I am particularly grateful to Eqbal Ahmad, who began to study the Tunisian trade-union movement shortly before I left Tunis, for many stimulating discussions and fruitful collaboration. Thomas Hodgkin stimulated many of my thoughts about single-party regimes when occasionally in the course of our travels we met. I should also like to thank Philip Birnbaum, then in the Tunis AID Mission, for his explanations of the intricacies of Tunisian economic development. Lastly, let me express my gratitude to two of my mentors at Harvard, Professor Rupert Emerson and Professor Carl J. Friedrich, and to Professor Roger Le Tourneau, for having suggested useful revisions of an earlier draft submitted as a doctoral dissertation. Of course I take full responsibility for any remaining errors of fact or of political interpretation.

Of a different but equally important order is the assistance that the Ford Foundation rendered me during three years of study and research at Harvard and in Tunisia under its very generous Foreign Area Training Fellowship program. I am also indebted to Eric Levine for his careful preparation of the index, and I wish to acknowledge the assistance of Pristella Schoeppner and Susan Schreiber of the Department of Political Science and the services of the Institute of International Studies of the University of California, Berkeley, in typing the final manuscript.

C. H. M.

Berkeley, California

CONTENTS

INTRODUCTION

CONTEMPORARY POLITICS in Tunisia should be of special interest to the student of comparative political development, because it provides one of the most successful illustrations to date of a politics of modernization based upon a single mass party. Independent since March 20, 1956, Tunisia was the first of a growing family of African states to consolidate a mass party regime.

Such a political system may, with respect to its party, be characterized by the following syndrome of traits:[1]

1. After winning independence, the party exercises a virtual monopoly of power, either directly or indirectly through the new state administration that it staffs, though weak opposition parties may persist.

2. While depending for its cohesion after independence mainly upon the personal power and prestige of a leader-hero, the party is a national symbol sharing his prestige as founder of the new state.

3. The party is open to (almost) all nationals.

4. Its leaders and cadres are selected primarily on the basis of their loyalty and political achievements rather than social position.

5. Its well-articulated structure, supplemented by a network of ancillary organizations, actively sustains a mass following and aims at integrating the society.

6. Though the party does not have a total ideology, it communicates a broad message of social and economic modernization.

This syndrome of traits may serve to define the concept of a mass party regime and distinguish it from other models of political organization associated with the more general notion of a "single-party system." Thus, unlike totalitarian regimes, the African mass party regime is open to almost everybody and lacks the sort of ideology that might justify systematic repression. Of equal importance is the distinction between a mass party regime and the nominal single-party regime, based on a caucus or patron-type party,[2] that imitates the forms of

[1] For a fuller discussion incorporating much of what follows, see my "Mass Party Regimes in Africa," in H. J. Spiro, ed., *The Primacy of Politics in Africa* (Random House, forthcoming).

[2] For this distinction see Ruth Schachter, "Single-Party Systems in West Africa," *American Political Science Review*, June, 1961, pp. 294-307, and Thomas Hodgkin, *African Political Parties* (Penguin, 1961), pp. 68-75.

mass party rule without the organizational or symbolic substance. The nominal party is not an effective national symbol; it lacks an effective organization and does not attempt to integrate a new national community; its leadership tends primarily to rely upon ascribed social status. The mass party regime ought also, by virtue of its concentration of power, to be distinguished from political systems characterized, as in India or Mexico, by a "dominant" party that practices much of the substance of constitutional democracy.

Tunisia was studied in part to test the proposition that the mass party type of regime might more effectively than the nominal single-party type meet the challenges of social and economic modernization without precluding the development of constitutional democracy. If the party could retain its organizational vitality and mass appeal after independence, it would probably avoid the instability that has paralyzed fledgling constitutional regimes that lacked adequate political structures. Moreover, in contrast to totalitarian regimes, politics within the mass party, its ancillary organizations, and the state bureaucracy could conceivably stabilize ground rules of political competition akin to constitutional norms.

With this possibility in mind, it seemed important not only to describe Tunisian structures and policies relating to modernization but also to discover how the political system performed the tasks of recruiting a political elite, politically educating the people, representing their opinions and their interests, and integrating the new nation. These four tasks could not, of course, be conceived as functional requisites for the maintenance of a mass party regime, which is probably a transitional phenomenon; but the way they were performed might suggest whether it would evolve toward a totalitarian, a nominal single-party, or a pluralist model of political organization.

The question of recruitment becomes especially interesting in a mass party regime after the party has consolidated its rule and placed its people in the government and bureaucracy. Does the party itself harden in a bureaucratic mold, becoming an oligarchy of privileged officials who curtail mobility among the youth of the post-independence generation? Under these circumstances can the state bureaucracy become an independent avenue of mobility? What types of secondary leadership are encouraged—administrators and technocrats or the political agitators of the pre-independence era?

Political education is significant at two levels. At the mass level it may stimulate broader political participation while mobilizing the people when their support is needed for specific government projects.

In the absence of survey research,[3] however, it is virtually impossible to ascertain the true impact of the party's political education at this level. More interesting, perhaps, at Tunisia's stage of political development, is the impact of political education upon the party's more sophisticated, internal audience. How is the party educating its own cadres? Are they internalizing the relatively democratic norms of party deliberation that exist in the statute books?

Representation and integration are two somewhat incompatible functions for any mass party to perform. Where national integration is desperately needed, effective representation and political participation are likely to be minimized. The party which had been relatively successful before independence in integrating the nation may afterwards find it possible to permit a greater variety of opinions and interests to be represented. But in any transitional society the process of integration is of necessity a continuing one. The mass party and its ancillary organizations perform this task to the extent that they (1) induce cohesion and a consensus on basic national values and objectives among the elite, (2) transmit the consensus to the people, and (3) provide new local structures to replace the traditional order. The important question, of course, is whether the party's means are compatible with its representational role.

Representation may take many forms, especially in a transitional society where there is no clear agreement on the meaning of politics. So far as it is envisaged as a spectacle of collective unity rather than a means of achieving concrete ends, a party and its leader may be representative solely by virtue of their role as symbols of unity. The meaning of such activities as elections and mass demonstrations may be primarily symbolic. Yet politics may also have more concrete meanings both at the local level and within the relatively modern sectors of society. At the local level, where people may have specific aims and grievances, sometimes mediated through traditional family or tribal structures, free elections and self-government may be encouraged by the ruling party. At the national level, modern interests and the opinions of the educated elite may be represented through the party, its ancillary organizations, and even such formal channels as a national parliament.

[3]Careful use of the questionnaire method might produce interesting results in both Tunisia and Algeria, societies comparable in many respects. But interviewing would necessitate a substantial staff of trained, indigenous social scientists and the coöperation of the government—two conditions notably absent in Tunisia in 1961, when Douglas Ashford tried to distribute a questionnaire to party cadres. With Tunisia's new Institute of Applied Social Science, it may in the future be possible to apply survey techniques.

Within the spectrum of mass party regimes, a very tentative distinction can be made between those that stress national integration and those that encourage fluid patterns of representation. The former, best exemplified by Guinea and Mali, might be termed neo-Leninist; the latter, best exemplified by Tunisia but perhaps also including Senegal and the Ivory Coast, might be termed "permissive." In terms of the six traits listed above that define the mass party regime, the distinction can be drawn as follows:

1. The neo-Leninist regime exercises its monopoly of power primarily through the party; the government and the state bureaucracy are the simple executors of party decisions. The permissive regime, in contrast, relies more heavily upon the organs of state for decision-making.

2. The neo-Leninist regime makes a cult of party supremacy, whereas the permissive regime emphasizes the cult of personality, the leader-hero's title to rule.

3. The permissive party allows greater freedom not to participate in its various organizations than does the neo-Leninist party.

4. Relative to the neo-Leninist regime, advancement in the permissive regime is determined to a greater extent by technical and administrative criteria and to a lesser extent by criteria of political loyalty and nationalist achievement.

5. The neo-Leninist regime maintains a more intensive rhythm of party activity, though the permissive type may maintain an equally well organized party apparatus.

6. Political discourse in the neo-Leninist regime tends to be more ideological and more replete with revolutionary imagery, though the objectives of the permissive regime may be equally revolutionary (in the sense of transforming the social and economic order) and articulate.

As this study of Tunisia will indicate, these distinctions are not in practice as clear-cut as they might appear; indeed, Tunisia may presently be slightly shifting toward neo-Leninism, while Guinea, at the other extreme, may be developing somewhat permissive characteristics. As ideal types, however, each pattern has interesting implications concerning recruitment, political education, integration, and representation. These may be elaborated into a set of hypotheses about the nature of the politics of modernization practiced under the respective systems.

Given the importance of the government as well as the party, technically and administratively minded officials may have a greater chance to influence politicians in the permissive regime. This fact, as well as the personality of the leader-hero, helps to account for the relatively less ideological character of the regime. Its policies may be more technically effective in launching the profound social and economic transformations that all mass party regimes desire. Economic development may receive more attention than such purely political matters as "the struggle against neo-colonialism." But the permissive regime runs the risk of succumbing to an overly rational view of modernization. The initial *élan* stemming from the independence struggle may be lost, and the mass party, no longer serving as the prime instrument of recruitment, may wither away. The neo-Leninist regime may find it easier to absorb the politically minded members of the post-independence generation and maintain the ritual, even if not the substance, of revolutionary *élan*.

Political education is presumably more effective under the neo-Leninist system, sparked by the effervescent mass party. Yet one may question the virtues of such education and its relevance to profound social change. Mass mobilization, unless it entails forced labor, may simply extend to the people the affective significance of politics without instilling its more instrumental meanings. Without rational communication, the profound changes in attitude implied by social change may be lacking. In the long run, the rationality of the more permissive regime's messages to the people may prove more effective.

The neo-Leninist party, in contrast, may have greater success in educating its cadres, by inculcating both a relatively simple ideology and the rules and procedures of democratic centralism. It is perhaps more difficult for the less ideological regime to train responsible cadres, because the content of such education is more complex. The rules of the political game, too, are more diffuse where the centers of power are more diversified, the patterns of influence more complex than in the neo-Leninist model.

Both types of regime vigorously pursue the task of integration, by generating consensus and stimulating new local structures of political activity. By demanding more intensive mass participation, the neo-Leninist regime may appear to force a more rapid pace. Its concentration of power within the party, in contrast to the dispersion of power that characterizes the more permissive regime, may also further integration. But there are probably limits to any regime's ability to create consensus from above. The permissive regime is perhaps better equipped to take advantage of any spontaneous, preexisting consensus, simply by providing more diversified outlets at the national level for political participation. In both regimes, the preeminence of the leader facilitates effective decision-making even when there is no consensus.

The cult of personality in the permissive regime suggests a serious problem. The very presence of the leader-hero may retard the development of political institutions, even though providing more flexible avenues of representation than the neo-Leninist apparatus. To maintain his monopoly of power, the leader cannot afford the emergence of stable countervening centers of influence, within either the party or the bureaucracy. There is no evidence yet, however, that the neo-Leninist party can more effectively resolve succession crises.

An over-all evaluation of the politics of modernization suggested by the permissive model must await the facts of the Tunisian case. The contrast with the neo-Leninist model is an intriguing one, although, as the Tunisian experience will illustrate, any real mass party regime, to survive the challenges of modernization, must probably partake of both models. The neo-Leninist pattern would tend to pursue the political priorities of modernization at the expense of technical ones, whereas the permissive model would sacrifice political fervor for administrative efficiency. In each case, without a blending of the other model's strengths, the mass party is apt to become a bureaucracy and thereby fail in its tasks of recruitment, education, integration, and representation—without which a balanced politics of modernization would seem unlikely.

Chapter I tries to explain the historical conditions that made permissive party rule possible in Tunisia. It is assumed that a successful permissive pattern of modernization presupposes a higher degree of national integration before independence, rendering unnecessary the more self-conscious methods of integration utilized in the neo-Leninist pattern. Though other African countries have established permissive mass party regimes, the relative success of the Tunisian experience may be due more to special historical circumstances than to any inherent virtue of the permissive model.

In Africa all mass party regimes were the product of colonial situations, but in Tunisia it was an especially intensive colonial experience within a peculiarly homogeneous society that elicited this reaction. The intensity of the colonial situation—measured by such indices as its duration, the directness of foreign rule, economic development, the spread of modern education, and the number of colonial settlers—stimulated the full play of what might be called a colonial dialectic.

The full play of the dialectic requires time for two concurrent processes to unfold before independence. On the one hand, for the nationalists dialectically to oppose the colonizer, they had to assimilate his political style and modernist outlook. On the other hand, the nationalist elite had to mobilize mass support in order to reflect the general

will of the nation and thereby justify its claim to rule. This involved a
struggle with that part of the traditionalist elite that indiscriminately
fought both colonialists and modernity. When, in other countries, a
modernist elite did not succeed in displacing an old elite, the goals of
the nationalist mass party were apt to be vague, conducive neither to
a national consensus nor to modernization (for example, in Egypt
during the interwar era of Wafd predominance). When, however, as
in the Tunisian case, the colonial dialectic was able fully to unfold,
the resulting integration of the nation rested on more solid foundations
than a mere coalition against foreign rule would provide.

Chapters II and III focus upon the leadership of Habib Bourguiba,
both as a leader-hero and as a politician who must operate within the
context of mass party regime. To what extent is the party a political
force distinct from its leader? What were Bourguiba's means of consolidating personal power, and what implications do his style of leadership have for the future of party rule? The Tunisian political system
is so dependent upon one man that it seemed necessary to devote considerable space to his leadership.

Chapter IV is focused upon the party as distinct from its leader and
analyzes the institutional relationships, so far as these are discernible,
between party and the state administration at the national and regional levels. The permissive pattern of party-state symbiosis is thus illustrated in institutional terms that contrast with those of the neo-Leninist
solution. Despite the gains in political recruitment, however, the cost
of these arrangements may be seen at the level of grass-roots politics,
discussed in Chapter V, which reveals increasing political apathy within the party. A healthy and somewhat democratic local politics persists,
however, under the tutelage of the party and the state administration.

In Chapters VI and VII, respectively describing the party's ancillary
organizations and their relationships to national decision-making, an
interesting though diffuse pattern of interest representation is described. It operates under the tight control of the party and, especially
in crucial issues, under the tutelage of Bourguiba. In conclusion, the
alternatives confronting the mass party regime are discussed and
weighed in light of its performance to date of the tasks of recruitment,
education, integration, and representation.

I THE ROOTS OF CONSENSUS

Tunisia's ruling Neo-Destour Party[1] has achieved possibly the most effective regime in the Afro-Asian world for leading its people toward a modern society. In terms of the criteria discussed above, single-party rule in Tunisia seems relatively permissive. More by persuasion than by force, it is educating, integrating, and representing the Tunisian people. Before analyzing party rule since independence, however, it seems necessary to discuss the underlying historical and social factors that made permissive single-party rule possible in Tunisia.

The key to subsequent Neo-Destour success lies not only in its hero-leader or elaborate organization—factors common to many nationalist parties—but also in the nature of the consensus achieved by the nationalists before independence. Unlike so many newly independent countries, Tunisia in 1956 had already developed a broadly based political elite. It was agreed not only on the desirability of independence but on the need for modernization through coöperation with France. Unlike the Muslim nationalists a generation earlier in the Near East, the Tunisian elite was wholehearted in its aspirations for a modern society; it did not merely seek modern techniques for enhanced power or prestige. Moreover, the consensus was shared not only by most French university-educated Tunisians; many of the less privileged Tunisians had assimilated new ways of thinking.

The Tunisian consensus was largely the product of a farsighted leader, Habib Bourguiba, and the efforts of his party to introduce a new sense of mission to the people. But politics alone does not explain why the society was so receptive to the new ideas and style of the Neo-Destour. The underlying consensus facilitating subsequent single-party rule was also the product of a peculiarly homogeneous and adaptable society, an intensive colonial situation, and fortuitous timing that permitted the full development of its potential before independence. For an understanding of the Neo-Destour regime, these background factors require elaboration, although a full social and political history of the Tunisian Protectorate (1881-1956) will not be attempted.[2]

[1]Its full name, in translation, is the Tunisian Liberal Constitutional Party. It emerged in 1934 as an offshoot of an older party having the same name, hence the prefix "neo." Destour (Dastūr) is the Arabic word for constitution.
[2]The best history of Tunisian nationalism is to be found in Charles-Andre Julien,

The Traditional Society

Natural homogeneity is not a sufficient condition for the building of a modernist consensus, but it may facilitate the spread of modern attitudes and help to maintain a consensus once achieved. By homogeneity here is meant the objective geographical, historical, social, and cultural factors that tend to unify the population of a given area.

Tunisia's very size is significant. Only slightly greater in area than New York State, Tunisia did not have a serious problem of internal communications. Even before the French built an impressive network of railroads and highways, there were sizable annual migrations within the country. Moreover, the population was small, totaling little more than a million in 1881 and approximately four million in 1963.[3]

Tunisia's geographical location also encouraged communications both within the country and with the outside world. Tunisia faces the Mediterranean to the north and especially to the east, where its hospitable coastline has sheltered a ribbon of civilization continuous both in time and in space. The extended Sahel, running from Bizerte southward to Gabes, is a 300-mile coastal axis upon which all of Tunisia's important cities are located. Upon its northern half lie the two foci of Tunisia's cultural heartland, the capital of Tunis (including its famous suburb, Carthage) and, a bit to the south, the fifty miles of coast adjacent to Sousse and Mahdia that comprise the Sahel proper. It was the interaction between the intellectual center of Tunis and the villages and towns of the Sahel that would create and define modern Tunisia.

Historically, Tunisia was almost two countries—the "thousand cities" of the extended Sahel and the seminomadic tribes of the interior. In dislocated times the tribes would raid the shrunken coastal enclaves; in times of peace the cities would extend order and agricul-

---

L'Afrique du Nord en Marche (1952). See also Félix Garas, Bourguiba et la Naissance d'une Nation (1956). The definitive work on Tunisia on the eve of the Protectorate is by Jean Ganiage, Les Origines du Protectorat Français en Tunisie, 1861-1881 (1959). The most useful and interesting social and intellectual history of twentieth-century Tunisia, to which the author is indebted for many insights, is by Leon Carl Brown, "Tunisia under the French Protectorate: A History of Ideological Change," doctoral dissertation, Harvard, 1962.

[3]The Tunisian Government estimated the population in 1867-68 at 1,007,200, but Ganiage, op. cit., thinks that the estimate, based upon taxation statistics of the qaids (who were essentially tax farmers), was conservative. In his "Old Families and New Elite in Tunisia" (see note 28 below), Henri de Montety maintains that the Tunisian population was at most 1,300,000 in 1880. The census of February 1, 1956, sets the total Tunisian population at 3,601,792, and Tunisian planners estimate the subsequent annual rate of increase at 2.1 per cent. See Perspectives Décennales de Développement, 1962-71, p. 22.

ture westward. In the fourteenth century Ibn Khaldun was probably thinking more of his Tunisian homeland than of the Arab East when he devised his famous cyclical theory of government. The nomad's solidarity upon which government and therefore civilization depended lasted only as long—usually three generations—as the tribal dynasty avoided being corrupted by the splendors of civilization.

By the nineteenth century, however, Tunisia was a country more or less stably governed and at peace with itself. After the disastrous nomadic invasions of the eleventh century—which almost destroyed all that had remained of the extensive settled agricultural areas developed by the Carthaginians and Romans—Tunisia underwent a partial renaissance under the Hafsids. During more than three centuries of Hafsid rule (1228-1535), Tunis became an important intellectual center, and the mosque of Zitouna flourished as a center of Islamic studies. Ancient city life was restored along the extended Sahel, and Andalusian refugees helped to extend Tunisian agriculture in the north while bringing new handicrafts to the medinas. The Arabic language, spread more effectively by the nomadic invasions than by the original Arab conquest of the seventh and eighth centuries, penetrated virtually the whole countryside, in contrast to Algeria and Morocco, where important Berber-speaking populations have subsisted in their mountain strongholds.

Tunisian homogeneity was also furthered by religious uniformity. Except for a localized Jewish minority[4] and a native Christian population that had all but disappeared by the time of the Hafsids, Tunisians were Muslims. Moreover, except under Fatimid rule in the tenth century, the Maliki rite of orthodox Islam was unchallenged until the arrival of the Turks in the sixteenth century. The Ottomans brought with them a different rite of orthodox Islam, but, far from proselytizing, practiced it only among themselves and recognized the legitimacy of Maliki justice for the rest of the population.

During its three thousand years of history, Tunisia was ruled most of the time by foreigners—Carthaginians, Romans, Vandals, and Byzantines, then various Muslim dynasties that usually originated in other Muslim lands. The Hafsids were themselves at the outset only agents of the Moroccan Almohads. Similarly the Turkish Husainid dynasty of the eighteenth and nineteenth centuries ruled in the name of the Ottoman Empire.

[4]According to the February 1, 1956, census the Tunisian Jewish population amounted to 57,792. However, other people of native Jewish origin were included among Tunisia's 255,324 foreigners, for many had acquired French nationality before independence.

In fact, however, the Hafsids and the Husainids ruled as independent sovereigns, for the parent empires were too weak to exercise effective control. Thus, before the establishment of the French Protectorate, Tunisia had experienced more than six centuries, interrupted only by a period of foreign invasions at the end of the Hafsid era, as an independent political unit. Its boundaries, which under the Hafsids had included parts of Algeria and Tripolitania, roughly coincided under the Husainids with those of the French Protectorate. Tunisia, unlike many African colonies, had a tradition of national self-government. Its historical tradition as an organized entity was yet another mark of the country's homogeneity.

This does not mean, however, that Husainid Tunisia was a modern nation state. Like all traditional medieval Islamic societies, Tunisia was a fragmented society. But its size, geography, and historical tradition made it less fragmented than most neighboring Islamic societies. Only Egypt, united by the Nile and a long history, displayed a natural cohesion comparable to that of the extended Sahel.

The Husainid Bey had all the powers of an absolute monarch, limited only by the flexible canons of Islamic jurisprudence (*shari'a* law). In affairs of state he had legislative as well as executive authority, and he appointed the chief religious leaders in charge of judicial affairs. In fact, however, his power was limited by the very nature of traditional society. Government was hardly supposed to do more than keep the peace and collect taxes; other social institutions performed the welfare functions usually associated with modern government.

However absolute in theory, the Bey's authority rarely encompassed the whole country. Taxes were collected without much difficulty along the extended Sahel, where roughly half of the population lived, but the tribes of the interior often displayed their independence; even annual military expeditions did not always succeed in bringing in the taxes. However, the Bey exercised more effective control over his outlying tribes than did the rulers in Algeria and Morocco over theirs. And, too, Tunisia's sedentary coastal population was proportionately much larger than that of its Maghrebi neighbors. The only part of the country to remain consistently independent of the central authority lay in the isolated, mountainous northwest corner inhabited by Khroumir tribesmen. Periodic tribal revolts in other parts of the interior were indications that the authority of the central government was felt.

The Bey ruled the countryside through agents whom he appointed: roughly sixty *qaid* and 2,000 subordinate sheikhs who were the natural leaders of the village or tribal fraction. The higher officials comprised an indigenous provincial aristocracy, the native *maghzen* families, for positions were generally passed on from father to son. Even when a tribe revolted, the rebel sheikh or qaid was usually allowed to remain in his position after compromising with the Bey.

Another important instrument of integration was the religious brotherhood. Diverse Sufi orders, each led by a self-appointed mystic or *marabout,* appealed to the Maghreb's rural Berber substratum and helped to reconcile classic antagonisms between city and countryside. Zitouna University educated the leaders of the mystic orders as well as the orthodox judges in the towns. Often the devout members of a religious order were the only literate members of a tribe, the only link between the tribe and the Islamic tradition of the settled areas. In the villages of the Sahel they were respected educators. Each of the nineteen principal orders in Tunisia had a network of centers; the *zawiya,* or brotherhood center, for educational and often for devotional purposes, had an important influence. One author[5] estimates that there were 500 zawiyas, with a membership of roughly 300,000 An early colonial administrator commented that "in Tunisia most of the natives belong to a religious order, more or less as every Frenchman considers himself a follower of this or that political party."[6] The brotherhoods thus mitigated the traditional opposition between the Sahel and the interior; the heads of the important brotherhoods in Tunis were, like the orthodox religious leaders, respected pillars of the ruling elite, present on ceremonial occasions at the Beylical court.

But whatever the natural homogeneity of traditional Tunisian society, a sense of national solidarity was lacking. Though communications were relatively good, the society was compartmentalized geographically and tribally as well as by classes, and political stability under the Husainids was due mainly to the society's fragmentation. Its various sectors, allowed a fair degree of autonomy, peacefully coexisted; stability was more a habit than a political design. At the pinnacle of the society the Beylical family, though theoretically exercising absolute power, remained isolated from the indigenous population. To staff the army and central ministries, it imported *mamlouk* (slave) officers from the Ottoman Empire. They formed Tunisia's aristocratic ruling caste, and married only among themselves. Socially they gravitated about the court of the Bey, upon whose whim their careers depended, and had little to do with the natives apart from policing, administering, and taxing them. Even the provincial maghzen officials, the qaids who came into direct contact with the population, were of indigenous rather than manlouk origin. Today the various quarters of

[5]Julien, *op. cit.,* p. 66.
[6]Charles Monchicourt, *La Région du Haut Tell en Tunisie* (1913), p. 313.

the Tunis medina bear witness to the compartmentalization of Husainid society: the palatial residences of the mamlouk notables are all within a single quarter near the kasbah.

The indigenous elite was also compartmentalized. Apart from the maghzen families were the *baldi,* a distinctive class of big merchants and the heads of the handicraft guilds.[7] They had common customs and dress, and family histories of at least several generations in Tunis. They had little contact with the Beylical court but mixed somewhat with the otherwise isolated Maliki *ulama* families. Even the *souk, or* market, reflected social fragmentation in Tunis as in other medieval Islamic cities. Each craft or type of commerce had its appointed location; there was no intermixing of goods and services, and, indeed, the *chechia* (a type of headgear) makers had higher social standing than the *babbouche* (a kind of footwear) makers!

Thus the social order had its own built-in political stability. The baldi were happy to stay out of politics, and the Bey and his maghzen families respected baldi interests and did not interfere with the work of the ulama. Even the bedouin countryside was satisfied, for its natural elite was integrated into the ruling structure. The mutual isolation of the various classes served to mitigate the rigid hierarchical ordering of the closed society and to veil animosities that might otherwise have arisen between the indigenous elite and the foreign ruling class. The provincial maghzen families, too, served as a useful buffer against the traditional disdain of the baldi for the *afaqi,* or provincial outsider. Curiously, in the old cities, and even in villages, of the extended Sahel an upper class also called itself baldi and similarly disdained the peasants. In old Tunisia almost everyone could point to a contemptible outsider, for the settled peasant likewise considered himself the superior of the bedouin—and vice versa—but fortunately communications were too limited for social conflicts to erupt between the various classes.

The conflicts that did arise concerned individuals, villages, families, and tribes rather than classes. The most important conflict of the nineteenth century was the revolt of 1864 against the doubling of the *mejba,* or capitation tax. Its very extension reflected the underlying unity of the society, while the patterns of conflict emphasized the importance of longstanding local rather than class rivalries.

The rebel slogan of "No mejba, no mamlouks, no Constitution" explained the ostensible grievances. Earlier beys, impressed with the

[7]In the Maghreb, unlike Egypt, the guilds were organizationally independent of the religious orders. See L. Golvin, *Aspects de l'Artisanat en Afrique du Nord* (1957), p. 33.

modern European technology that had conquered Algeria, had virtually bankrupted the state in naive efforts to modernize it—much like their contemporaries, the khedives of Egypt. Active European consular officials thus acquired sufficient influence over the Bey to encourage the promulgation of a liberal constitution in 1861. The constitution benefited primarily the mamlouk elite, some of whose more influential members were reaping huge profits from foreign loans as well as the usual tax farming. It seemed as if the revolt of 1864 might be a "national" revolution against foreign rule, and, indeed, one scholar suggests that there was danger of the revolt becoming a *jihad* against the Christians whom the mamlouks blamed for the objectionable innovations.[8] The revolt extended to a large number of tribes throughout the country and even to the settled villages of the Sahel, impoverished under the weight of existing taxation.

But actually the rebellion was far from constituting a national front. The checkerboard nature of the loose rebel alliances reflected only traditional local rivalries. The tribes had been divided since the early eighteenth century into vague geographical blocs, the Bled et-Trouk and the Bled el-Arab, corresponding to sides taken in a Husainid family dispute over the succession and to the degree of control exercised by Tunis. By 1864 most of the relatively more independent Bled el-Arab tribes had been brought to pay their taxes, and it was they who launched the rebellion. Bled et-Trouk, therefore, remained loyal to the Bey. In the Sahel the taxation issue also revived the earlier dispute over the Husainid succession, as rival villages took opposing sides in the revolt. Clearly, for a modernist consensus to take root in Tunisia, the traditional compartments had to be removed; otherwise, collective social action would be doomed to dissipate in petty rivalries.

Fortunately the traditional obstacles to a sense of nationhood were relatively minor in Tunisia. The latent opposition between Bled et-Trouk and Bled el-Arab could hardly, in Tunisia's geographical setting, take on the dimensions of the divorce between Bled el-Maghzen and Bled es-Siba in Morocco. Through various channels the tribesmen of Tunisia were integrated into a single society with a long collective history.

Moreover, at least half of the population lived along the highly civilized coast, open to influences from abroad as it had always been. The Sahel would be the axis of a modern integrated nation emerging from the impact of a colonial situation. The villagers from the densely populated area of the Sahel proper would be especially open to new ideas and capable of implementing them. Indeed, the traditional

[8]Ganiage, *op. cit.*

characteristics of this core area account in large part for Tunisia's great capacity to adapt itself to the new ideas and problems of the modern world. Because of the Sahel, Tunisian society was not only homogeneous but receptive to colonial innovations. This receptivity was not the result of preponderant colonial influence in the Sahel, for it remained virtually free of European settlers.[9] Rather, certain features of the traditional society explain the Sahel's unique contribution to modern Tunisia.

The Sahel villager rather than the Tunis baldi constituted Tunisia's third estate. In the traditional Sahel society a genuine middle class had developed, based not on commerce but on olive-oil production. An ethos of gain pervaded the society, and social status was measured primarily by the number of olive trees one owned. Moreover, all the cultivators lived together in villages rather than on isolated farms. The Sahel village displayed a kind of solidarity lacking in a fragmented medieval city like Tunis. In the off-season, the villagers led a collective life that blurred any social distinctions between the owners of many and of few trees. Each village had a sense of identity, the product of common worship in the mosque, local self-government, and collective defense against both nomads and intruding land speculators from richer villages. Within every village family rivalries persisted, but not in the face of external danger. Unlike the fragmented elite of Tunis, the Sahelian stood by his fellow; and, unburdened by the weight of traditional hierarchy, he was more open to new influences. To the peasant virtue of thrift he added that of a pragmatic temper in keeping with an old Mediterranean civilization. The traditional Sahel would give birth to a new national elite when the colonial situation disrupted the old order.

The Colonial Situation

French rule in Tunisia had the unforeseen consequence of creating the social conditions for its successful overthrow. In this respect the Tunisian experience was similar to other colonial situations where new elites challenged foreign rule in the name of the occupying power's value of selfdetermination. What distinguished Tunisia from most other colonial societies, however, was the extent of social transformation effected by French rule—a product of the intensity of the colonial

[9]While settler farms flourished in the Tunis area and on the great northern plains, only two colons survived in the whole of the intensively cultivated Sahel. See P. Lunet, "Aspects sociaux du Sahel de Tunisie," *L'Afrique et l'Asie*, IV (1954), 55-63. In some respects a southerly extension of the Sahel, the Sfax olive orchards originally financed by colons were largely (6/7) in Tunisian hands by 1940. See Jean Despois, *La Tunisie Orientale: Sahel et Basse Steppe* (1940), p. 436.

experience. Tunisia's colonial situation irrevocably disrupted the old order and encouraged the formation of a new elite that accepted the new values of liberal France. Yet French influence was not so all-pervasive as to destroy through assimilation the identity of the potential modern nation. It encouraged, instead, the full play of what we shall consider as a colonial dialectic.

Intensity may in part be measured by the duration of colonial rule. The French Protectorate lasted seventy-five years, from 1881 to 1956, and the Tunisians did not gain internal autonomy (self-government in their domestic affairs) until 1955. With the exception of Algeria, no other Mediterranean country underwent foreign tutelage for so long a time. Elsewhere the three-phased dialectic, requiring at least three generations of development, was impossible to fulfill.

Intensity is also in part a function of the number of colonial settlers. In 1881 there were roughly 700 Frenchmen and 11,200 Italians (mostly workmen); by 1911 there were 134,000 Europeans; and by 1956 their number had almost doubled, representing a constant 7 per cent of the total population.[10] Nowhere outside North Africa in the Afro-Asian world, with the sole exception of South Africa, was there so high a concentration of European population. Yet Tunisia, unlike Algeria, was never officially considered an integral part of France. Though the settlers helped to shape a modern Tunisian society, they were never sufficiently numerous or powerful to threaten to "assimilate" the indigenous society.

The existence of a settler society in Tunisia had a number of consequences that mere foreign rule probably would not have brought about: urbanization, new patterns of land tenure, secular jurisdiction, the creation of a modern economy, the development of a settler politics, and new educational opportunities. Together these factors served not only to stimulate the spread of new ideas and ways of living but also to create within the native society sets of alienated individuals and classes.

To be sure, similar phenomena occurred elsewhere in other colonial situations. Direct as contrasted with indirect colonial rule is a measure of intensity giving rise to a colonial dialectic. Economic development, too, may occur in the absence of a large unmber of European settlers; in this respect the Belgian Congo, where extractive industries employed roughly one-quarter of the adult male population, was far more advanced than less richly endowed Tunisia. But the existence

[10]See A. Basset et al., Initiation à la Tunisie (1950), p. 282, and Recensement Général de la Population de la Tunisie du 1 Février 1956 (Service de Statistiques), p. 101.

of a substantial settler minority in Tunisia produced a more balanced set of social changes, transforming values and social structure as well as the economy.

It is not even certain, in the absence of settlers, whether colonial rule in Tunisia, where an organized state existed, would not have been indirect rather than direct. The French established their Protectorate primarily to safeguard Algeria's eastern flank and to forestall an Italian take-over.[11] The French treaty with the Bey, while imposing French military occupation "to reëstablish order and security," did not challenge the latter's domestic jurisdiction, though the La Marsa Convention of 1883 committed the Bey to undertaking "financial, judicial, and administrative reforms that the French Government will judge useful." Like Marshal Lyautey in Morocco, some of the earlier French colonial administrators in Tunisia favored policies of indirect rule that would safeguard native customs. Even in 1922, when paternalism was no longer possible, one highly respected and scholarly senior official exhorted: "Let us regain in all its plenitude our role of older brother, whose task it is, *in accordance with native customs*, to direct and to defend all the members of the family. . . ."[12]

The private secretary of the first French Resident General had earlier noted the existence of a class of bureaucrats happy to serve the new administration and more capable than their Turkish or Egyptian counterparts.[13] These sons of the mamlouk families, who already wore European dress and had assimilated many European techniques before the French arrived, were one of the early mainstays of the French presence. The provincial maghzen families of qaids, along with the local sheikhs, were also for the most part (though in reduced numbers) maintained by the French. In the north the seminomadic tribes were rapidly sedentarized, but the ruling armature of old families was preserved in the new fixed geographic setting.

The French carefully supported the religious orders because of their importance in local society. High colonial officials kept on good personal terms with the leaders of the orders, while the government named the zawiya directors and hence could play off local rivalries.[14] The Resident's influence with the Bey assured the speedy dismissal of any traditional political or religious leader disapproving of the

[11]Even French colonization was officially encouraged primarily to counterbalance Italian migration.

[12]Rodd Balek, *La Tunisie après la Guerre 1919-21* (1922), p. 318 (italics mine). Rodd Balek was a pseudonym for Charles Monchicourt.

[13]P.H.X., *La Politique Française en Tunisie* (1891), p. 341. P.H.X. was the nom de plume of Baron d'Estournelles de Constant, private secretary to Paul Cambon.

[14]See Monchicourt, *op. cit.*, p. 318.

French presence, but most of the old ruling elite were submissive in the face of preponderant French power. France's policy toward the natives was essentially that of indirect rule, papering over cracks in the old system rather than fundamentally altering it.

But alongside the old system the French installed a modern administration to deal with the problems of the settler society. The new ministries at first had so little to do with Tunisians that the native prime minister ceased countersigning their French directors' decrees. Similarly, the French encouraged the creation of city councils, chambers of commerce and agriculture, and other consultative bodies primarily as organs of expression for the settler community. Although allowed a minor role in some of these bodies, Tunisians received less official training in modern self-government than the natives of other French colonies where no settler community existed to monopolize whatever representative organs the authorities permitted. However, the settlers introduced to Tunisia modern concepts and a rhythm of political activity that the nationalists would later copy.

Symptomatically, even before the First World War, the few Tunisian Muslims appointed to the Consultative Conference[15] were voting with the "anticlerical" Republican Left against the conservative settler element.[16] The existence of a vocal French Left in Tunisia would influence greatly the form nationalism took in the 'twenties and 'thirties. The Tunis branch of the French Socialist Party (SFIO) never numbered more than a few hundred members, but it represented a second France that was not colonialist, an anticlerical France that would suggest to Tunisian nationalism alternatives to an anti-Christian *jihad,* and above all a sympathetic humanitarian outlook that would induce nationalists to articulate their moral assumptions. Indigenous tradeunionism, too, would develop, long before independence, out of the settler trade unions organized as early as 1906.

The settler community also created the social climate in which nationalist politics could operate. In 1956 roughly 162,000 of Tunisia's 255,000, Europeans lived in Tunis and its suburbs. An additional 43,000 were concentrated in Bizerte, Menzel-Bourguiba (formerly Ferryville, a part of the Bizerte naval complex), Sousse, and Sfax; but no other center had more than 2,000 European inhabitants on the eve

[15]Originally established for the settlers in 1892 and expanded in 1896 to represent all French citizens in Tunisia, the Consultative Conference was to advise the Resident General primarily on budgetary questions. In 1907 it was enlarged to include fifteen Muslims and one Jew in addition to thirty-six Frenchmen; only the latter were elected.

[16]The phenomenon was noted unhappily by André Servier, *Le Nationalisme Musulman en Egypte, en Tunisie, en Algérie: Le Péril de l'Avenir* (1913).

of independence. Apart from a few agricultural towns, like Beja and Le Kef, that were mostly settler creations, the Europeans lived in a few cities of the extended Sahel, and especially in Tunis. They built modern European cities surrounding the old Arab medinas and indeed dwarfing them.

Even before the Protectorate, Tunisia was distinguished for its village and city life along the extended Sahel. In 1921, the first year for which reliable statistics are available, 23 per cent of the Tunisian population inhabited agglomerations of more than 1,000 inhabitants. By 1956, however, the proportion had jumped to 37 per cent, mainly because of the spectacular growth of the city of Tunis and its suburbs. In 1956, about one-tenth of the native population lived in the capital. From 1936 to 1946 alone, more than 150,000 miserable refugees from the desiccated Center and South flocked to Tunis as to paradise in search of food and jobs. Numbering 93,500 Muslims in 1936, the city counted 189,000 in 1946, and during the same period the suburbs doubled their Muslim population as the bedouins clustered in sprouting *bidonvilles*.[17] This permanent migration—tremendous for a country as small as Tunisia—was only in part a by-product of the Second World War;[18] by then the colonial impact had disrupted traditional life even in the outlying countryside.

Disruption was caused partly by the strain on a subsistence economy of rapid population increase. Adhering to a normal colonial pattern, the Tunisian population doubled during the last thirty-five years of the French Protectorate. But disruption of the traditional order was in even larger measure the result of rural colonization.

It was estimated in 1937 that Europeans owned roughly 725,000 hectares of Tunisia's best land—or one-fifth of the total area suitable for modern agriculture.[19] Originally they had alienated even more land that successful Tunisian farmers bought back. It is not true, as some French apologists have maintained, that the settler land had previously been unoccupied wasteland. Tens of thousands of natives were evicted or made agricultural workers when the property on which they lived changed hands. Most of the land was, however, poorly worked, being leased out to tenants by the rich Tunis landowners. Typically the tenant (*khammes*) worked for a miserable fifth

[17]For statistics see Salah-Eddine Tlatli, *Tunisie Nouvelle* (1957), pp. 54, 84-85.
[18]Most of Tunisia was an active theater for war operations from November, 1942, to May, 1943.
[19]Paul Sebag, *La Tunisie* (1951), p. 42. Of 9,000,000 cultivable hectares—including state forest domains as well as settler farms—7,200,000 ha. remained in the hands of Tunisians. However, 4,125,000 ha. were suitable simply for grazing or for esparto grass. See *ibid.,* p. 101.

of the produce, and the mamlouk owner was interested only in his steady income.

Modern European farming was only rarely a model that Tunisians imitated. The one exception was in the Sfax area, where the French successfully introduced new dry-farming techniques for the extension of the olive-tree forest, and the Tunisians tended the trees and used half of the profits to buy out the French investment. In the fertile northern plains, however, few Tunisians imitated the *colons* to become business-like modern farmers. Credit was a serious problem, and entrepreneurial skills and techniques were in even rarer supply. Of the 2,167 farmers in 1938 enjoying significant credit facilities—one index of big modern enterprise—only 242 were Tunisians.[20] The Tunisian *fellah* may be less backward than his Syrian or Egyptian counterparts, but there was little exchange between the colons and the natives.[21] The latter were often brought into the market economy as agricultural workers, but few learned new techniques or acquired any education.

Colonial implantation did, however, introduce a new attitude toward property and a new legal system—the first step toward rural renovation. Traditionally, property had been of three sorts: *melk, habous,* and *arch.* Melk was simply private property. The habous were foundations set up for purposes of religion or social welfare either directly (public habous) or indirectly after the extinction of family heirs (private habous). Like the arch, or collective tribal lands, these were inalienable properties. Most of the private habous—totaling more than 1,500,000 hectares in 1956—were even more poorly cultivated than the melk of absentee landlords. Tenants leased them annually at auctions, unless (after 1905) they could afford an *enzel* of twenty years' rent for a permanent lease.

The French in 1885 had the Bey promulgate a land registration act, so that settlers could acquire recognized property deeds. As a result, many Tunisians acquired Western conceptions of property and legal procedure. They were drawn into the new property system, either because of disputes with Europeans buying their melk or to protect their property from the claims of others. By 1956 almost two million hectares were registered, including the lands of some 11,230 Tunisians.

This new attitude toward property made headway even among the bedouins living on the arch. Some tribes discovered modern values when Europeans or the state expropriated their land under the act of 1885. Others, gradually sedentarized under the new administration,

[20]*Ibid.,* p. 106 n.
[21]P. Marthelot makes this point in "Disparités géographiques et sociologiques," *Cahiers de Tunisie,* No. 25 (1959), 123-140.

were more fortunate, as the Protectorate aided them to develop their land. The tribesmen rapidly acquired the notion of private property that their neighbor settlers were putting into practice.[22]

The Islamic institution of the habous was severely undermined by the French presence, though it survived until independence because the French did not desire a head-on collision with Islam. In 1898 a law was passed whereby the public habous administration was to hand over 2,000 hectares annually to the State Domains administration, which sold it to settlers on easy credit terms. The state could take over private habous lands by enzel, register them, and then sell them as private property to settlers. Though most settler land had originally been melk,[23] the habous under certain circumstances were no longer inalienable. Moreover, the Protectorate in 1926 attempted to provide native squatters and tenants with legal rights on the vast habous estates. Until the old elite families owning the habous persuaded the Resident in 1935 to have the law revoked, much litigation, affecting some 60,000 hectares, opposed landlord to squatter.[24]

The litigation brought many Tunisians, even backward bedouins, into European law courts and thus away from the traditional system. It was significant also for emphasizing the importance of lawyers—rather than the natural traditional rulers—as protectors. Moreover, young Tunisian lawyers were encouraged to take sides: at the beginning of his political career, Habib Bourguiba was defending the squatters, while many of his future rivals were big habous landowners or their allies. And whatever the outcome of a case, the loser could blame the colonial situation. Either the French were stealing private habous land away from the proper owners or they were collaborating with the owners to preserve the colonial *status quo*.

The development of modern city life, based on the export crops of the colons and a few extractive industries, created a modern economy existing alongside a disrupted traditional subsistence economy. Except in the Sahel, where increased olive-oil production and exportation kept pace with the new market economy, Tunisian agriculture re-

[22]At least one instance of economic inequality became apparent after a generation of sedentary cultivation. See the very interesting case study by A. Bessis *et al.*, *Le Territoire des Ouled Sidi Ali Ben Aoun* (1956).
[23]The writer could find no over-all statistics on the origins of settler domains, but in one typical colon stronghold, Medjez-el-Bab, 55,000 ha. of the 67,981 ha. of European land had previously been melk, according to Victor Mottes, *La Colonisation Française et la Propriété Indigène dans le Contrôle Civil de Medjez-el-Bab* (1925).
[24]See L. Carl Brown, "Colonization—A Second Look," *Institute of Current World Affairs* pamphlet, May, 1961. The following point is also taken from Brown's article.

mained inefficient and the bedouins fell victim to the Malthusian law.

Yet the development of a modern sector did provide some jobs for the swelling native population. By 1956 about 160,000 Tunisians were employed in it, although Europeans had virtually all the better jobs. Almost half of an industrial proletariat of 100,000 was employed in construction and public works, which could hardly have existed in the absence of a booming European economy. The large modern tertiary sector, too, depended upon European cities and a top-heavy *fonction publique* on the French model. In contrast, the traditional handicraft industries, which even in 1956 employed almost 100,000 workers, had been submerged under the competition of cheap manufactured imports.[25] Both traditional artisan and modern clerk or industrial worker could be expected, even more than the displaced bedouin or impoverished landowner, to harbor grievances against the colonial order.

The modern influences exerted upon the society by the colonial situation were brought to bear upon a new elite through the educational system. The Tunisian colonial experience was not unique in this respect, but the educational system was better developed than that of either Algeria or Morocco. In 1931-32 there were 151 North African students in French universities: 119 Tunisians, 21 Algerians, and 11 Moroccans.[26] Actually, the Protectorate, which was hardly a welfare state, did relatively little to educate the Muslim population, but the network of schools for Europeans whetted the traditional Tunisian appetite for education. Before the Protectorate every village had its *kouttab*, or primary school; and a Tunisian historian maintained that the country had 1,250 kouttabs and that about 13,000 students were pursuing traditional secondary or university education.[27] Muslims were slow to enter the new government schools; there were fewer than 3,000 in 1908 and only 10,690—one-quarter of the total school population—after the First World War. At first Muslim families distrusted the French education; then lack of government funds was the obstacle. Only after the Second World War did the Protectorate spend important sums on native education; by 1955, one-quarter of the Muslim children of school age were in school.

During the Protectorate era various types of education coexisted in cultural confusion. Hardly changed in curriculum until 1950, traditional Zitouna education flourished. The Grand Mosque had less than

[25]Tlatli, *op. cit.*, pp. 53-54, 132.
[26]Annual *Bulletin,* North African Muslim Students' Association, 1932, quoted in an unpublished draft doctoral dissertation, "Le Néo-Destour," by Moncef Dellagi.
[27]Sebag, *op. cit.*, p. 175; Tlatli, *op. cit.*, p. 220. The historian was Ben Dhiaf, who lived in the nineteenth century.

a thousand students in 1881, but by independence had expanded to 15,000. This sort of education was ill-adapted to the modern world, and relatively few sons of the old elite (even sons of the ulama!) attended the university after the First World War. As early as 1938, two-thirds of the student body came from outside Tunis and the Sahel, and only 0.5 per cent were from the elite families that had monopolized the institution two generations earlier.[28] Directed by the old ulama families, Zitouna remained the citadel of Muslim conservatism, but most of the students were of impoverished (largely rural) parentage or were not qualified to enter the better modern schools. Even before the Second World War they constituted an intellectual subproletariat that political parties could use.

The most important indigenous educational institution was Sadiki College, founded in 1875 by a modernist prime minister, Khaireddine. It flourished under the Protectorate, first as a training center for interpreters used by the French administration and then as the incubator of a modern university-educated elite. Khaireddine had intended Sadiki to be a modern secondary school, disseminating a bilingual culture that included the new sciences as well as Arabic studies. The idea succeeded beyond his dreams, for the Franco-Arab education of Sadiki provided the beginnings of cultural synthesis for the new nation that the Neo-Destour was to represent. The elite was small,[29] but its outlook has dominated Tunisia since independence.

At the elementary school level, a similar Franco-Arab style of education developed in both the government and private Quranic schools. The latter, launched in Tunis in 1906, soon spread into villages avid for modern education, wherever the Protectorate authorities could not be persuaded to provide public education. By 1950 there were ninety of these institutions, founded on local initiative and educating one-quarter of the school-going Muslim population. Emphasizing modern studies as well as the Quran, they were far superior to the traditional kouttabs, and prepared students for modern secondary schools. Most of them were concentrated in Sfax and the Sahel—respectively the centers of the modern commercial and political elites.

After the First World War education was increasingly the key to social status even for the old ruling families. The French *politique des grandes familles* had granted only the form of political power to the old elite, while undermining its substance. Even in the traditional ad-

[28]Henri de Montety, "Vieilles familles et nouvelle élite en Tunisie" (1940), by courtesy of the author.
[29]In 1939 Sadiki had 410 students enrolled in five grades; by 1955 it had 1,350 students, out of a total of more than 6,000 Muslims in modern secondary schools. See Tlatli, *op. cit.*, p. 230.

ministration the old families were losing their importance, though they continued to receive the top appointments. For recruitment to intermediate positions the French instituted examinations that virtually eliminated the sons of old families. Even the cream of the old aristocracy recognized the value of modern education by allowing their daughters not only to go to school but to marry educated young administrators who had no standing in the old society. Because of its superior language training, Sadiki became the key means of access to the modern administration and enhanced social status. With the development of primary school education outside of Tunis, however, Sadiki increasingly became a school for Tunisian *parvenus* from the provinces. In the 1939 contest for admission, only 15 out of 80 successful candidates were from the old Tunis aristocracy of mamlouk or baldi families. Half of the new class was from the Sahel, and one-quarter had received Quranic school instruction.[30] The upper classes attended French secondary schools, though by the 1930's provincials were coming into even these institutions. By 1955 more than a thousand Tunisians were studying in French universities or in the Institut d'Hautes Etudes in Tunis, and relatively few of them were of upper-class origin.

The new elite based on modern education overlapped to some extent with the elite of old families. The latter in 1939 comprised a third of the new *khalifas*,[31] three-quarters of the Muslim lawyers, half of the doctors, and almost half of the pharmacists. More significant, however, was the rise of obscure sons of the middle and lower classes to these prestige occupations. The trend would be completed by independence, when the new professional upper class would have increased more than eightfold.[32] Only the old families— in accordance with the French *politique des grandes familles*—were permitted in the various consultative organs of modern government. In 1939 the old families monopolized the Muslim sections of the municipal councils (90 per cent), the chambers of commerce and agriculture (95 per cent), and the successor to the Consultative Conference, the Grand Council (85 per cent)—because they were appointed by the government or elected by colleges of notables.

The core of the new elite came from the towns and villages of the Sahel, supplying half of Sadiki's entering class in 1939 and more than one-third of Tunisia's university students even under the vastly expanded scholarship program of the independence regime. These stu-

[30] De Montety, *op. cit.*
[31] The highest office recruited by examination in the traditional administration.
[32] In 1939 de Montety counted 30 Tunisian lawyers, 40 doctors, and 14 pharmacists. Tlatli, *op. cit.*, p. 54, counts 700 Tunisians in the professional classes by 1956.

dents perhaps had a greater incentive, for many of them were very poor—in an era when university education was neither encouraged nor paid for by the government—and their thrifty families made great sacrifices to send them to Tunis and then abroad. Collective self-help was something of a Sahel village tradition that followed the young graduates to Tunis. It was not uncommon for a Sahel doctor practicing in Tunis to buy equipment for a young pharmacist who would later repay him. Moreover, the educated Sahelian was mobile once he had left his village. He traveled anywhere, married a French woman, but kept contact with his native village and especially with his colleagues in Tunis.

As a group, however, the Sahelians were considered *parvenu* by the old Tunis families, and in many respects they had more in common with the French intellectuals. Even before the Protectorate, Sahelians had a tradition of government service; many of the Beylical functionaries and officers came from Monastir (Bourguiba's birthplace). Yet the French officials kept natives out of prestige positions in the administration; indeed, some Residents harbored a positive dislike for those natives who had assimilated too much French education. The colonial situation had thus produced an uprooted class, a counter-elite at home neither with official France nor with the traditional order.

Within fifty years of the establishment of the Protectorate, modern society had been created, centered on the colons; yet a traditional society, in part disrupted, existed alongside, unassimilated to the new order. Many sectors of the old society were alienated, once the Protectorate had upset the former balance. The old elite was no longer sure of itself, the artisans were impoverished, most of the landowners were failing to modernize, the Zitouna students were jobless, and landless bedouins were encamped on the outskirts of Tunis. New classes were emerging that were alienated in a double sense, in both societies: the educated counter-elite, the students, and an industrial proletariat, a clerical class, and even a rural proletariat of agricultural workers on colon farms. Furthermore, in Tunisia the settlers would be sufficiently strong to undercut all French Government efforts at reform, thus ensuring the political tension necessary for the unfolding of the colonial dialectic.

The Colonial Dialectic

Dialectic is the hallmark of an intensive colonial situation, but its proper fulfillment before independence presupposed a homogeneous precolonial society and a national core—such as the Tunisian Sahel—

that was relatively undisturbed by the colonial situation. If the dialectic fully unfolds, a modernist elite absorbs most of the alienated sectors under its nationalist banner, while overpowering recalcitrant traditional sectors; by virtue of its long and difficult political conflict with the colonial power, it absorbs modern political styles and values, just as an inexperienced army assimilates the techniques of its adversary in a protracted war. Through the workings of the colonial dialectic, a modern political system was able to develop in Tunisia before independence.

The course of the dialectic can be traced in three stages. The Young Tunisians before the First World War represented a small Western-educated elite that had wholeheartedly accepted modern values and wished to transmit them to their society. Although they formed a political party in 1907, the accent was on educational, cultural, and economic matters. So far as they were political, the Young Tunisians accepted the French Protectorate as a good modernizing influence, while attacking the racial arrogance of some of the settlers. The Young Tunisians—modeled on the Young Turks—were mostly of mamlouk families; before 1914 there were fewer than fifty Muslim university graduates in Tunisia, and most of them were mamlouk. So far as they identified with forces outside Tunisia, they looked to the Ottoman Empire.

The Young Tunisian movement was very important for implanting early seeds of modern liberal thought in Tunisia's nationalist tradition. It carried on the work of the Ottoman minister Khaireddine, who had tried, after it was already too late, to modernize the country by sound fiscal methods. His books, *Le Plus Sûr Moyen de Connaître l'Etat des Nations,* expressed his desire to adapt European techniques, education, and culture to Tunisia. The sweet reasonableness of the Young Tunisians was perhaps due to the fact that Tunisia had been rapidly, bloodlessly, and unalterably colonized. Except for repressing a brief flurry of rebellion in the summer of 1881, the French in Tunisia, unlike those in Morocco and Algeria, had little pacification to perform. There was virtually no primary resistance to distract the new elite from the problem of modernization to more narrowly political concerns. In the wake of a visit by Mohammed 'Abduh to Tunis, the old families in 1885 presented a petition of political grievances to the Bey, but there were no political aftereffects. Tunisians, it seemed, were so stunned by French power that the reaction of the educated class was to assimilate French ways. Early Tunisian liberalism was the product of admiration for and docility toward the foreign ruler. It had few roots in the country.

After the First World War Tunisian nationalism became political. The effects of the war were far-reaching: some 65,000 Tunisian soldiers (of whom 10,000 were killed) and 30,000 workers went to France to help the war effort, and Tunisia, like other Islamic countries, was exposed to the Wilsonian idea of self-determination. A new group of Tunisians entered politics with a growing sense of grievance against the colonial regime. These were the dissatisfied members of the old elite who had found no place in the new order—some of the mamlouk, ulama, and baldi families. Symptomatically, the issue that sparked the founding of their Destour Party in 1920 related to the private habous possessions of the old landowning class. The French passed a law whereby these stagnant lands were to be developed at the expense of partial expropriation. The "Old Turbans," as the traditionalists were called, rallied to the nationalist cause and financed a delegation to Paris to plead for a Tunisian constitution.

As an acute French observer in 1913 had predicted, "Our veritable adversaries in Tunisia are the sons of the old [baldi] bourgeoisie" who resented their loss of privileges and could whip up the "religious fanaticism" of the peasants.[33] The small group of modernists—remnants of the Young Tunisians—in the Destour was submerged by newcomers who shared similar social origins but few of their modernist attitudes.[34] The leader of the Destour, Sheikh Abdelaziz Taalbi, spoke hardly a word of French. He was a Zitouna sheikh, although he was a Muslim reformist in the Egyptian Salafiyyah tradition, unlike most of the more conservative Tunis ulama.

Like its contemporary the Wafd in Egypt, the Destour was essentially the party of an old indigenous elite. It could mobilize the masses for demonstrations, but the party did not have a mass membership or an articulated modern structure. When Taalbi in Paris published his famous indictment of the colonial regime, *La Tunisie Martyre*, one of his collaborators reported: "This book has acquired a great reputation, but the popular and middle classes . . . have gathered only what the upper class has told them [about it]."[35] Old Destour leaders today admit that they had never tried to recruit the masses into the party; rather, they focused on the intellectual elite, which in old Destour terms meant the traditional Zitouna-educated elite of Arabic and Islamic culture. Party leadership was almost entirely in the hands of the

[33]Servier, *op. cit.*, p. 64.
[34]Interestingly, the mamlouks more than the baldi had acquired a Western education, while the baldi were dominant in the Destour.
[35]"Origine et circonstances des poursuites," a French legal document explaining the circumstances of Taalbi's arrest in July, 1920. The quotation is from a letter from Sheikh Salah Ben Yahia to Taalbi, January 14, 1920.

old families (Taalbi being the brilliant exception), while the modest
grass-roots organization of village committees was the concern of
only the more important local families.

The Destour was the antithesis of the Young Tunisian movement.
It marked the rejection by nationalists in the name of anticolonialism
of many of the innovations introduced by French rule. To the author
of *La Tunisie Martyre*, the Protectorate had brought only servitude
and exploitation; the era preceding the Protectorate was looked upon
as the golden age of Muslim rule to which Tunisia must return. Although the Destour's Eight-Point Program[36] of 1920 was moderate and
implicitly accepted the existence of the French Protectorate, Taalbi's
vision of the good society would become inflexible. Islamic society
perhaps required a measure of reformation to recapture its ancient
imperial grandeur, but modern European influences and domination
were considered brute obstacles, not catalysts, to any Muslim renaissance.

Yet the Destour was a positive contribution to Tunisian nationalism
in that it marked the first coherent and broadly based political reaction to the colonial situation. The Young Tunisians' ideas had been
too modernist and moderate to reach beyond a narrow cultivated
elite into the society as a whole. With the Destour the modernist idea
of assimilation was unequivocally rejected, and the first groping gestures were made in search of a national identity.

The price the Destour had to pay—in a society still largely traditional—was an ideological vagueness unsuited to the dynamic colonial
situation. The Destour's political style reflected its social composition
by its very conservatism. The leaders, even those who were not lawyers, had a lawyer-like approach to political activity. They presented
their claims to the Bey and to the French authorities much as a lawyer
would plead his case in court. There was no thought of making compromises. Politics was to be pure, a matter of ideals, rather than the
practice of the art of the possible. Illustrative of the Destour's approach, the party appealed to French jurists to decide whether a
Tunisian constitution would be legally compatible with the existence
of the Protectorate. The jurists' affirmative answer was sacrosanct,
much like the *fetwa* of a Muslim *mufti*, or judge.

[36]The eight-point petition to the Bey called for a deliberative assembly of Frenchmen as well as Tunisians, elected by universal suffrage, and a government responsible to the Assembly. It included such demands as equal access of Tunisians
to all administrative positions on the basis of talent and intellectual qualifications,
equal salary for equal functions, popularly elected municipal councils, liberty of
the press and of association, and participation of Tunisians in the buying of government land.

The Destour was known more as a party for urbane conversation than for mass activities. However radical and reactionary its rejection of the colonial influence, its leaders, good gentlemen that they were, were often noted at the receptions of the French Resident and occasionally were not above confidential discussions with him.

In its heyday (1920-1922) almost everybody sympathized with the Destour: the discontented upper classes of Tunis, Sfax, and Sousse; the village notables of the Sahel; the entire Arabic press; the café-sitters, the youth, and the intellectuals of Tunis; and the literary clubs forming in other towns after 1918. But the Destour's *élan* rapidly dissipated after the departure of its charismatic leader, Taalbi, on a fifteen-year tour of Islamic countries. Through a clever French Resident, Lucien Saint, the Destour was politically neutralized. Within the native society it was also neutralized, locked in the traditional order that it represented.

Perhaps the best example of the Destour's inability to adapt to new situations was its failure in the crisis of 1925 to support Tunisia's first autonomous native trade-union movement. In late 1924, thousands of Muslim workers, probably with some Communist support, broke away from the Socialist CGT to found an autonomous CGTT (Confédération Générale des Travailleurs Tunisiens). Their leader, Mohammed Ali, became a national legend. Born near Gabes, he is said to have obtained a doctorate in Germany and was at one time the chauffeur of Enver Pasha. Back in Tunis, he had an ambitious plan for developing consumer cooperatives, but shifted to trade-unionism in 1924 when discontent was ripe among the longshoremen, most of whom were Metouias from a southern oasis near Gabes who had recently moved to Tunis and maintained a strong sense of solidarity. By 1925 the new CGTT had won the support of Tunis dockers, tramway workers, employees of the municipality and central market, and textile, cement, and construction workers. It also had centers in Sfax and Bizerte, and was attempting to spread its organization to Mateur, Ferryville, and the phosphate mines of Gafsa and Metlaoui. But in February, after barely six months of numerous strikes and demonstrations, the colonial authorities dissolved the CGTT. The Destour, pressured into silence, was awarded modest political reforms.

To the workers the Destour's fault lay not in its traditionalism—for the modern proletariat was equally religious and respectful of tradition—but in its modern bourgeois betrayal of the people. Actually, the Destour disdained the workers more for their bedouin origins than because of any Marxist class bias. Modern methods of political agitation, too, were hardly in accord with the Destour's legalistic approach to politics.

The dialectic required a political force that could break out of a traditional social base into the modernizing society and combat colonialism on its own ground. Nationalism, to be effective in Tunisia's intensive colonial situation, had to develop new political techniques and to mobilize emergent classes such as the indigenous proletariat. Had France been as liberal in 1920 as Britain was in Egypt, the Destour might have been successful; but in Tunisia, with its large colon population, the stakes wcre too high to be won by legalistic methods.

The new force that pushed nationalism into its third stage of political development was, of course, the Neo-Destour Party. Founded in 1934, the party spent more than two decades in nationalist opposition. The cohesion induced by the struggle against foreign rule, dramatized by the periodic suppression of the party and the jailing of its leaders, was used to build a positive program and a modern national *mystique*. Moreover, the party vindicated a new political style and outlook in the face of obstruction by the older Destour. The older party accused the Neo-Destour leaders of being atheists, attacked whatever compromises the younger party effected with France, and challenged its nationalist credentials.

By 1938, the Neo-Destour could effectively demonstrate its greater mass following, and the postwar colonial period gave it time to consolidate a virtual monopoly of political power while devising the outlines of its independence program. Despite periods of incarceration, its leaders remained true to their modernist values and objective about French contributions to Tunisia, rather than developing an obstructionist mentality. Yet they contested the colonial *status quo* with far greater determination than their more conservative rivals.

The younger party marked the entrance of a new elite into nationalist politics. Virtually all its party leaders had a French university education, and very few came from old Tunis families.[37] The original animators of the party (Bourguiba, Mahmoud Materi, Tahar Sfar, Bahri Guiga) had returned from France in the late 'twenties to practice their liberal professions. By 1932 they were writing their own nationalist newspaper, *L'Action Tunisienne*, and in May, 1933, were admitted on the Executive Committee of the Destour. Even in this early period the ginger group came into conflict occasionally with the older leaders of the party, but not explicitly on matters of ideology.

[37]Henri de Montety observed in 1939 that, whereas old families comprised 70 per cent of the old Destour leadership, they comprised only 15 per cent of the Neo-Destour leadership.

Tactical differences, however, reflected an underlying divergence of attitudes. In 1930, Tahar Sfar, the "intellectual" of the group, was already attempting to demonstrate that the feeling of patriotism (*watan*) antedated Islam and was thus independent of religion, although patriotism might be a religious duty.[38] Later he tried to synthesize Islam and the modern secular world by relegating religion to the realm of conscience—an unorthodox stance even for a Muslim reformist.[39] The young generation was usually careful, however, despite its sympathies with French laïcisme, to avoid antagonizing the conservative majority. Dr. Materi did not dare in 1930 to join the Socialists in defending Tahar Haddad, who was being persecuted for advocating women's emancipation from obsolete religious laws.[40] Bourguiba had earlier defended the custom of the veil, though on nationalist rather than religious grounds.

As one scholar has noted,[41] the great contribution of the younger generation of nationalists was a new sense of mission, a heightened feeling of individual responsibility toward the cause of emancipation. Their intensity of commitment was perhaps a result of the younger generation's sense of alienation. To the French society as a whole they were not quite equals, and their social origins granted them only a second-rate place in traditional society. But the new sense of mission was the product, also, of the modern view of politics as a creative process.

Bourguiba and his colleagues, by dint of their very exposure to French intellectual and political life, were deeply influenced by the attitudes and style of the French Left, the liberal France sympathetic to nationalist aspirations. Although they felt the intricacies of the Marxist dialectic to be both inhuman and irrelevant to Tunisia, they shared the Left's view of political activity as a door to a new and better society. Whereas the older generation wished merely to restore a preëxisting order, the new elite aspired to a new social order. The Destour looked to a traditional state, but the new generation took it upon themselves to create a new nation, hence a new society. While

[38]*Voix du Tunisien*, November 4, 1930.
[39]See Tahar Sfar, *Journal d'un Exilé* (1960).
[40]Tahar Haddad had incurred the wrath of his Zitouna University colleagues by writing a book, *Our Women in Religion and Society*, which suggests that some Islamic practices were obsolete in modern social conditions. Under pressure, the Tunisian prime minister removed Haddad from his teaching job. Materi claimed that this decision was justified, though he would have protested any government decision to ban the book. Materi also criticized the Socialists for their attacks on the "Muslim fanaticism" of Haddad's adversaries. See *Voix du Tunisien*, December 12, 1930.
[41]Brown, *op. cit.*, chap. VII.

he was still a member of the young group, Abdel Hac summed up their point of view: "One can say that the Tunisian nation was really born only when the French Protectorate geographically detached [it] . . . from the rest of the Islamic world. If Tunisian nationalism existed, it should have found, in a country having *de facto* independence, an excellent occasion to manifest itself when France occupied Tunisian territory."[42] The Tunisian nation had to be created before lawyers could plead its case. Bourguiba drew the conclusion that it was his mission to create it; and this was a preeminently political task. Bourguiba and his colleagues focused upon a future that they thought they could make. Not only were they lawyers pleading a case; they had to be politicians and prophets to instill in the society a sense of nationhood.

More in a Jacobin than in a Marxist tradition, the new prophets appealed to the masses. In *L'Action Tunisienne* they identified themselves with the *guenillards*, the ragged, tattered ones at the bottom of society. For in the Republican tradition everyone had to be part of the nation, and the measure of citizenship was a sense of dedication rather than prestige or wealth. The "people" were the source of legitimacy, though they had to be educated as patriots before the nation could take shape. The categories of the old society were only barriers to the new sense of solidarity that had to be aroused. By the 'thirties the old families were losing touch with the modern society.

Ironically, the issue precipitating the split between the older and the younger generation on the Destour's Executive Committee concerned the burial of naturalized French Muslims in Muslim cemeteries. The modernists rather than the old guard took the ostensibly reactionary position that any Muslim who accepted French citizenship ought to be excluded from the Islamic community and from Muslim burial. An activist follower of Bourguiba supported the Mufti of Bizerte who made a fetwa to this effect. *L'Action Tunisienne* proceeded to foment demonstrations in Tunis when naturalized Muslims died, and especially when the rector of Zitouna issued a contrary fetwa at French request. The editors also expressed their solidarity with the Zitouna students' strike against the rector's curriculum reforms and his fetwa. Whatever their Muslim convictions, the older generation was apparently not eager to pursue the naturalization issue; *L'Action Tunisienne* criticized their "strange attitude" and regretted having earlier credited them for some of the demonstrations.[43]

[42]Quoted by Félix Garas, *Bourguiba et la Naissance d'une Nation* (1956), pp. 69-70. Abdel Hac was the pseudonym of Chadly Khairallah, the director of *Voix du Tunisien*.
[43]*L'Action Tunisienne*, April 18, 1933.

The nationalists—in the face of the repressive colonial decrees of May 6, 1933—were reconciled soon thereafter at the Destour's unity congress, but the naturalization issue led to a definite rupture a few months later. Eager to capitalize upon a demonstration in Monastir against the burial of a naturalized child, Bourguiba led a delegation of the demonstrators to the Bey. When the Destour's Executive Committee censured him, Bourguiba resigned. Bahri Guiga was expelled for exposing a confidential conversation between the Resident and some of the Destour leaders. The other members of the team then resigned to join Bourguiba in creating a new party, or rather, as good tacticians, to call a Destour congress and try to capture the party apparatus. The congress of March 2, 1934, marked the birth of the Neo-Destour.

The paradox of the modernists espousing a religious cause was apparent. The old guard, with some justification, accused the young upstarts of being atheists who were trying to use religion for political purposes.[44] Like the Egyptian Muslim Brotherhood, the Neo-Destour occasionally called for tobacco boycotts, and it often used mosques and zawiyas as meeting places. It called upon the people to pray five times a day for various "martyrs" to the national cause. But religious devices did not mask an obscurantist ideology like that of the Brotherhood. The modern notion of national solidarity required mass mobilization, and in the transitional society Islam was a common vocabulary, though the jihad was to be for modern political ends. As a fair-minded French administrator put it:

The Neo-Destour often has been reproached for its two faces: western and democratic before westerners, Islamic and xenophobic when it addresses its troops. The theorists of the party are nonetheless sincere in their love of Cartesianism. But, in a party of the people, they must speak the passionate language of the people, with the risk of being dragged beyond the balanced borders that these men of two civilizations imagine.[45]

Part of the secret of the Neo-Destour's effectiveness as a mass mobilizer lay in its ability to manipulate the religious symbols of the old society, though in their revolutionary spirit rather than in accordance with the orderly canons of medieval tradition.

The early task of the party was not only to mobilize "the people," but also to discipline them, to direct the spontaneous energies that its appeals might arouse. It had to educate them politically by articulating specific grievances, in order to minimize the need for a quasi-re-

[44]See *El Irada* (official Destour organ), February 16, 1934.
[45]Henri de Montety, "Les données du problème tunisien," *Politique Etrangère*, January-March, 1952, p. 452.

ligious style of agitation that was not in keeping with modern secular values. Bourguiba was fond of telling the peasants of the Sahel that the colonial government was exploiting them by taxation without representation. After 1934, as the effects of the world depression and continued drought were felt in Tunisia, the party emphasized economic rather than religious issues for building the needed political solidarity.

To educate the people and develop a disciplined following, the Neo-Destour from the outset emphasized organization, though never as successfully as did European Communist parties. Some sixty delegates from forty-nine of the Destour's eighty local committees attended the constituent congress,[46] but Bourguiba's followers exercised unchallenged control over few of the committees. By 1937, however, the Neo-Destour had more than four hundred branches. Unlike the old guard, the new leaders barnstormed the country whenever they were not in jail or under house arrest. They not only captured most of the Destour apparatus but built in its place a solid structure that on paper, at least, closely resembled that of the French Socialist Party.

It was not by accident that the first congress was held at Ksar-Hellal, the center of the forty-mile axis between Sousse and Mahdia that defines the Sahel. The Sahel gave the party a core of mass support as well as a flow of student recruits to the new elite. Moreover, Bourguiba's main source of financial support, Mohammed Chenik,[47] had business connections with the creditors of a number of weavers from Ksar-Hellal. But the party rapidly won support from other regions and social classes. Groups like the Metouia, whom the Destour had shunned, were welcomed into the party; this tribe of longshoremen constituted one of the party's oldest and most active branches in Tunis. Bourguiba also went to the countryside for tribal support; he took advantage of the drought by contacting the camps where the authorities had placed some of the bedouins on relief. He renewed contacts, too, with tribes whose property he had defended as a young lawyer. Although his tribal support was not widespread in 1934, it emphasized the party's image as a democratic force interested in all Tunisians, however poor and ignorant. For the first time in history the peasants of the Sahel and the bedouins of the interior were entering

[46]Dellagi, cited in note 26, above. Dellagi had access to the congress' report. Of the 49 committees, 13 were located in Tunis, 3 in the North, 2 on Cap Bon, 19 in the Sahel, and 12 in the Center and South.

[47]A year earlier, despite protests from the old Destour leadership, Bourguiba had come to the defense of Chenik, a Grand Councillor who had previously collaborated with the Protectorate and amassed a fortune, when the authorities discovered financial irregularities involving the Tunisian Credit Cooperative, of which he was President. See Roger Le Tourneau, *Evolution Politique de l'Afrique du Nord Musulmane 1920-1961* (1962), pp. 75-76.

politics. Those who showed political promise could aspire to responsible positions in the highly structured party apparatus, regardless of their social origin.

The new party represented not only a palace revolution among the elite but a transformation within the society. Even at the local level, the supremacy of the notables was challenged. The impoverished artisans of the medina, too, were breaking the bonds of the medieval guild system to join the party. Zitouna, the citadel of conservatism for the old elite, lost the loyalty of a majority of its students to the party, offering a bold and vigorous leadership unlike that of the old sheikhs. The students of Sadiki, the *lycées,* and French universities were more closely attuned to the new ideas of the new elite. But at least half of the local cadres of the party by 1937 were Zitouna graduates. The Sadiki education of the top leaders formed an effective link between the two cultures represented in the party. At the grass roots the Zitouna training of many of the activists gave them some of the oratorical and literary skill that the people respected and that effectively countered the cultural pretensions of the older party.

By means of its disciplined mass support the Neo-Destour was able not only to manifest the popular basis of a new nation but to pursue the anticolonial struggle in truly dialetical fashion. Bourguibist tactics were tailored to the colonial situation and utilized political values and style that a French public could readily comprehend. When the French Government was sufficiently strong and liberal to pursue a policy of gradual colonial emancipation, Bourguiba was prepared to make compromises toward the goal of independence. When the government was either weak or intent on an illiberal policy—often, under the pressure of the settlers—Bourguiba was ready to use advanced techniques of political agitation and subversion. The political machinery of Neo-Destour was sufficiently developed after 1936 to give the leaders the necessary tactical flexibility. The periods of repression and compromise, too, oscillated to the rhythm of nation-building; in periods of repression, the masses could be mobilized in political jihad; in periods of compromise, the cadres could develop their understanding of politics and sense of discipline. As the process unfolded, the rank and file absorbed the attitudes of the educated elite. Thus a truly modern party evolved in direct antithesis of, and as an alternative to, colonial rule.

By challenges from within, the nation acquired a greater sense of cohesion than party organization alone could provide. Before independence the Bourguibists had to defend their ideas to the public against the Destour and the Communists. The Destour, though organizationally weaker than its offshoot, presented a serious challenge in July, 1937, when Taalbi returned from fifteen years of exile. It soon became apparent that Taalbi wanted to reincorporate the Neo-Destour into the Destour under his leadership, and the battle of the Destours entered its final phase. At stake, really, was whether a modernist party could survive in a Muslim society that had found a charismatic leader. To the slogan "Down with false *zaims*," the Neo-Destour proved its superior organization by disrupting Taalbi's meetings. Taalbi lost much of his prestige by having to seek colonial police protection. When the Neo-Destour published his testimony against Bourguiba, after the latter's arrest in 1938, he was discredited to all but an emaciated Destour following. The old elite was no longer a dangerous political force, so long as the Neo-Destour paid lip service to Islam. The Destour survived, but only to become an antique in independent Tunisia; its main force was spent with the demise of Taalbi.

The other antagonist, the Tunisian Communist Party, was never an important force except in the labor movement after the Second World War. Nationalist labor leaders, intent on creating an autonomous Tunisian union, had to combat the Communist-dominated CGT for the support of Tunisian workers. In 1944 Farhat Hached, the Bourguiba of Tunisian labor, led a group of unions in Sfax out of the CGT. With the support of other unions in Tunis and the General Federation of Tunisian Functionaries he was able in January, 1946, to found a new all-Tunisian federation, the General Union of Tunisian Workers (UGTT). The Neo-Destour supported Hached and provided political organizers who became top-ranking trade-unionists. The UGTT was rapidly recognized by the colonial authorities and attracted a majority of Muslim workers away from the European-dominated union. The latter, however, after changing its name to become the USTT, survived until 1956 and sometimes embarrassed the UGTT by attacking its compromises with the Neo-Destour and its subordination of trade-union interests to the exigencies of the independence struggle.

In 1950 the nationalists underlined their desire for trade-union autonomy and their distrust of international communism. The Neo-Destour dismissed from its Political Bureau a long-time member and fellow traveler, Slimane Ben Slimane. After breaking with the Communist-dominated World Federation of Trade Unions, the UGTT affiliated itself with the International Confederation of Free Trade Unions. Thus the Communist issue was settled once and for all within the nationalist ranks before independence. European Communists had served primarily to cement an alliance between the Neo-Destour and a new and powerful Tunisian trade-union movement.

The development before independence of the national organizations was another sign of Tunisian cohesion under the Neo-Destour. The party was of great assistance to the UGTT. The experience of Mohammed Ali had shown that Tunisian trade-unionism could succeed only with the backing of the dominant nationalist party in a common front against colonial domination. Hached and the UGTT, while working for limited professional gains, considered self-government a necessary condition for achieving social justice. When the party was driven underground in 1952, the UGTT was not suppressed, mainly because of its international links. Hached served, however, on the Neo-Destour's clandestine Political Bureau until his assassination[48] in December, 1952.

Although the Neo-Destour did not create the UGTT—Hached had been a CGT leader rather than a party man—it did engineer the other national organizations, the Tunisian Union of Shopkeepers and Artisans (UTAC), the General Union of Tunisian Farmers (UGAT), and the General Union of Tunisian Students (UGET). Even before the war the party built up an organically linked group, the Neo-Destour Youth, to keep public order at party rallies and provide young militants for the party. Other groups, like the Muslim Scouts, the Muslim Youth, and the Graduates of Sadiki were also covers for party activity. Thus, before independence a virtual political system already existed—the *pays réel,* to use a French and Neo-Destour expression—outside the formal institutions of the Protectorate—or *pays légal.* Unlike most emerging nations, Tunisia already had its modern interest groups to articulate the special grievances of various sectors toward the colonial regime. Moreover, they had a history of coöperation with the dominant party that would be a vital precedent in the pursuit of national interests above group interests after independence.

In the postwar era the Neo-Destour was outlining the basic elements of its independence program and thus clarifying the nationalist consensus. The man who became a director of the Tunisian Government's steel company in 1962 was already, in 1948, writing in the Neo-Destour newspaper, *Mission,* of the need for Tunisian steel production. A future minister of finance was then underlining the importance of Tunisian economic planning.[49] The future minister of education, at the time a schoolteacher and trade-union official, was devising the broad lines of educational reform that he later carried out. Although

[48]Though Hached was seen to enter willingly the car of his supposed assassins, it seems farfetched to suspect his political colleagues of the killing. The inquiry of the *juge d'instruction* was quietly dropped, and it is generally assumed that the Main Rouge, a quasi-official terrorist organization, was behind the plot.
[49]See *Mission,* June 16 and September 15, 1948.

the Neo-Destour and UGAT dared not attack the habous institution for fear of raising a religious outcry, there was general agreement on the need to reform land tenure to encourage private ownership.

Perhaps even more important than any specific program was the sense of national identity produced by two decades of Neo-Destour activity and personified by Bourguiba. The leader's exceptional gifts were crucial in forging a new national consciousness, but shortsighted colonial policies also worked to Bourguiba's advantage. On June 19, 1942, five months before the Germans occupied the country, Moham-med el-Moncef became Bey of Tunisia. As French authority col-lapsed, he formed an independent government and succeeded in rally-ing all sectors of Tunisian opinion behind him. In the well-informed opinion of one historian, "undoubtedly, had Bourguiba been there [he and many of his colleagues were in Vichy prisons], he would have deferred to him like everyone else."[50] Fortunately for Bourguiba, how-ever, the revival of the monarchy was cut short in 1943 when Moncef Bey, unfairly accused of collaborating with the Germans, was exiled after the Allied liberation of Tunis. The mystique of Moncefism per-sisted until his death in 1948, but his successor, handicapped by being considered illegitimate while Moncef lived, lacked the skill and energy to mobilize nationalism in support of the monarchy. By deposing Mon-cef, the French created a vacuum that invited the building of a new type of authority. But one has only to contemplate Morocco, where Mohammed V became the symbol of triumphant nationalism and neu-tralized the inspirational appeal of Allal al-Fassi, to imagine a Tunisia similarly divided by conflicting principles of authority. France inad-vertently permitted Bourguiba to win by default.

In the absence of a strong monarchy, the Tunisian sense of identity could embrace a whole party unified under heroic leadership. The party's history became that of the emerging nation. When the storm clouds of repression became visible at the end of 1951, Bourguiba spoke of a third trial of strength. On January 18 the storm broke, and *Mission* republished an article Bourguiba had written fourteen years earlier. The party was the repository of the shared experiences of anti-colonial struggle. It articulated the symbols of national identity, all the more comprehensible for the cyclical rhythm of repression and compromise that characterized party history.

Tunisia's place in the world—identity with regard to others— was also clarified before independence. The country that before the First World War had looked with the Young Tunisians to the Ottoman Empire for inspiration had in the 'twenties and 'thirties shifted its gaze

[50]Le Tourneau, *op. cit.*, p. 97.

to Egypt. Kemal Attaturk seems to have alienated the conservatives by his lack of respect for Islam and the modernists by his authoritarian methods. By the late 'forties Egypt, too, had lost its luster for the Neo-Destour. Bourguiba witnessed the Palestine debacle and was disappointed in Pan-Arabism after receiving less than full support from the Arab League. While the Zitouna sheikhs and the old Destour leaders remained committed to the Pan Arab ideal, the modernists saw only the political instability and chaos of the postwar Orient and wished to avoid similar experiences. The French-educated progressive, indeed, saw the shadows of incompetent archaic Destour politicians in the Egyptian politicians of the Farouk era. Tunisia—and possibly the Maghreb—would modernize more successfully, the new elite hoped, because, if less numerous, it considered itself to be better educated and its people to be more *évolué* than the downtrodden Egyptian fellah.

When Bourguiba returned from Cairo in 1949, the romantic attitude of a few of the Neo-Destour leaders towards the Orient fell out of fashion.[51] In its place had developed a new national myth that viewed Tunisia more as a French historian might depict it. In the columns of *Al Mabahith* (1944-1947) the French-trained Arabists of the Neo-Destour placed Tunisia in the context of Mediterranean civilization.[52] Not only could the emerging nation look back with pride at the relics of its Carthaginian, Roman, and Arab periods. It could also continue its tradition of cultural interdependence with other Mediterranean nations and assimilate the best of civilization from each. The Mediterranean perspective gracefully allowed Bourguiba to pursue a policy of cooperation with France without fear of losing Tunisia's identity. When he subsequently asserted that it was more to Tunisia's benefit to cooperate with an advanced country like France than with Egypt, such an un-Arab view was nonetheless in accord with the Mediterranean image. Tunisia identified with the mainstream of classic civilization and shared a vision of interdependent free nations.

By the time the Neo-Destour attained self-government, its synthesis seemed relatively complete. The party had imposed upon the naturally

[51]See Ali Belhaouane's earlier columns in *Mission*. "Oriental Tunisia naturally tends toward the Orient. Mistress of her destiny, she would be able to serve as a link. . . . To the modern world the Orient gave Ghandi and the West, Hitler. . . . We still think that it will be the Orient that will save humanity. . . . The misfortune of Hitler was to say aloud what each people of the West thinks to itself," (April 21, April 28, May 5, May 12, 1948). But Belhaouane later supported pro-Western Bourguiba in his showdown with Salah Ben Youssef, whose slogans were Pan-Arabist.
[52]See Brown, *op. cit.*, Chap. VII.

homogenous society a new modernist consensus of a Western-educated elite. The consensus not only survived the challenges of the traditionalists and the Communists; the long struggle with France also assured that the consensus penetrated through the party to the society as a whole. Divisions, of course, remained: traditional modes of thought still permeated the uneducated population, and economic problems of underdevelopment were unsolved. The modernist intellectuals had devised no permanent solution to the problem of Islam in the modern world, and Tunisia still lacked a coherent cultural identity. However, perhaps more than in any other emerging nation, the colonial situation in Tunisia had set up the conditions for stable and permissive single-party rule after independence.

II THE LEADER AS A NATION-BUILDER

THE deep historical roots of Tunisian consensus suggest that its post-independence regime, far from being the work of one man, was the result of a complex of peculiarly Tunisian circumstances. Yet in any single-party system, whether of the neo-Leninist or the permissive variety, the leader usually plays a preponderant role. Tunisia is no exception. Indeed, Bourguiba, when recently asked about Tunisia's political system, exclaimed, "The system? What system? I am the system!" Were this literally true, one might expect Tunisia to lapse into chaos after Bourguiba's eventual departure from the scene. A precise assessment of his role is thus of crucial importance.

The leader of an emergent nation may be viewed, first, as founding father, or nation-builder, who stimulates and articulates a consensus on the identity and purposes of the new nation. Second, unlike the classic Legislator who retires from the political scene after founding the *polis*, he remains the nation's chief executive and dominates the political process. In this chapter Bourguiba's first role, that of articulating new social values, is described. In the following chapter his second, more narrowly political role will be discussed in a preliminary fashion, apart from other aspects of the system subsequently to be explored.

Bourguiba's Personality and Ideas

Bourguiba was born in 1903 at Monastir, one of the Sahel's most ancient cities. He came from a respectable family of low-ranking civil servants of modest means. At an early age, after his mother died, he was sent to Tunis to study at Sadiki's elementary school annex, then at Sadiki College and Lycée Carnot. Though his studies were interrupted by poor health, he left Tunis for Paris in 1924 to study law and political science on what funds an older brother could muster. In Paris he found time to study French literature and, perhaps with politics in mind, became interested in pathology. He also learned to dance the Charleston, attended the theater frequently, and acquired a French wife and son before returning in 1927 to a law office in Tunis.

Even in 1927 Bourguiba was hardly a typical Tunisian, though very much a product of the colonial situation. Self-help and family solidarity rather than a family fortune had allowed him to acquire a Paris university degree. Few Tunisians in those days studied abroad, for the wealthy did not need European higher education and the poor could not afford it. In the context of Tunis society, however, Bourguiba was an outsider, an afaqi, or provincial. He did not come from a family esteemed in the old social order, but was considered a social climber. In French liberal circles, however, his education made him an equal. His ambiguous social position, his background of a motherless childhood and delicate health, perhaps encouraged his ambitious nature along the path of revolution. His education focused within him the dialectic of the colonial situation.

Bourguiba was introduced to politics at an early age. In 1922 he joined the Destour; in Paris he had contacts with the French Left and became a close friend of Dr. Materi, who had broken with the Communist Party. Not until 1930, however, did Bourguiba embark upon his political career. The Eucharistic Congress, which suggested a new Christian crusade, provided the final shock pushing him to a career of nationalist opposition to the colonial regime. He contributed to nationalist newspapers written in the French language, became a regular columnist for Chadly Khairallah's *Voix du Tunisien*, and then formed his own newspaper, *L'Action Tunisienne*, with the small circle of fellow university graduates who in 1934 became the nucleus of the Neo-Destour Party.

In September, 1934, Bourguiba and his friends were thrown into prison for the first time. Bourguiba spent ten of the next twenty years in French prisons (1934-1936, 1938-1943, 1952-1954); but during his battles for Tunisian independence he never shut the door to negotiations and to a future of coöperation with France and the West. When he returned to Tunis in 1949 after four years of disenchantment with Egypt and Eastern Arabism, sympathetic French observers noted an increasingly conciliatory and moderate style in his political manners. But his "moderation" is partly myth. Many observers were shocked when he exploded the myth by provoking the Bizerte crisis of 1961; even then, however, Bourguiba was acting true to form. He never would have mobilized a nation and achieved Tunisian independence if he had been simply a moderate lawyer-politician. Politics to him is rational calculation, a Cartesian activity tempered with common sense, but the man is a fiery bundle of passions and theatrical gestures. It is not only intelligence but determination and personal magnetism—so focused on politics that he addresses private individuals as though they are public audiences—that make him an inspirational leader. Like all great actors, Bourguiba, who seems always to be on stage, is able to calculate his gestures and to release the warm spontaneity which draws audiences to him. Untypically Tunisian, his deep blue eyes and commanding jaw are major assets that lend dignity to a short and stocky frame. His intelligence, his education, and his experience as a political organizer and an unofficial diplomat taught him to use his natural charm for carefully thought out objectives. His reputation as a statesman seems justified. He never wrote a treatise on political theory, but through experience he developed an articulate set of ideas to guide his impetuous disposition and the destinies of his country.

"Bourguibism," as the ideas came to be labeled by French journalists, is a set of tactics rather than a political ideology. A man of action, Bourguiba disdained all rigid doctrines. At the root of Bourguibism, however, lies a certain political orientation based on the man's education and practical common sense.

Bourguiba's political inspiration came from Rousseau, Lamartine, and Hugo—the romantic strain of French nationalism rather than Karl Marx. For Bourguiba Marxism was a theory about industrialized nations, not Tunisia. "Tunisia is a country of middle classes and peasants, those which the Radical represents in France and which socialism is trying to capture by battering the brain of Karl Marx."[1] Although he wrote those lines in 1931, the Neo-Destour "socialism" he devised in 1961 could be better understood as an expression of socially oriented nationalism than as an offshoot of Marxism.

The fixed values emerging out of Bourguiba's political career were simply those of the French Republican tradition—liberty, fraternity, equality—adapted to the purpose of making Tunisia not only an independent but a modern country. All Tunisians were to be equal as citizens having human dignity. They were to be brothers in the family of the Tunisian nation. They were to be free so far as their liberty did not conflict with the liberty of others or with the general interest. Human dignity required bread and possibilities of employment, education, and health services as well as civic liberties; therefore the nation, existing as a good only so far as it furthered the dignity of its citizens, had to be modern as well as free. Bourguiba's nationalism, though emphasizing the need for disciplined solidarity, has always had a humane orientation. Consent elicited by Bourguiba was to bridge the gap between the individual's dignity and the needs of the nation.

Bourguiba's methods, applying Western ideals to a Muslim society, were more original and carefully articulated than the ideals themselves. Bourguibism is essentially the art of rational persuasion, which he believes to be the source of all great political, social, or economic

[1]*Voix du Tunisien*, April 10, 1931.

transformation. Implicit is the assumption that change can never really be forced, whether the goal be political independence or the modernization of Tunisian society. A good child of the Enlightenment, Bourguiba has always had confidence in the eventual triumph of his "rational" proposals, whether about Ramadan or the evacuation of French bases on sovereign Tunisian territory. But from the Romantics he also learned that appeals to the heart were sometimes necessary before the voice of reason might be heard. Reminiscing about the nationalist struggle, Bourguiba once explained:

There was the need for a driving force (*élan vital*): a product of the heart and sentiment that would force men to endurance and action, create enthusiasm and maintain it in spite of the vicissitudes and failures of a long and unequal struggle.

On the other hand there was the need for intelligence and reason, to direct and channel this struggle toward our objective.

. . . Both were necessary: the motive force and the steering helm.[2]

In Bourguiba's personality the two needs were linked: his energy—the actor and demagogue in him—provided the *élan vital,* and his aptitude for political calculation provided the "steering helm." Unlike most demagogues, Bourguiba had little respect for political extremists; he once said of the Pan-Arabists in Tunis and Cairo that "their Oriental mentality does not allow them to understand that politics is the art of attaining the possible."[3]

Bourguibism is best known as a style of political negotiation for transforming a colonial situation, a combination of intransigence upon principles with flexibility in the choice of means to implement them. Willing to advance by gradual stages, Bourguibism patiently accepts compromises which lead toward his goal. Bourguiba's sharp distinction seems dubious, however, between goals or principles, which are not negotiable, and means or modalities, which are. No political formula can express an immutable principle. Bourguibism has thus sometimes proved a more rationalization for political opportunism. Bourguiba once explained his famed tactics of negotiation:

In the Middle East Bourguibism has been interpreted to mean one thing only, and even that is misunderstood: take what is offered and then ask for more. This is equivalent to saying that one should accept anything. As an illustration, the example is given of a debtor who out of a debt of a hundred millimes agrees to pay back one only. That is better than anything, it is said, and the creditor has only to go on asking. No, that is not Bourguibism.

[2]Speech, June 24, 1961.
[3]H. Bourguiba, *La Tunisie et la France* (1954), p. 246.

In point of fact, Bourguibism only accepts a partial compromise insofar as it offers the possibility of taking everything owed.

A better example could be taken from the art of strategy. Imagine you are in the position of someone who is trying to take a fortress held by an enemy who is stronger than you and from whom you cannot take everything at one blow. If he offers to let you have, say, a path which is useless, there is no point in accepting the compromise. But if he abandons a strategic position capable of becoming a point from which the whole system of fortifications can be taken, it would be criminal to refuse. So long as I feel myself incapable of taking the whole citadel by force, I would be failing in my duty and harming the cause of my country if I refused to take a point which would enable me later on to take all the rest.[4]

When favorable compromises with France were not possible, Bourguiba switched from negotiation to the tactics of mass agitation to persuade French opinion of the instability of the Tunisian *status quo*. Intransigence and violence, carefully controlled, were designed as pressures to induce favorable compromises. In 1938, he preferred to agitate the mobs against paying their taxes rather than to continue negotiations with a weakened Popular Front government. In 1954, even after two years in prison, Bourguiba decisively rejected the Voizard reforms, which called for a Tunisian parliament of settler as well as indigenous representatives, because the implicit idea of Franco-Tunisian co-sovereignty threatened future political advance. Instead, the *fellagha* (guerrilla) movement was mobilized, and Bourguiba was willing to negotiate with France only after Mendès-France promised internal autonomy.

Simultaneously with the constructive compromises and prison terms for agitation which characterized Bourguiba's experiences with the Protectorate, he was engaged in building a nation to accord with his conception of nationhood as a shared and living solidarity of popular sentiment. During periods of agitation, the masses could be inspired with an *élan vital,* a reflection of the Islamic reflex of jihad. During periods of tranquillity and compromise, with their concomitant of tacit public liberties, the masses could be organized and educated as modern nationalists. Like French governments, the Tunisian masses had to be stimulated to listen to Bourguiba; rational appeals were not sufficient to induce solidarity. Although Bourguiba did not generally appeal to the masses in a religious vocabulary, the image of shared struggle against colonialism struck a familiar Islamic chord.[5]

[4]Speech, April 6, 1961.
[5]In 1938 Bourguiba wrote: "It is really the march toward deliverance which is now going on. Every militant is convinced that he is participating in a grandiose epic, in a doubly sacred work for national liberation both social and political." *La Tunisie et la France,* p. 171.

As a technique of effecting basic social transformations by persuasion and rational strategy, Bourguibism fitted the colonial situation in Tunisia. But the technique is perhaps easier to exert on people who share political values and uneasy consciences, like colonial rulers, than on a transitional society modernized only in part by an intensive colonial situation. The question remained after independence whether Bourguiba's rational appeals, however emotionally articulated in fiery speeches, could persuade Tunisians to shift their energies from anticolonialism to the battle against underdevelopment. One possible means of making them change their attitudes, modify their traditions, and accept the economic sacrifices necessary to achieve his dream of a modern Tunisia was through the exercise of charismatic leadership.

Bourguiba and Charisma

It is rare that the events that make up the landmarks in the life of one man are integrated into the history of a people to such an extent that the man seems to incarnate his whole people. If this transposition has been brought about, it is because the man was able to be the sincere and disinterested spokesman of the nation's conscience, and because he fought so much and so well for the people's cause that the movements in the life of each were brought to merge with one another.[6]

The "modest man who is talking to you," as he put it, was Bourguiba talking about himself and his nation's history on the solemn occasion of the promulgation of independent Tunisia's constitution. He was only stating accepted facts already enshrined in the nation's political mythology. As the Supreme Combatant for independence, Bourguiba seemed to be the unquestioned and inspirational leader. Might not his personal prestige be sufficient not only to give Tunisia political stability but also to urge it forward on the path of modernization?

However great his prestige, Bourguiba is not a charismatic leader if *charisma* is taken to mean "a certain quality of an individual personality by virtue of which he is set apart from ordinary men and treated as endowed with supernatural, superhuman . . . powers or qualities."[7] The worship of marabouts (local saints) was once an

[6]Speech, June 1, 1959.

[7]Max Weber, *The Theory of Social and Economic Organization* (1947), p. 358. For an excellent though highly involved critique of the concept of charismatic leadership, see Carl J. Friedrich, "Political Leadership and the Problem of the Charismatic Power," *Journal of Politics,* 1961, pp. 3-24, and, by the same author, *Man and His Government* (1963), chapters 6, 9, 10. Friedrich would reserve *charisma* to apply to properly religious as contrasted to merely inspirational leadership. This distinction is especially important to make in the context of Islamic culture where the traditional synthesis of politics and religion has broken down. As long as the popular identification of politics and religion lingers, *charisma* in Friedrich's strict sense is potentially of the highest political significance. So is its lack.

important factor in local cohesion. Religious superstition, however, was discredited in most parts of Tunisia (unlike Morocco) when the colonial authorities tried to use the various sects to their advantage. Orthodox Islam, too, had been stronger in most of the country than in the isolated mountainous Berber-speaking regions of Algeria and Morocco. Whatever his reputation as the Supreme Combatant, Bourguiba (unlike the King of Morocco) could hardly claim authority on the basis of supernatural powers in a society most of which was opposed to such a conception of authority. If some Tunisians thought of Bourguiba as a holy man, the phenomenon was not widespread.

Bourguiba's oratory, though replete with religious imagery and passages from the Quran, used the vocabulary of modern nationalism. He appealed to Tunisians' reason and common sense rather than to superstition, and clothed his messages, spoken in colloquial Arabic, in vivid images of everyday life. Rather than suggesting the distance of a supernatural leader, Bourguiba always emphasized close physical contact with the masses, to whom he was simply Si Lahbib. As Head of State he became "Your Majesty the President," but the man's direct style remains.

Although not a truly charismatic leader, Bourguiba is more than a popular political figure. His boast that he incarnates the nation has an element of truth. The man's great popularity seems in a measure to reflect the Tunisian marabout tradition. People flock to see him, to hear his voice, to feel his presence. Bourguiba is the providential figure—the Legislator of Plato or Rousseau—who created the nation and its regime. He sometimes claims his leadership to be a "gift of God." Like the Legislator, Bourguiba is a moralist as well as a politician. His speeches are more like exhortations of a social reformer than briefings or fireside chats of a practical politician. Every two or three weeks Bourguiba steps into his role as the nation's father, and gives advice on such matters as personal cleanliness, decent housing, the importance of sports, or the desirability of sedentary village life.[8] In the past five years his speeches have dealt with religion as much as they have with Neo-Destour socialism. They are important channels of national communication, for, on his frequent tours, his speeches are heard on the radio by an audience of the entire nation. The talks are rebroadcast several times and are heard in the Arab cafés of the most

[8]In the couple of years following independence, Bourguiba addressed the nation once a week over the radio, usually on a Thursday so that what he said could be echoed in the mosques on Friday. These speeches were generally brief reports on political progrss. As the regime stabilized, however, Bourguiba apparently felt less need for frequent contacts with the masses on political matters. He made fewer but longer speeches, of more general interest, dealing with specific problems.

isolated villages. Usually extemporaneous, they seem to be a needed outlet for Bourguiba's personal energy as well as a welcome distraction for the people from their narrow daily routine.

Bourguiba, however, can hardly be considered charismatic even in the attenuated sense of possessing a special, generally recognized moral quality. He articulates his nation's values, but what he teaches is not unquestioned. Educated Tunisians, especially the young, may agree with the modern tenor of his ideas while reserving the right to disagree with specific political measures. Uneducated people, in contrast, may lack the background necessary for judging a particular national policy, but they question the new ethos, especially when it affects their religion. Bourguiba's past political successes have not given him the authority to decide what is good and what is bad for people in their private lives. Probably much of Bourguiba's moralizing effort—though it lies at the core of his tactics of persuasion—is heard in apathy by a large sector of Tunisian society. Although respected for his political accomplishments, the man is widely reputed to be an atheist. For a ruler to be considered a bad Muslim is perhaps not incompatible with Islamic theories of legitimacy; but in the popular culture, where no clear-cut distinction is made between religion and politics, Bourguiba's image is hardly "charismatic."

Besieging the Islamic Bastion

To be sure, there was a time, in the flush of independence, when most Tunisians recognized in Bourguiba a special moral quality, or *charisma* in an attenuated sense. The very title of Supreme Combatant (*mujahid al-akbar*) by which he was popularly known connoted a special Islamic virtue. "Whoever does not believe in the word of Bourguiba," an old Zitouna sheikh was reported to have said, "does not believe in the word of God or his Prophet."[9] But the logic of Bourguibism as a strategy of modernization carried with it the unforeseen deterioration of his *charisma*.

Although Bourguiba's "revolution" had no predetermined timetable of reforms, the first task in the building of a modern society was to transform popular attitudes toward change, rather than immediately to decolonize economic structures and engage in full-scale planning. The new government had to be firmly established, the necessary administrators found, and studies and statistics produced. Moreover, political crises with France, exacerbated by the continuing Algerian war, occupied the Tunisian Government's attention for the first five

[9]*Le Petit Matin,* October 1, 1958.

years of independence. Yet, even after 1961, when economic planning became the focus of national effort, the psychological dimension of modernization was still emphasized. As Bourguiba summarized his strategy:

A new need must be taught [to the people]: the need for dignity. Just as we gave our Tunisian compatriot in the Center and South of the country a feeling that his dignity was wounded when a French Resident in Tunis humiliated a minister or a civil controller oppressed his compatriots, it is necessary that he feel the need to improve his living standards by work, that he aspire to dress better, to eat better, to look after his family decently, to educate his children, to look after his health, in a word to live honorably as advanced people do.[10]

Bourguiba's psychological offensive, however, was bound sooner or later to erode any *charisma* he might once have been thought to possess. For the transforming of people's traditional attitudes entailed an assault, however skillfully executed, upon religion as devout Tunisian Muslims understood it.

Bourguiba's initial reforms were brilliantly timed and supported by a rationale that originally convinced most devout and patriotic Tunisians. Although nourished on French anticlerical political culture, Bourguiba did not openly advocate secular reforms. Rather, his ostensible aim was to reform Islam in Tunisia by putting its activities under the control of his new state apparatus and by reorienting decadent practices which no longer accorded with their religious source. The *laïcistes* in France had never thought of infiltrating the Catholic Church. In Tunisia, however, Bourguiba tried to use religion, to remold it to suit his modernist ends. For in the Islamic tradition there was neither a clergy nor a rigorous separation of Church and State. In times of Muslim grandeur, on the contrary, Church and State were one.

Bourguiba tried to project himself as a great Muslim reformer in the traditions of Mohammed 'Abduh. "The objective of this pioneer movement is to restore liberty to human intelligence, to free it of the shackles which dogma had imposed. What they (reformers like 'Abduh) wanted was to open the way to free inquiry, to permit the man, the Muslim of intelligence and knowledge, to submit everything to the light of his thinking, to admit nothing and to do nothing which he did not in his conscience believe to be valuable and useful." One loyal Bourguibist, a young trade-unionist professor, tried to justify the President as a Muslim reformist. Laws were in accordance with Islam,

[10] Speech, June 24, 1961.

he argued,[11] if they were in the spirit of the Quran and traditions, and accorded with the universal consensus (ijmā) of the umma (community). Bourguiba was obviously more representative of the Tunisian umma than were the religious sheikhs, and—there being no classic division between spiritual and temporal power—could speak for it on religious matters.

Religion was to be a positive force, "the means of enlightening consciences and breaking chains." The religious customs and practices which Bourguiba was to attack were not an intrinsic part of Islam as he interpreted it. Religious conservatives might argue that Bourguiba, with his emphasis upon man's intelligence, reason, and the virtues of free enquiry, was more nearly a non-Muslim child of the European Enlightenment than a Believer. But who has yet clearly defined the Muslim in the modern world?[12]

Bourguiba's first step was to abolish the inefficient and semi-autonomous public habous administration. Its lands, some 150,000 hectares which financed the mosques and other religious and charitable institutions, were turned over to the State Domains administration. Effected immediately after independence (May 31, 1956), this reform seemed an uncontroversial measure to consolidate the authority of the new sovereign government. The old habous administration had been tainted by collaboration with the Protectorate authorities; for many years since 1898 it had sold 2,000 hectares per year to European settlers, and scandals of corruption had discredited it. The reform served, however, to bring most religious activities under direct state control.

Bourguiba's strategy of reforming rather than attacking Islam was implied in Article 1 of the constitution, which was passed at his request on April 13, 1956: "The Tunisian State is free, independent and sovereign. Islam is its religion and Arabic its language." Though it was also promised in the constitution that the state would tolerate the practice of other religions, it was clear that Tunisia was not to be a secular state. The principle of separation of church and state was

[11]L'Action, October 15, 1956.
[12]As von Grunebaum has pointed out, "The decisive factor in successful adaptation [of Islam] is . . . not the . . . scholarly terms in which an attempted reinterpretation renders the meaning of founder and sacred texts, but the conviction it is able to generate in the minds and the hearts of contemporary believers that it answers to their needs as would the Founder's words were he still in their midst. . . . To make the ijma an active instrument of adjustment or even a tool of planned change, nothing is needed but a shift in public opinion sufficiently marked to compel its formal recognition by the learned in terms of a restatement of the consensus. . . ." See his Modern Islam: The Search for Cultural Identity (1962), pp. 9, 11-12.

rejected, despite the idea of at least one French jurist that the notion of a modern state necessarily entailed secularism.[13]

The Code of Personal Status, ratified on August 13, 1956, was one of Bourguiba's most daring innovations. It attacked Tunisia's social structure at its very roots, the family, by abolishing polygamy and making marriage a voluntary contract by which the woman as well as the man acquired rights. By setting a minimum age for marriage and requiring the bride's consent it outlawed the custom of selling off young girls. It thereby encouraged the modern idea that marriage was more a relationship between two people than between two families. The husband was no longer permitted arbitrarily to divorce his wife; she, as well as the husband, was given the right to institute divorce proceedings. The whole tenor of the new law ran counter to traditional Muslim jurisprudence.

Bourguiba was hailed by the modernists in his party and administration as the great emancipator of women. By taking the legal step which the French Protectorate for political reasons had never dared, Bourguiba helped to complete the revolution in family customs introduced by the colonial situation. As Henri de Montety observed, "After the short waves of modernism from 1925 to 1950, a groundswell silently formed under the crust of tradition which would break open with the national revolution. . . . With the passionate élan of triumphant nationalism, the revolution of customs could be accomplished with good conscience and with the support of legality.[14]

Although Bourguiba could rely upon his great prestige in the summer of 1956 as the father of Tunisian independence, he had felt it necessary carefully to prepare the ground for his reform. In late April, in a move which had been apparently long contemplated, Tahar Ben Achour was appointed rector of Zitouna.[15] He had infuriated the nationalists even in 1933 by giving an ambiguous fetwa concerning the naturalization of Muslims as French citizens, but he was an important Maliki sheikh, from a distinguished family of religious scholars, and in previous periods as rector of Zitouna had fathered moderate reforms. Less conservative than many of the other old sheikhs, he was persuaded to support Bourguiba's reform.

In late April, too, the Ministry of Justice reshuffled the sheikhs who

[13]See Lavau's article in *L'Action*, February 3, 1958.
[14]Henri de Montety, "Mutation des moeurs familiales en Tunisie," *Cahiers Nord Africains*, ESNA, No. 77, pp. 25-26.
[15]*Le Petit Matin*, April 26, 1956; rumored in *L'Action*, December 19, 1955.

sat on the shari'a courts.[16] All were to sign a petition against the new
Code of Personal Status, but five of them, including the two new
cadhis, were willing to accept positions as judges to apply the code
when, on August 3, the courts were integrated into Tunisia's modern
legal system.

By these moves the Bourguiba government obtained partial support
for the controversial reform from the influential circle of ulama. He
courted the Enniffers as well as the rival Ben Achour family, and had
Chadly Enniffer appointed to the Constituent Assembly.[17] Before producing the final draft of the code, Bourguiba persuaded the Bey to
pass a decree stating that his seal was no longer necessary for government decrees to be valid. Bourguiba also persuaded the Maliki Sheikh
El Islam, Mohammed El Aziz Djait, to accept the principle of the
reform.[18]. One of his relatives, Abdelaziz Djait, later accepted the
honorific position of Mufti of Tunisia, thereby giving the government
an aura of religious legitimacy without curtailing its modernist objectives.[19] A head-on clash with the sheikhs of Zitouna was postponed
for two years while Bourguiba consolidated his power.

[16]Divided into the two orthodox rites of Maliki and Hanafi, the two six-man courts
were the highest religious and legal authority on matters concerning Muslim personal status. Each was headed by a Sheikh El Islam and reorganized to include
one cadhi and four muftis. In a reversal of the old hierarchical distinctions, the
cadhi was given more effective authority. Two new cadhis were appointed, Mohammed El Hedi Bel Cadhi for the Hanafi court, and Fadhl Ben Achour, the son
of Tahar Ben Achour, for the Maliki court. One mufti retired; another, Mohammed El Moktar Ben Mahmoud, was suspended and brought before a council of
discipline for having paid insufficient attention to his work. (See *Le Petit Matin,*
April 28, 1956.) The rise of Fadhl Ben Achour was as interesting as that of his
father, for the son also had a political past as a Zitouna youth organizer and occasional ally of Farhat Hached. After his break with Salah Ben Youssef in 1950 he
and the Neo-Destour became bitter rivals. One of Tunisia's most distinguished
Islamic scholars and a reformist, he clashed also with Mahmoud Messadi, the
brilliant Arabist *agrégé* who subsequently became secretary of education.

[17]Although Chadly Enniffer had often collaborated with the Bey, he had allowed
the Neo-Destour before independence to infiltrate his Zitouna youth organization,
the rival of a similar organization, the Muslim Youth, headed by another Enniffer.
Of the three Enniffers who remained as muftis on the Malekite court, two
brothers resigned in August rather than become modern judges, but the third,
Chadly's brother, for a time accepted being a judge.

[18]The Sheikh was reported by *L'Action* to have said, "As long as one conserves
one's faith, religion can adapt; the main thing is to respect the spirit of Islam"
(September 3, 1956). The Ministry of Justice consulted him in the preparation of
the code. Tahar Ben Achour also backed the reform. Djait was later persuaded by
other conservative sheikhs to repudiate his support and sign a petition attacking it
in the old Destour newspaper *Istiqlal.* He denied to *L'Action* that he had ever
supported the government reform (Letter and Answer, September, 1956).

[19]Abdelaziz Djait had long been rector of Zitouna and had also been a Sheikh El
Islam before 1956.

Bourguiba's attack on outmoded Islamic traditions was next aimed at the 1,500,000 hectares of private habous land. Not even the party had suggested the elimination of the system, for many influential families in the cities profited as heirs. But in the summer of 1957 Bourguiba was strong enough to defy the wrath of the old elite. His law of July 18 simply eliminated the institution; mixed habous, so far as they were public, reverted to the state, while private habous were to be divided among the heirs in such a way as to give women their fair share. The *de facto* rights of tenants who had long occupied the land were also respected, and the government helped them acquire the lands as private property. By his daring initiative Bourguiba liberated a potentially important economic asset—land which had remained outside the modern commercial circuit.

Bourguiba waited until 1958 before embarking upon the most difficult of the early reforms, that of the educational system, which lay at the heart of his strategy of modernization. As he explained:

When we were in opposition, living outside legal institutions and harassing the Protectorate regime to obtain recognition of our rights, I told myself that if the state apparatus passed into our hands, we would give priority to the problem of education. This indeed concerns the motor element, the brain which permits man to rise above the animal condition. . . . [With] useful knowledge the human being is capable of miracles; but if the content [of education] is retrograde, the whole society falls back to the level of the herd.[20]

Political tactics rather than technical problems account for the two-year delay. The reform, when it took effect in October, 1958, constituted a final assault on that bastion of conservative religious learning, Zitouna University.

The reform had two main aims: to establish a "coherent, unified system" and drastically to expand education.[21] Bourguiba, the leaders

[20]Speech, June 25, 1958.
[21]See *Nouvelle Conception de l'Enseignement en Tunisie* (Secrétariat d'Etat à l'Education Nationale, October, 1958), p. 17. Expansion was primarily a technical and financial problem. Universal primary education was to be achieved in ten years by reducing the number of hours of class and by subtracting a year from primary education. The use of Arabic was to be greatly increased, but French, after the second year, remained the language of instruction for most purposes in middle and secondary education. The new system was designed not only to conform to French university standards but also to provide specialized technical cadres; middle education, for less gifted pupils, prepared them for specific practical careers. Education became Tunisia's most important investment; it constituted, respectively, 18, 18.7, and 20 per cent of the regular budgets of 1958-59, 1959-60, and 1961, which themselves had increased by almost one-fifth in the three years. The Ten-Year Perspectives foresaw a total investment in educational facilities of $210,000,000 for the period 1962-1971; in addition, the annual operating expenditures would more than triple during this period.

in his party, and the UGTT Federation of Teachers had all agreed before independence on the priority they would give to education. Mahmoud Messadi, who had drawn up reforms in the late 1940's to present to the French authorities on behalf of the UGTT, was put in charge of the Bourguiba reform. The integration of Zitouna into the system of national education meant the suppression of the former and the revival of old personal animosities. For years Messadi had been on the blacklist of the Zitouna professors, who considered his modern ideas "atheistic," although the Neo-Destour and the UGTT before independence had tried to placate the influential sheikhs in order to sustain a common national front against the Protectorate. As de Montety observed, in 1951, no "Tunisian would dare openly to counter the Zitouna movement, because it has an irresistible backing, the prestige of Islam."[22] But the Neo-Destour leadership educated in French universities had never respected Zitouna's tradition of religious learning. Now, as President of the Republic, Bourguiba no longer had to placate the sheikhs. Outlining the new reform, he said of Zitouna: "[It] had the merit of opposing the current of Frenchification. This was not progress, only resistance. . . . But today this is no longer sufficient. We have to be demanding. We have to advance and no longer be content with fixed positions. We are now free to adapt our education so as to catch up with the procession of civilization."[23] Messadi admitted that even gradual liquidation of Zitouna was a risk, for the venerable university's 16,000 students and 500 professors might have helped revive political opposition to Bourguiba.[24] Most of them had no place in Tunisia's new unified system, for religious instruction had been cut to one or two hours a week in primary school and was virtually eliminated in secondary education.[25]

Although the full effects of the education reform would not be felt until the early 1970's, when all children would be going to school, and more than ten thousand students would be attending the univer-

[22]Henri de Montety, "Révolution moderniste à l'Université Ez-Zitouna," L'Afrique et l'Asie (1951), p. 33.

[23]Speech, June 25, 1958.

[24]Interview, December 2, 1961.

[25]Three years later, slightly more emphasis was accorded to religious instruction, made compulsory two hours a week in secondary schools. Zitouna graduates with the *alimia* (university level) diploma were to be recruited as religious instructors in the schools or as preachers to educate the masses. Bourguiba said that they "could even contribute to form the youth by renovated Islamic principles." Like engineers or doctors, they would now have a "mission of progress" (June 29, 1961). But the Zitouna system of education was eliminated; all that remained was a faculty of theology, under Fadhl Ben Achour, integrated into the modern University of Tunis.

sity, Bourguiba attempted in other ways to accelerate modernization. In his weekly speeches he tried to further the psychological impact of the Code of Personal Status by urging women to take off their veils. "It is unthinkable," he once said at a religious festival in ultra-conservative Kairouan, "that half the population be cut off from life and hidden like a disgraceful thing."[26] On a different occasion he added: "If we understand that middle-aged women are reticent about abandoning an old habit, we can only deplore the stubbornness of parents who continue to oblige their children to wear a veil in school. We even see civil servants going to work in that odious rag. . . . It has nothing to do with religion."[27] In Sfax, Bourguiba went so far as to prohibit " that odious rag" in the classroom.

Bourguiba repeatedly stressed the theme of human dignity. Speaking to miserable seminomadic tribesmen, he said: "Man's dignity requires him to strive for comfort and to take pride in his appearance. Even the Prophet said that one must pay attention to this. It is by his appearance, his cleanliness, and his standard of living that one measures the evolution of a man." For the women, he continued, "There should not be these differences in dress in the diverse regions. . . . We must do away with this dark *melia* [bedouin veil]." As for the men, "You must not neglect your work, pretending that this work is unfamiliar to you. . . . Follow the directions of your Government so that your children and grandchildren may accede to city life. . . . Either you decide to work and carry out instructions . . . or else you can remain attached to a primitive type of life, which condemns you to vegetate on the margins of society." Bourguiba was appealing to the nomads to settle down to a sedentary peasant existence as gardeners: "Even if we do not take into account the influence of the schools, of trade unions, of local Party branches, the very fact that men live in a village, around a mosque, a school, a dispensary, and a market is in itself a factor of progress."[28]

The regime was trying to generalize the healthy village society of the Sahel. In the South a pilot project was launched whereby the cave dwellers of Matmata were eventually transferred to a new village specially constructed for them in 1961. Caves, it was thought, were not fit habitations for modern man. Change the dwelling and perhaps the man's attitudes will also change. "A decent standard of living cannot be envisaged without decent housing."[29] The three-quarters

[26]Speech, October 1, 1957, quoted in *La Femme Tunisienne* (Secrétariat d'Etat à l'Information, 1960), p. 20.
[27]Speech, December 5, 1957.
[28]Speech, May 19, 1960.
[29]Speech, May 27, 1960.

of the Tunisian population living in "miserable mud huts" were to be encouraged—and "when necessary" forced—to build new houses in conjunction with vast government efforts over a period of years. In 1960 Bourguiba declared: "The task that will be accomplished with state control in the next three years is destined to efface the mud huts, which mar our countryside, and rid our local population and tourists from this depressing sight. . . ."[30] He announced a massive "popular lodging" program, beginning in 1961.

In 1957 Bourguiba personally encouraged the formation of the Union Nationale des Femmes de Tunisie (UNFT) to pursue the task of female emancipation. In the spring of 1957, for the first time in Tunisian history, women were given the vote in municipal elections, and continued to vote in all subsequent elections. The UNFT by 1960 claimed 40,000 members and 5,000 Neo-Destour girls, organized in 85 sections throughout Tunisia's urban centers.[31] It encouraged women to vote, sponsored conferences to teach them their new rights and duties, and carried out welfare projects such as establishing kindergartens.

Having neutralized Zitouna by his reform of education, Bourguiba attacked the strongest of the traditional five pillars of Islam—the hallowed custom of fasting during the month of Ramadan, the one clearly visible manifestation of Islamic social solidarity. Even the Tunisians most deeply influenced by Western education and values adhered to the fast in their country, at least in public. Yet Bourguiba dared to attack it on the grounds that it paralyzed economic and administrative activity during a whole month. "At a time when we are doing everything possible to increase our production, how," he asked, "can we resign ourselves to give up our efforts and permit the production level to descend to the zero mark?"[32]

More than three weeks before Ramadan, on February 5, 1960, Bourguiba launched his campaign before the nation's political cadres. He outlined his new plan to provide full employment on government work sites and insisted that this mass mobilization not be impeded by "religious barriers."

I do not believe that religion should be able to impose such a sacrifice. . . . This is an abusive interpretation of the religion. When fasting, man's physical forces are so depleted that he is obliged to cease all activity. No dogma is justification for such a rhythm. . . . All practices of this religion are issues

[30]Ibid.
[31]La Femme Tunisienne (1961), p. 46.
[32]Speech, February 5, 1960.

of logical intentions. But when they become incompatible with the necessary struggles of this life, this religion must be amended.

Although, in the original extemporaneous Arabic, Bourguiba's speech was said to be even more virulently opposed to fasting than the translated text suggested, he was careful to present his new policy as a reform rather than as an attack on religion. He claimed to have consulted the Grand Mufti, Abdelaziz Djait, and Tahar Ben Achour, the rector of Zitouna, before making the speech. "I am not asking the people to give up the fast. . . . But I am saying that if the fast risks endangering your health or interrupts the activity which is your means of living, . . . then Si El Aziz Djait is there to give you the authorization to break this fast, which you will execute later when you are on vacation or retired." Working hours during Ramadan would remain unchanged. Cabarets and "indecent spectacles" that had previously made night life during Ramadan a grand popular holiday would be prohibited. Bourguiba concluded with an appeal for national progress: "We are obliged to throw out the worst customs. We must be devoted to progress and not lose sight of our goal."

One week later Djait made the promised fetwa, but it was not what Bourguiba had expected. Fasting remained a religious duty, to be excused only in cases of illness or military jihad. Djait praised Bourguiba for closing the nightclubs, the real cause of fatigue during Ramadan, and urged the faithful to work hard. But they were not to receive a dispensation. Djait and Ben Achour soon lost their official positions.

On February 18, Bourguiba made another appeal to the public in which he gave his own interpretation of the Quran. "As Head of a Muslim state, I also may speak in the name of religion. . . . If I asked advice from these professors [Djait and Ben Achour], it is because our action must benefit from unanimous agreement. . . . Unfortunately our professors belong to a certain category of people who refuse to reason and judge according to past experience and the teachings of the Quran." Underlining the challenge of the explosion of France's first atomic bomb in nearby Algeria, Bourguiba asserted that economic development was Tunisia's true jihad. He concluded: "In so far as the young prove to be incapable of coping with the effort of work and fasting, we must be tolerant. They can then break their fast with a quiet conscience. This is my fetwa."[33]

Bourguiba modified working hours of the administration and on government work sites, but adhered to his earlier stand in the face of

[33]Speech, February 18, 1960.

widespread opposition among the men of religion, troubled consciences within his own party, and doubt among some of his ministers.
In his political stronghold of Sousse, where most party militants were
religious conservatives, he addressed another meeting on the subject
of Ramadan, and he described his opponents as being "those slightly
hit by the regime—revoked qaids, retired teachers, dishonest civil
servants, clients of the *Haute Cour* who have lost their lands or jobs.
All this attractive crowd claim to constitute the last stronghold for the
defense of religion. Their real motives are, however, quite clear."[34]
"Divine law," he argued, "is not a monopoly. We also know how to
interpret it." Bourguiba told his party militants about antinational in-
terpretations of the Quran which the old scholars had made during
the Protectorate.[35] He concluded with a warning: "I do not want
those who are able to fast and keep up with their daily work to provoke or scorn those who are not able to do so. Such mockery will be
punished by the police force and by the national courts. . . . We must
not force hypocrisy on those who cannot stand the fast."

Bourguiba's campaign had few immediate results. Most Tunisians
continued to fast, except in Tunis, where civil servants and students
were no longer ashamed to eat in public. Perhaps the most significant
effect of the campaign, apart from emphasizing the new "struggle
against underdevelopment," was to present the problem of fasting as
a matter of personal conscience rather than social reflex. Some Muslims, even those who fasted, were coming to feel that they had a right
to personal interpretation of their religion.

In 1961 Bourguiba reiterated his appeal, though "many of my friends
have advised me against bringing up the subject, for fear of upsetting
public opinion."[36] Bourguiba admitted that, while the "overwhelming
majority of Destourians" understood his position, there were still "some
misgivings and apprehensions." He was more modest about asserting
his point of view, for, while arguing that the Quran should be liberally
interpreted to allow for Tunisia's vitally needed economic development, he said: "I am putting this forward as my personal opinion.
You are under no compulsion to share it. . . . I am certain that the
youth of the country will adopt my opinions. . . . Sooner or later my
views will prevail." Bourguiba had pressed the psychological revolu-

[34]Speech, February 26, 1960. The Haute Cour was a special tribunal set up in
1956 to try Bourguiba's political opponents.
[35]In 1917, when Tunisians were mobilized for agricultural work in war-torn
France, the Sheikh El Islam gave them dispensation from fasting because "these
workers have gone to accomplish their mission . . . not of their own free will but
under compulsion from another and by order of their sovereign."
[36]Speech, February 8, 1961.

tion as far as possible, and by Ramadan of 1961 there were signs that
much of Tunisian society had remained impervious to his claims as a
religious reformer. It would take many years and the full force of
Bourguiba's educational reforms over a period of time to change the
old conservative mentality.

Religious leaders had in small ways demonstrated their disapproval
of Bourguiba's Ramadan policy in 1960. In Kairouan they had celebrated the beginning and the end of Ramadan one day later than
Tunis had. By this gesture they rejected Bourguiba's scientific determination of the lunar month and followed Cairo's lead. The religious
leaders in Sfax followed Kairouan, and the party in these areas was
internally divided and not sufficiently powerful to persuade the people
to obey the government policy. In 1961 the head imam of the Zitouna
mosque, one of the Enniffers, was discharged for wishing to celebrate
the end of Ramadan one day late. (He was replaced by the brother
of the governor of Tunis.) Natural disasters, such as floods, insufficient
rains, and a slight earthquake near Monastir, were interpreted as
signs of Allah's disapproval of Bourguibist heresies.

Popular discontent was focused in Kairouan with incidents on January 17, 1961, one month before Ramadan. Mobs shouting "Allah is
great, he will not depart" converged on the governor's official house
in what seemed to be an attempt to lynch him. Cars were burned and
some of the mob penetrated the residence. The police, the National
Guard, and army detachments quelled the rioting only after twenty-
four hours of fighting.[37] This was the first serious protest against the
regime since Bourguiba had consolidated power.

The immediate issue which had precipitated the riots was the governor's decision to transfer a teacher, Abderrahman Khelif, from Kairouan.[38] As second imam of Kairouan's most important mosque, he had
delivered sermons castigating the religious policy of the regime,
especially its attitude toward Ramadan (he had also criticized the
government for permitting an Italo-American film company to shoot
scenes in the mosque). The masses, considering their religion in jeop-
ardy with the removal of this popular imam, protested.

Three weeks after the riots, in his conciliatory speech about Ramadan, Bourguiba gave a more complex explanation relating to Kairouan's social structure, In the first place, religious leaders like Khelif

[37]About eight were killed when the authorities opened fire, and some of the mob
seem to have been armed, for one National Guardsman was killed.
[38]Khelif had been a sufficiently distinguished student at Zitouna to be appointed
director of Zitouna's annex in Kairouan, when it was controlled by Zitouna
authorities. When the government in 1956 took charge of the annexes, Khelif was
demoted, though he remained a schoolteacher in Kairouan.

"feel nothing but hatred" toward the regime. "In order to oppose the State, they seize on the religious pretext by which they can stir up simple people. . . . Their grievance [of the real instigators] against Governor Amor Chechia is based on much more serious considerations: on the government's orders, he attacked certain strongholds of privilege, and he has not been forgiven for this."

Bourguiba singled out the Mrabet family for attack. They had owned huge tracts of land which the government progressively had taken away. Much of it was private habous, which in part, by virtue of the 1957 law, reverted to the bedouin cultivators rather than to the landlord. Then by virtue of a law passed on May 7, 1959, concerning "insufficiently exploited" land, large remaining tracts were confiscated by the government.[39] Other rich Kairouan landowners were also hurt by the regime, because they were no longer allowed to exploit their tenant debtors. The old bourgeois families were the natural allies of religious families. Indeed, the two were often the same family, and constituted a tenacious elite opposed to the regime. They could, as Bourguiba suggested, use their religious prestige for personal interests. But in the last analysis the Kairouan events showed that religious symbols had greater mass appeal than the Neo-Destour's political symbols, at least in Kairouan. The same was probably true also of Sfax, where olive-oil riches and piety were twin attributes of the elite but where the rich had not been as hard hit by the regime's land legislation.

In the short run Bourguiba's psychological offensive at modernization had only limited successes. Most Tunisians—probably in increasing numbers since 1960—continued publicly to observe the fast.[40] Most of the women even in Tunis continued to wear the veil, though their daughters in school did not. Politically, Bourguiba had been able to go very far—the reorganization of justice, the Code of Personal Status, the land and educational reforms were important and original achievements in a Muslim country—largely because by careful diplomacy he had neutralized the old religious elite. But the outcome of his Ramadan policy showed the obstacles which remained before Islam could be used as a positive instrument or social change.

[39]Bourguiba omitted, however, to mention less fortunate aspects of government land policy in Kairouan. During the previous autumn 5,000 ha. of land taken over by the government had been sold cheaply to Hassen Ben Abdelaziz, the famous fellagha leader of the Sahel. When he tried to expel Bedouin squatters from his land, he needed the armed intervention of the National Guard. Though the government later withdrew the land from the fellagha, its progressive populist orientation in land distribution could be questioned.

[40]Nevertheless, in 1964 Bourguiba tried to set an example during Ramadan by drinking a glass of orange juice at a public rally!

The Heritage of Internal Opposition

Widespread religious discontent was too diffuse and disorganized to threaten Bourguiba's political position. But Bourguiba as the educator and emancipator of his nation was challenged also on more specifically political grounds within his own party. Even before independence, the new nation almost fell apart under the explosive impact of the Youssefist opposition.

"Youssefism," so named after Salah Ben Youssef, Bourguiba's chief aide as general secretary of the Neo-Destour Party until 1955, is significant in the present analysis primarily for illustrating the fragility of any leader's popular appeal in the Tunisian milieu. It suggests that *charisma*, even watered down to mean the gift of political popularity, may often prove an empty concept. More concretely, the Youssefist appeal showed Bourguiba, who previously had always had the crowds spontaneously on his side against the colonial adversary, that he could not rule without a political instrument subservient to his will.

Bourguiba's welcome home on June 1, 1955, after a final three years of prison and exile, had seemed a living national plebiscite not only for the man but for the Franco-Tunisian Conventions upon which he had staked his career. These Conventions, a compromise granting Tunisia home rule but not independence, contained much, especially concerning internal security and the police, that was rankling to the nationalists.[41] Bourguiba, however, managed to keep control of the party apparatus and gain the support of most of the veteran leaders, along with that of young Ahmed Ben Salah's powerful UGTT. By the end of the summer, when a new all-Tunisian transitional government was being formed to apply the Conventions, Salah Ben Youssef and Bahi Ladgham were the only important holdouts.

In exile in Cairo since 1952, Ben Youssef was exposed to the extremist climate of the Arab Maghreb Liberation Committee. Not sur-

[41]The police was to be headed by a French national for ten years, and certain key police jobs were to remain in French hands for twenty years. French security services would continue their activities, and the French would maintain borders, airports, and a number of military installations. Thus the French Resident, henceforth to have the title of High Commissioner, and the commander of the French armed forces in Tunisia were to wield considerable influence in Tunisia's domestic affairs. Moreover, there were objectionable provisions designed to protect the vital interests of the French settlers. For five years, until mixed courts could be established, existing French courts were to have jurisdiction over the 180,000 French citizens in Tunisia. In townships having a substantial European minority, this minority was to be given roughly proportional representation on the elected town councils. Consultative economic organs, such as mixed chambers of commerce grouping both Tunisians and Frenchmen, were to remain unchanged. In the civil service the positions of Frenchmen with tenure, some 8,000 out of 13,500, were guaranteed; thus rapid tunisification appeared out of the question.

prisingly, the Algerians and the Moroccans, still waging guerrilla warfare, were opposed to any lessening of political tensions in Tunisia.[42] Moreover, even though he had been Bourguiba's closest collaborator since the mid-thirties, Ben Youssef, seven years younger, was ambitious. Most Tunisians who knew him would probably agree with this description of his abilities:

A redoubtable polemicist, intelligent and passionate, primarily a political animal, he had an instinct for diatribe, for debate, for assertion and for compromise. A prolific and skillful talker, he knew in conversation how to seduce in trying to convince. He also possessed the art—by his lucidity, sincerity, tricks, calculations, and skillful dosing—of electrifying a crowd by utilizing the resources of dialectic as well as the arsenal of passionate slogans.[43]

Perhaps there was not room in the Neo-Destour for two Bourguibas! Personal jealousy of Bourguiba more than Cairo Pan-Arabism seems to have been at the root of Ben Youssef's intransigent rejection of the Conventions.

After repeated invitations by Bourguiba, still hoping for a reconciliation,[44] Ben Youssef returned to Tunis on September 13 and resumed his duties as general secretary, but only to lambast the Conventions as "a step backward" and publicly to attack the Political Bureau, the party's supreme executive organ.[45] As a democrat Bourguiba had once argued that "the existence . . . of several *tendances* in the nationalist movement proves at least that our party is not totalitarian . . . ,"[46] but the Political Bureau could not allow one of its members flagrantly to contradict it. On the evening of October 8 it voted to strip Ben Youssef

[42]After the Conventions were signed, Al-Fassi of the Istiqlal Party called them "a big betrayal" of the Maghreb's anticolonialist cause; the Algerians, having begun their armed uprising on November 1, 1954, were bitterly opposed to any Neo-Destour compromise with France. Nasser until 1956 had little interest in North Africa, but remained on good terms with the Maghreb bureau.

[43]*Afrique-Action*, August 19, 1961.

[44]Recalling his own return from exile in 1949, when the shoe was on the other foot, Bourguiba said he hoped that Ben Youssef would "do the same to disappoint our adversaries who expect everything from a scission." *Le Petit Matin*, September 13, 1955.

[45]The last regularly elected bureau had been constituted in 1948; of the ten members, only Bourguiba, Ben Youssef, Slim, Fares, and Belhaouane were members in 1955. New leaders had been coöpted in Ben Youssef's absence. Taieb Mehiri, who when not in prison had been the acting director of the party since 1952, was officially appointed to this position. Ahmed Tlili, important for his connections with the Gafsa fellaghas and the UGTT, was appointed treasurer of the party. Sadok Mokaddem and Mohammed Masmoudi were appointed to the new Political Bureau, giving Bourguiba and the Conventions a clear majority in any showdown with Ben Youssef.

[46]*Le Petit Matin*, June 1, 1955.

of his office and expel him from the party. Ladgham, who meanwhile had returned from exile, became the new general secretary in return for his support of Bourguiba and the Conventions.

But Ben Youssef—like Ben Bella in an analogous context at Algerian independence seven years later—was politically isolated only at the top of the party hierarchy. Public opinion was in his favor where it counted most: Tunis. Those who supported the Conventions were on the defensive and could only argue, in apparent paradox, that they were a practical means of attaining independence. Within the party many militants, having worked closely with Ben Youssef in the past, were unhappy about his exclusion from the party. After all, he had controlled it during Bourguiba's absence from 1945 to 1949, and had placed many of his own followers in the apparatus. He had virtually created UTAC and UGAT and enjoyed close relations with Hached and other UGTT leaders. Outside the party Ben Youssef's intransigence appealed to four main groups. Coming from Djerba, he had the unquestioned support of most Djerbans. These formed a powerful class of small shopkeepers and large retailers who virtually monopolized the food trade throughout Tunisia.[47] Ben Youssef had a sympathetic audience also among the urban youth and masses who were politicized—ready to respond to extremist slogans—without being effectively organized. From their ranks his faction could recruit shock troops with Djerban money. The traditionalist arch-enemies of the Neo-Destour, too, were potential Youssefist allies or sympathizers. Significantly, Ben Youssef delivered his opening attack on Bourguibist policies in the Zitouna mosque.[48] A fourth group supporting Ben Youssef were landowners in UGAT who feared the rise to power of a coalition of Bourguiba and the UGTT.

Another factor favoring the Youssefist campaign was public impatience with the new government.[49] Mongi Slim, as the new minister of

[47]The few Djerbans who did not back Ben Youssef were experienced party militants whose loyalty to the Neo-Destour proved greater than regional attachments.
[48]The old Destour barely existed as an organization, but continued to exercise influence among the old families and opposed the Conventions, complaining that the unification of French and Tunisian courts would imply a secular legal code incompatible with Islam! See the communique of Salah Farhat, general secretary of the Destour, in *Le Petit Matin*, August 27, 1955.
[49]Its composition differed little from that of the previous transitional government. Tahar Ben Ammar, an independent landowner with a moderately nationalist reputation, remained as prime minister. The four Neo-Destour ministers, Slim, Masmoudin, Nouira, and Mokaddem, were joined by Fares and three party sympathizers, but the government remained heterogeneous. On October 7, in an effort to dam the disorderly flow of impatient demands upon the new government, the Political Bureau went so far as to make a public appeal for "stopping all agitation concerning schools, private and collective lands" and asking militants to use legal channels to solve their problems.

interior and key Neo-Destour channel, was submerged in a flood of rising political and patronage expectations. Old militants—veteran fellagha[50] and terrorists who had "fought so that you can occupy your present comfortable position while we get nothing"— constantly harassed Slim, who in applying the Conventions was involved in continuous negotiations with the French. Slim was under fire even from the Bourguibist press[51] for not proceeding rapidly enough in replacing antinationalist qaids with good Destourians. The country's administration was verging on chaos because the Tunisian civil servants of the old regime, to whom the French had transferred power, had little authority over the Neo-Destour activists in the countryside.

Bourguiba, Ladgham, and Mehiri, however, prudently remained outside the unpopular government. They scheduled the party's long-awaited congress for November 15 in order to allow themselves time to organize it without giving Ben Youssef enough time to set up an effective apparatus inside the party. The choice of the site was also astute; the Political Bureau avoided Tunis, where Ben Youssef's popular appeal was greatest, for Sfax, whose business community had never tolerated the infiltration of Djerban merchants.

Ben Youssef's reactions to the Political Bureau's offensive were clumsy. First he argued that the party's statutes did not permit the Political Bureau to expel the secretary general. Then he said that he would contact the rank and file before November 15 and try to change the party's policy at the congress.[52] Pressed for time two weeks later, he asserted that only the secretary general had the right to convene the party's congress and that he would schedule it for early 1956.[53] He called on the Neo-Destour branches to boycott the November 15 meeting.

The Political Bureau exploited its major organizational assets; despite Ben Youssef's mass appeal in Tunis, the Bourguibists held on to the Tunis Federation[54] and could neutralize Ben Youssef's speaking

[50]The fellagha, or guerrilla fighters, were those who had taken up arms against the French in the spring of 1954. When they disbanded in late 1954, under an agreement between the Neo-Destour and the French authorities, 2,500 of them were counted. Including terrorists, those classified as "resistants" numbered 7,047, and it was many months before the government could award property or business concessions to these restless heroes.
[51]L'Action, November 7, 1955.
[52]Le Petit Matin, October 14, 1955.
[53]Ibid., November 1, 1955.
[54]Ali Zlitni and Tahar Amira, who had accompanied Ben Youssef to Bandung, had been elected, respectively, president and vice-president of the federation in the autumn of 1954, while in exile. During their absence Ben Djaffar, the secretary general, had exercised effective leadership with Taieb Sahbani, another officer of the federation. Zlitni and Amira, when they returned with Ben Youssef in Sep-

tours. In Tunis the Bourguibists even set up secret security committees to find out who was attending Youssefist meetings and who could be influenced to favor the Political Bureau. At the Sfax congress a majority of the Tunis delegation supported Bourguiba and, in conjunction with the UGTT, pushed for the acceptance of radical social and economic principles.

While Ben Youssef tried to outline what opposition to the Conventions might entail—"It doesn't mean one must take up the battle again with sticks and scythes"—Ben Salah spoke eloquently for the Conventions and the pressing need for democratic institutions.[55] In Kairouan Ben Youssef delivered a diatribe against the Conventions when UGAT offered its locale as a speaking place, but the Political Bureau mobilized militants from other parts of Tunisia to heckle Ben Youssef with cries of "Yahia Bourguiba" and to block him from visiting neighboring tribesmen. Ben Youssef gained little from the trip because he could have counted anyway on the support of the conservative religious and landowning families of the medina. Like Taalbi eighteen years previously, he was made to look ridiculous because public authorities had to protect him from the mobs. On a trip to the northern provinces his appeal was neutralized by the party's mass organization. Conversely, even in hostile Kairouan the masses, conveniently augmented by youth groups from other party federations, were on Bourguiba's side when he made a fighting speech to counteract Ben Youssef's trip. When Ben Youssef wanted to tour Gabes and the south, the federation and national organizations were persuaded to cable him not to come for fear of tribal incidents.

The Neo-Destour congress confirmed the success of the Political Bureau's tactics. Ben Youssef's boycott failed. Of the 1,314 regular delegates, only 54 did not show up.[56] Even Tahar Amira, one of Ben Youssef's sympathizers, participated with the Tunis Federation and gave the congress a representative flavor.

On the opening day, Bourguiba forcefully expressed his point of view. Tunisia was to be an Arab and Muslim nation, but this would not hinder it from coöperating with France and constituting a link between two civilizations. Bourguiba promised, however, that he would

---

tember, enjoyed great prestige as veteran militants, but it was Ben Djaffar and Sahbani who had daily contact with the branches. At meetings they subtly sabotaged the efforts of Zlitni, who tried to present himself as the moderator between Bourguiba and Ben Youssef. Sahbani and Ben Djaffar remained unequivocally Bourguibist and systematically influenced the federation's militants.

[55] *Le Petit Matin*, October 25, 1955.

[56] *National Congress of Sfax* (published by the Neo-Destour Party, 1956, available only in Arabic), p. 50.

ask France for revision of certain Conventions, notably for the creation
of a national Tunisian army. French technicians in the government,
too, would be replaced as Tunisians were trained. Bourguiba hinted
that he would soon achieve Ben Youssef's goal of total independence
by negotiations with France. Referring to Ben Youssef's ties with the
old Destour, he concluded that "this disagreement [is not] . . . a scission, but we esteem simply that some elements have come to join the
partisans of the old party.[57] To allow the congress to judge the conflict between the two men, he suggested that it invite Ben Youssef to
explain his position.

Ben Youssef's reply to the telegram took the Political Bureau by
surprise. On the eve of the congress Ladgham had phoned Ben Youssef to invite him, and the latter had categorically refused. But his
answer to the congress' telegram was to thank it for thereby recogniz-
ing his status as secretary general and to ask for a week's postpone-
ment so that he could bring cell representatives from his newly formed
federal secretariat to the congress.[58] Ben Youssef's answer dampened
the momentum of the congress, for many delegates, desiring party
unity above all, were tempted by his suggestion. Work in the political
commissions flagged in an atmosphere of hesitation.

Bourguiba broke the stalemate by abruptly presenting the congress
with a political resolution. By dint of his strong personality and
theatrical flair, he persuaded the delegates to vote and to ignore the
few Ben Youssef sympathizers who objected to the irregular procedure. Unopposed, the resolution approved "without reserve" the policies of all the Political Bureaus since 1952 and expressed its confidence
in Bourguiba and the Political Bureau "for the complete realization of
the democratic work of political, social, and economic emancipation,
which remains the aim and *raison d'être* of the Neo-Destour."[59]

The general-policy resolution effectively stole Ben Youssef's slogans
by proclaiming that "total independence remains the final goal," and
suggesting the means to attain the goal: "the rapid application [by
the government] of all the Conventions." In the subsequent elections
for the Political Bureau, the congress ratified a Bourguibist slate.[60]

[57]*Les Congrès du Néo-Destour* (1959), p. 72.
[58]*National Congress of Sfax*, p. 48.
[59]*Les Congrès du Néo-Destour*, p. 75.
[60]All the members of the provisional bureau formed in June— Fares, Slim, Belhaouane, Mokaddem, Tlili, Mehiri, Masmoudi—were easily elected. Ladgham received the largest number of votes, and was Bourguiba's choice to replace Ben
Youssef as secretary general. Hedi Nouira, a member of the Political Bureau before 1954 and one of Bourguiba's closer associates, was easily elected. For the
tenth place on the Political Bureau, Abdallah Farhat, who had also been assisting
the old bureau, was elected against Ahmed Mestiri, Taieb Slim (Mongi's brother),
and Tahar Amira, who received the smallest number of votes.

Ben Salah and his close friend Mustapha Filali achieved a significant victory, the fruit of the UGTT's alliance with Bourguiba. Filali's progressive economic report[61] was enthusiastically adopted by the congress, and Filali received the most votes in the subsequent elections by the congress of National Council members. Ben Salah's strategy, that the UGTT give Neo-Destour policy a progressive social and economic content, seemed successful. In a special resolution the congress called for respect of trade-union rights, and notably the "right to strike in all sectors of work."

The congress marked a turning point in the struggle between Bourguiba and Ben Youssef, for Bourguiba had won the political battle on a ground of his own choosing. Ben Youssef weakly argued that the congress was illegal because only the secretary general had the right to convene a congress, but, to the disciplined party militant, Bourguiba and the Political Bureau now clearly represented the Neo-Destour's true orientation. As if to justify Bourguiba's hopes for Franco-Tunisian coöperation, it was at this time that the exiled Sultan of Morocco was allowed to return home. Anticolonialist violence no longer made sense in either country.

But, after Sfax, Ben Youssef defied all rules of political logic and brought Tunisia to the verge of civil war. Wherever a Neo-Destour branch existed, he tried to find a few friends to set up a rival branch which claimed to be the true branch of the party in the area.[62] By the end of November, urban terrorism erupted.[63] In January, Youssefists under Tahar Lassaoued resorted to guerrilla warfare in the mountainous regions of west-central Tunisia. Neo-Destour branches were raided, leaders assassinated, money extorted, and village populations inducted into the Youssefist organization. Lassaoued was able to re-

[61]The report called for the revision of the Convention protecting large foreign companies, nationalization of the public habous, limitation of private habous, transformation of collective lands into coöperatives, and fragmentation of large irrigated holdings—policies which Bourguiba's government subsequently carried out, but only after it had neutralized the UGTT.
[62]By mid-January his secretariat claimed to have set up 747 branches loyal to Ben Youssef.
[63]In Tunis a journalist who had taken pictures of Ben Youssef was shot dead. In nearby Cap Bon armed fighting broke out between Neo-Destour and Youssefist branches. The party's old terrorist bands which had remained loyal to Bourguiba were mobilized to counter Ben Youssef, and his chauffeur was assassinated in the heart of Tunis on December 1. Near Kairouan, Youssefists machine-gunned a party branch headquarters. On the following day Moktar Ben Attiya, a Djerban in UTAC who had been closely involved with the Political Bureau's clandestine efforts in 1953, was one of several individuals to be assassinated, perhaps because he had wished to remain neutral. Two weeks later a joint communiqué of the Tunisian Government and the French High Commission revealed the existence of a Youssefist 150-200-man armed gang with assassination plans.

cruit a number of Algerians into his bands, though the FLN had ordered their bands to remain neutral.

The Neo-Destour had cause for alarm. Many party cadres were new members who had entered in 1954. Notaries, sheikhs, and school-teachers, they were respected members of their local communities but had not been reliable militants filtered through the party's youth apparatus. Isolated from the masses, they were obeyed more out of habit than by conviction. Furthermore, within the branches and federations, local rivalries facilitated Youssefist penetration.[64] Perhaps the greatest danger was that the cells were no longer effectively mobilizing the youth, who were running in large numbers to Ben Youssef.[65] The Arabic press, except for the official Neo-Destour daily, sympathized with the political renegades.

The government was in a quandry because it did not exercise control over public security, still largely in the hands of the French.[66] Only in mid-January did it finally crack down on Ben Youssef. When he was refused permission to hold a congress, he answered: "We go to war with the Government." Mehiri then explained at a Neo-Destour meeting that conciliation with Youssefism was no longer possible. On January 28 the police launched a three-day operation during which 120 Youssefists were arrested; Ben Youssef himself was tipped off and managed to escape to Tripoli.

At the end of January it was estimated that there were 600 neo-fellagha throughout Tunisia. Although grouped mostly in the west-central plateaus, 140 were said to be in the Sahel, normally Bourguiba's stronghold.[67] The ambush of local Neo-Destour leaders continued, and one distinguished federation leader, Husain Bouzaiane, was assassinated in his home town of Gafsa late in March, immediately after being elected to Tunisia's new Constituent Assembly. In the Tunis area the last of the Youssefist terrorists were not caught until mid-

[64]Local vendettas having only an incidental relation to national politics were the cause of violence in some villages, especially in the Sahel. In some areas, Neo-Destour leaders may have used Youssefism as an excuse to discredit their rivals. In Thala important local landowners were accused of Youssefism when in fact they were simply afraid of mistreatment by the victorious local Neo-Destour leader, who had been appointed qaid of the area by Mongi Slim.

[65]See the article in L'Action, December 5, 1955, analyzing the weaknesses of the party's organization which the Youssefist campaign was unveiling.

[66]In mid-December the French handed over the first mobile security units to the Tunisians, but the transfer was gradual and the French were unwilling to take the responsibility for arresting Youssefists. The loyalty of the French police to the Tunisian government was far from certain, and in early 1956 there were incidents suggesting the complicity of some policemen with both Youssefist and colon terrorist groups.

[67]Le Petit Matin, January 29, 1956.

May. Whole tribes in the center and south joined Tahar Lassaoued's guerrilla "army," and only in mid-June, after a full-scale French military operation in Matmata, did the last of the Youssefists lay down their arms—three months after Tunisian independence had destroyed whatever rationale the movement had once had.

Resort to violence seems to be a chronic Tunisian reaction to political competition. Had the French not been in full control of the police in 1937, the dispute between Taalbi and Bourguiba might have verged on civil war. For twenty years the Neo-Destour was an underground organization more than half of the time, and the experience of revolutionary violence helped as much to shape the political habits of the party militants as did the liberal principles voiced by its leaders. Violence, too, was encouraged by the absence during these transitional months of Tunisian history of a coherent administration for law and order.

Whatever its explanation, Youssefism by its unfortunate memories crucially influenced subsequent Tunisian political development. In the short run its failure enhanced the prestige and political power of a new political generation that had combated Youssefism: the young Bourguibists in the party apparatus led by Taieb Mehiri and the UGTT led by Ahmed Ben Salah. In the long run Youssefism demonstrated the overwhelming need in Tunisia for strong organization. The liberal and orderly competition of different political groupings was no longer a realistic alternative to one-party rule.

Bourguiba's faith in the rationality of the average Tunisian had been severely undermined. Hitherto the crowds had always been on his side, and national unity had been reflected in the enthusiastic faces at party rallies—easily organized whenever the French had permitted political activity. But during the Youssefist campaign these enthusiastic crowds showed how easily they could be turned away from Bourguiba. As one Neo-Destour leader lamented, "If you put them in a bottle they will take its shape." Any demagogue could sway them, regardless of the justice of his cause, to violence if necessary. The lesson was clear: never again could a demagogue be tolerated who might oppose Bourguiba.

The idea of a loyal neutralist and Pan-Arab party opposing Bourguiba's pro-Western orientation was proved by bitter experience to be utopian.[68] Furthermore, Ben Youssef's popularity showed Bourguiba how dangerous religious and Pan-Arab slogans might be. Although the Neo-Destour had existed for more than twenty years, Youssefism

[68] *L'Action* had expressed a hope for a loyal opposition party on October 24, 1955, just after Ben Youssef's expulsion from the Neo-Destour.

revealed the durability of the old Destour's extremist orientation in public opinion. Stable consensus did not yet exist in Tunisia, and its absence was all the more dangerous, given Bourguiba's international position as the leader of a small nation in a hostile world. Relations with France remained strained even after full independence was achieved, until the end of the Algerian war six years later. The Youssefist threat continued, however, as long as Ben Youssef, who took refuge in Cairo, remained politically active. Alliance between him, Nasser, and the FLN was always a possibility until Ben Youssef's assassination in August, 1961. During its early years of independence, Tunisia by artful diplomacy successfully countered the threat of such an alliance by supporting the FLN while, through its good relations with the United States, avoiding a full-scale French invasion. Supporting the FLN, however, involved the toleration on Tunisian soil of Algerian forces superior to those of the Tunisians. Thus the threat of Ben Youssef returning to Tunisia ("on a FLN tank," as one Youssefist exclaimed in 1960) always remained possible. To survive at all, Bourguiba could forge only one weapon for beleaguered Tunisia: political cohesion.

III PRESIDENTIAL MONARCHY

UNABLE TO RULE merely on the basis of his own popularity or *charisma*, Bourguiba during the first three years of independence hastened to consolidate power. The political system that emerged might aptly be described as presidential monarchy.[1] This term conveys the dual nature of Bourguiba's style of leadership—reminiscent of that of the traditional autocrat yet depending mainly upon modern political structures.

Bourguiba as the Bey's Successor

Even while combating Youssefism, Bourguiba was taking steps that led to presidential monarchy. Between late 1955 and 1959, a new Tunisian regime took shape. The Neo-Destour had no consistent theory about the sort of state it wanted to organize. Its leaders all favored constitutional democracy, but they were faced with a situation to which French political scripts no longer applied. The end product, a presidential constitution promulgated on June 1, 1959, had the merit of blending democratic ideals with the realities of tightened single-party rule under Bourguiba.

The Neo-Destour had intended the Tunisian Constituent Assembly, elected on March 25, 1956, to serve as a tactical political weapon as well as a parliament for drawing up a constitution. Acting in the name of the people, the Assembly would have the merit of undermining the Bey's authority[2] while inducing further concessions from the French[3] and thus neutralizing the ostensible basis of the Youssefist appeal.

[1] I have borrowed this term from David E. Apter's concluding chapter of *Ghana in Transition* (1963). Although de Tocqueville also used it, I was tempted to employ the more contemporary French term, "republican monarchy," coined by Michel Debré (see Nicholas Wahl, "The French Political system," in Beer and Ulam, *Patterns of Government*, rev. ed., 1962, p. 402), to characterize the Tunisian phenomenon that Gaullism has turned out in many respects to resemble. Tunisia, however, does not have an analogous republican tradition.

[2] The Bey had been a tardy and hesitant collaborator for the nationalist cause. Although the Neo-Destour had usually, through friends at court, been able to manipulate him, and occasionally even to write his speeches, the Bey had acted more out of fear of mass disapproval than from conviction.

[3] The French Resident was not unaware of this possibility even in January, 1955, more than a year before the election actually took place. In a report to Paris he wrote: "Bourguiba will not allow himself to be outflanked by Salah Ben Youssef.

71

The Bey and his advisers were aware of the dangers of a popular assembly, though the Neo-Destour had always publicly expressed allegiance to the idea of constitutional monarchy. In late 1955 *L'Action* accused the Bey and his entourage, assisted by Prime Minister Ben Ammar, of a "dangerous plot" unilaterally to proclaim a constitution, sidestepping a Constituent Assembly.[4] In fact, if Bourguiba is to be believed,[5] the plot went even deeper. Alarmed at the prospect of Bourguiba taking over power, the Bey tried to persuade France not to hand over certain police forces needed by the Tunisian Government to combat Youssefism. When the French High Commissioner disclosed this information, Bourguiba threatened the Bey with exposure and pressured him to sign the decree for the Constituent Assembly. On December 29, after weeks of delay, the Bey declared: "The Constitution elaborated by the Assembly will be adorned by Our seal and promulgated as the Constitution of the Kingdom."[6] The Bey's surrender was unconditional, for laws had always hitherto been "submitted to" his seal.

With a minimum of consultation even within the party,[7] the electoral law was drawn up to ensure the selection of deputies by party headquarters. Bourguiba declared that elections would be by straight majority list voting in order to make certain that the Assembly would produce a strong government. Under pressure, the Bey ratified Bourguiba's decision one week later.

. . . We therefore have the right to suppose that the Conventions, once signed, will be challenged in one way or another. . . . The only question is to know whether the Tunisians in this regard will use the simulated democracy of an Assembly that will declare itself constituent. . . . That is why I have always thought that a constitution was necessary to give our Conventions a minimum guarantee, for one does not conclude a treaty with a 'state in the process of becoming'" (Pierre Boyer de Latour, *Vérités sur l'Afrique du Nord* [1956], pp. 99-100). The Resident General's analysis was shrewd. The Constituent Assembly would probably have unilaterally proclaimed Tunisia's independence if France had not recognized it just before the Assembly was elected. On March 17, 1956, news came from Paris of a breakdown in the negotiations between Bourguiba and the French premier, Guy Mollet. The Assembly electoral campaign was already in full swing, and the immediate reaction of one important National Front candidate (Ahmed Ben Salah) was to promise his future constituents: "Our Constituent Assembly at its first session will declare total independence." See *Le Petit Matin*, March 18, 1956.

[4] *L'Action*, December 19, 1955.
[5] Speech, July 25, 1957.
[6] *L'Action*, January 2, 1956.
[7] Even the Bourguibist press protested that the government should consult the national organizations about the electoral law and not lose sight of the party's rank and file. *Ibid.*, December 26, 1955.

Few articulate Tunisians were happy about the electoral law. Mohammed Masmoudi, despite the fact that he was a minister and member of the Political Bureau, allowed the weekly paper *L'Action,* with which he was closely associated, to attack the law for facilitating "monolithic" majority rule. Masmoudi's "liberal" wing of the party had wanted the elections to be based on proportional representation, so that the Assembly would reflect all interests and encourage Ben Youssef to stage a parliamentary rather than a subversive opposition. Tunisia's small Communist Party also publicly attacked the law, and leaders of the old Destour and the baldi elite grumbled because the law shut them out of political life. Criticisms of the law were all based upon standards taken from French political life. It was assumed that proportional representation would have been fairer and more democratic.[8]

Straight majority voting meant that the party's lists would sweep the elections. Without the possibility of *panachage,* independents had no electoral chances unless selected by the party. Moreover, the eighteen constituencies were large enough to put local personalities at a disadvantage.[9]

After some discussion[10] the Political Bureau was mandated to draw up electoral lists in consultation with the UGTT, UTAC, and UNAT, a new farmer's organization which had replaced the Youssefist UGAT. Various interests would thus be expressed in the new assembly, but only in the context of a National Front orchestrated by the Political Bureau. Cohesion would be both horizontal and vertical: horizontally the national organizations were to keep in step with the Political Bureau, while vertically the electoral law assured the Political Bureau of effective control over any local party leader not included on its list who might be tempted to run as an independent.

The elections of March 25 turned out to coincide with Tunisian independence festivities—providing an additional display of national

[8]The omission of *panachage,* the device whereby an elector can replace a candidate of the list he favors by an opposing candidate, was also criticized. The fact, too, that women were not accorded the vote was criticized by the liberals.

[9]Perhaps as a result of difficulties Bourguiba encountered on a tour of the South, where Youssefist tribal sentiment was later expressed in armed uprisings, he had the Bey reduce the nineteen circumscriptions decided by the Council of Ministers to eighteen, and combined Kebili, Matmata, Mednine, and Tataouine.

[10]Mehiri defended the law to the party's high-ranking cadres at a National Council meeting. The party, he explained, had to combat "the forces of evil," the reactionary elements relying on colonial rule (presumably the old baldi families having connections with the Beylical court, the Zitouna mosque, or the old Destour). Conciliation with Youssefism was no longer possible. The electoral law, Mehiri argued, was really democratic because it gave the electors a choice between two mentalities, that of the reactionaries and that of the Neo-Destour populists.

unity. Opposition was limited to twelve ineffective Communist lists and a list in Sousse of independent lawyers who were sympathetic to the Neo-Destour.[11] There had been talk[12] of other opposition lists in Le Kef, led by a Youssefist sympathizer, and in Beja, but these never materialized. The Neo-Destour swept the elections, in which Communists and Independents attracted a bare 1.3 per cent of the total vote. The most successful opposition list, that of the Communists in Beja, won only 1,877 out of 25,615 votes. The elections thus respected democratic forms while consolidating the power of the single party. The silent opposition which abstained—71 per cent in Youssefist Djerba, 41 per cent in Tunis—was more significant than the legal opposition.

The hopes of party liberals that the Assembly would quickly draft a constitution and give way to a freshly elected parliament were submerged in interminable constitutional deliberations, interrupted by a national crisis whenever they seemed on the verge of success. In retrospect, the three years of delay served to consolidate Bourguiba's own position as a presidential monarch, whether or not that was his original intention. After months of preparation in Assembly commissions, the constitution, so it was rumored in February, 1957,[13] was to be promulgated by April 8, the anniversary of the Constituent Assembly. On this anniversary there was still no constitution; instead, Bourguiba praised the work of the Assembly and tried to justify its delays: "The framing of a Constitution implies choices which are too serious to be made lightly. Between a monarchy and a republic, constitutional monarchy and a presidential regime, for instance, the choice is delicate and merits reflection."[14] Three months later the Assembly deposed the Bey and proclaimed Tunisia a republic. Bourguiba was named president and given the Bey's full executive and legislative powers. The Assembly's commissions reconvened to revise the draft of the constitution to accord with Tunisia's new presidential regime. By January, 1958, it appeared that the new constitution was ready for ratification, but plenary discussions in the Assembly were interrupted by the bombardment of Sakiet Sidi Youssef by the French, and in the ensuing battle for the evacuation of French troops the deputies were sent on vacation.

[11]The latter argued that one of the Neo-Destour candidates, Ahmed Bellalouna, was not eligible because he had been appointed *kahia* in January by Mongi Slim. Legally the withdrawal of one candidate would have entailed the withdrawal of the whole list, but the Neo-Destour argued that Bellalouna had not taken up his administrative functions.

[12]*Le Petit Matin*, March 8, 1956.

[13]*L'Action*, February 11, 1957.

[14]Speech, April 8, 1957.

Constitutional discussions were not resumed until late in the following autumn, after the Neo-Destour party organization had been overhauled. By this time such discussions had lost their burning political interest, for Bourguiba's regime had gained the time it needed for consolidation.

The crucial constitutional question, that of the relationship between the executive power and the "sovereign" assembly, was resolved in practice long before the constitution-makers ratified the solution. When, on April 8, 1956, the Assembly convened for its inaugural session, the transitional prime minister, Tahar Ben Ammar, resigned. The French drama of ministerial crisis commenced with the new Tunisian players, the Bey weakly playing the role of a Fourth Republic president. Within the party, after discussions including the Political Bureau and important leaders of the national organizations, it was decided, considering the Youssefist menace, that Bourguiba should be prime minister and commit all his prestige to the new government. After consultation with leading Neo-Destour figures who communicated this decision, the Bey officially invested Bourguiba. But the French script was not followed in its entirety: when Bourguiba finally presented his government and outlined his program to the Assembly, massive applause took the place of a debate and vote.

Subsequently Bourguiba neatly sidestepped parliamentary control. When Ahmed Ben Salah, a deputy with French Republican reflexes, demanded that the Assembly vote on the government's budget and on its economic, social, and foreign policies, Bourguiba presented an alternative motion, adopted unanimously, which vaguely called upon the Assembly to "inspect" and "supervise" the government's activities. The motion did not provide for debates or voting on laws or policies; rather, the Assembly—and even its commissions—was restricted to constitution-making. Bourguiba rarely took his seat in the Assembly and preferred to rule through use of the Bey's unlimited legislative powers.

The government did consult the Assembly about the 1957-58 budget, but "modifications in the budget made by the government subsequent to approval by the Assembly further demonstrated its advisory role."[15] There was no consultation on the budget the following year. Occasionally in times of Franco-Tunisian crisis, the Assembly was called upon to pass political motions for propaganda purposes. A French observer has accurately if unkindly described the Assembly on these occasions:

[15]William S. Lee, "The Government of Tunisia since Independence," *Parliamentary Affairs*, 1960, p. 377.

Before the session, the Political Bureau of the Neo-Destour fixes the line to follow and the goals to attain. Its orders are then taken up by the Bureau of the Assembly. . . . During the meeting some of the deputies make speeches, then Mr. Bourguiba mounts the tribune, gives his opinion, and makes a flowing discourse. No one then dares to contradict him. So great is his prestige that it would seem sacrilegious to oppose him.[16]

Government-Assembly relations were further clarified with the deposition of the Bey on July 25, 1957. The deputies on a roll call unanimously voted to abolish the monarchy and call the new regime a republic. At the suggestion of Djalouli Fares, president of the Assembly (and member of the Political Bureau), they then acclaimed Bourguiba as Tunisia's first president. But this was no time to discuss the modalities of Bourguiba's new rule. Instead, after a ten-minute break in which to word his proposal, Fares presented a four-point declaration. The last point, which had not been discussed, stated: "We entrust the Government with the execution of this decision and with taking the necessary measures for the preservation of the Republican system."[17]

Within four days it was clear that "necessary measures" included taking all the legislative powers formerly belonging to the Bey. Fares told the press that the President of the Republic had received all the Bey's old prerogatives,[18] and Bourguiba's law of July 29, 1957, specifically stated: "The Law, adopted by a Cabinet Council grouping the secretaries of state concerned, is promulgated by the President of the Tunisian Republic and published in the *Journal Officiel*." Instead of presenting his new government to the Assembly, he in the end gave a banquet for his new government and Neo-Destour party cadres (many of whom were deputies). The Assembly was split up into its constitutional commissions to revise its work in light of the new situation. It did not meet again in plenary session until January 18, 1958. Exasperated, *L'Action* complained that the deputies did not work, received fat salaries, and "participated in a succession of interminable monologues that one calls debates."[19]

Perhaps "the proclamation of the Republic was a pretext seized by Bourguiba to avoid, until the vote on the Constitution, the supervision of the Assembly. . . ."[20] This, at any rate, was the effect, and Tunisian politicians had two more years of nonconstitutional government to as-

[16]Charles Debbasch, "L'Assemblée Constituante Tunisienne," *Revue Juridique et Politique d'Outre-Mer,* 1959, p. 42.
[17]National Assembly Debates, No. 1 (my translation from the Arabic text), in *Journal Officiel de la République Tunisienne* (1957).
[18]*Le Petit Matin,* July 28, 1957.
[19]*L'Action,* October 14, 1957.
[20]Debbasch, *op. cit.,* p. 50.

similate the new political style of a presidential regime. By virtue of the July 29 law, even the Council of Ministers was abolished. To em-phasize the fact that Bourguiba was no longer simply a first among equals or limited by a parliamentary system, his ministers were hence-forth called secretaries of state. Except for Ladgham, who was in charge of coördination between the secretariats, they in effect assumed the power and status of high-ranking civil servants.

The Constitution of 1959

By 1959 Bourguiba's presidential rule had taken root, and all po-tential centers of effective opposition to his government, both inside and outside the party, had been removed. The two opposition parties still existed, but they were too small to endanger Bourguiba's authority. It was now opportune to embody the actual style and structure of power in a formal constitution.

The constitutional debates reflected the increasingly authoritarian practice of the regime. By 1958 the broad features of the constitution had been decided. The president and a National Assembly were to be elcted for concurrent five-year terms by universal suffrage. Members of the government were responsible solely to the president, who exer-cised a legislative veto that could be overruled only by a two-thirds majority. In the course of the first reading, however, the deputies under government pressure modified subordinate features of the draft to accord more power to the president.

The Assembly was limited to meeting only six months of the year.[21] Investigation committees were quietly dropped because they suggested parliamentary supervision of the executive.[22] Although deputies re-tained the right to initiate legislation, projects presented by the presi-dent were now to be accorded "priority."[23] Moreover, the president was given the power to make decree laws when the Assembly was not in session.[24] His new emergency powers, too, were virtually un-

[21]The draft constitution, published in L'Action, January 13, 1958, called for the Assembly to be permanently in session, except during vacations that it might de-cide. (Art. 38). In the definitive constitution, the Assembly may meet in regular session no more than six months during the year; special sessions are convened only at the demand of the President of the Republic or a majority of the deputies (Art. 29).

[22]See Le Petit Matin, February 7, 1959. In the draft (Art. 42) the Assembly had the explicit right to elect investigation committees that were guaranteed access to any documents or explanations requested of the executive.

[23]Compare draft Article 45 with Article 28 of the Constitution.

[24]A standing commission of the Assembly must, however, consent to the decree law, and once in session the Assembly must ratify it (Art. 31). In the draft, the Assembly was specifically forbidden to delegate its legislative competence.

limited.[25] Even the role of the Assembly in a succession crisis was curtailed.[26]

Draft articles giving Tunisian citizens ambitious social rights disappeared in the course of the debates, reflecting the weakened position of the UGTT after 1956. The right to strike, solemnly proclaimed by the party in 1955, was omitted in the final text. Articles affirming the obligation of the state to provide free primary and secondary education, work, and medical care for all citizens were set aside.[27] Many classic civil liberties were written into the constitution—subject, however, to definition by positive law. Duties such as taxpaying and military service were included in the final text.

There was no formal press censorship in Tunisia. But in practice the suppression of the semi-official party weekly, L'Action, in 1958 (see below, pp. 90-92) meant the end of independent journalism, at least with regard to domestic politics. After occasional suspensions for nonconformity,[28] the nonparty papers learned to echo the political line of the government's Information Department.[29] In the autumn of 1960 two newspapers were allowed to appear: the weekly Afrique-Action and the monthly Tribune du Progrès. The former was run by

[25]According to Article 32 of the constitution, in cases of "imminent peril menacing the institutions of the Republic, the security or independence of the country and hindering the normal functions of the public authorities," the president may take any "exceptional measures demanded by the circumstances." The "measures" cease to be valid when the "circumstances" end, but it is left to the president to decide when that might be. He merely has to inform the Assembly of his measures. The Assembly is permitted to delegate its legislative powers to the president "for a limited period and for a determined objective" (Art. 28).

[26]In the draft, the Assembly is to choose a successor to the presidency within forty-eight hours. He must be a deputy (Art. 69). In the final constitution, the members of the presidential cabinet choose an interim successor among themselves, and after four weeks the Assembly elects the president, who need not be a deputy (Art. 51).

[27]It was at first decided—with sixteen UGTT and liberal deputies opposed (L'Action, February 3, 1958)—to send the articles back to commission to be incorporated into the constitution's preamble as aspirations. Later, at Ahmed Tlili's suggestion, the Assembly inserted into the body of the constitution: "The State occupies itself with procuring instruction, medical care, and work for the citizens" (Le Petit Matin, December 26, 1958). But in the end, the "citizen's right to work, health, and education" was merely alluded to briefly in the preamble. The right to property, "within the limits of the law," was, however, affirmed in the final text (Art. 14) after seven deputies, including one minister, had opposed it (L'Action, February 3, 1958).

[28]Es-Sabah in 1957 and La Presse in 1958 were suspended for a number of weeks.

[29]In May, 1961, Masmoudi, who was then secretary of information, complained that the drab dailies merely echoed official declarations. He urged Tunisian journalists to "make news commentaries and criticisms, if necessary" (La Presse, May 28, 1961). But it seems that the advice was not immediately heeded, and Masmoudi himself (for other reasons) was retired to the political wilderness several months later.

many of the people who had previously staffed *L'Action,* but it dealt with African rather than Tunisian themes.[30] The *Tribune* alone focused on domestic politics, but was tolerated for more than two years, presumably because its transparently Communist line served to limit its influence.[31] One result of the Bizerte crisis of 1961 was that one of the three French dailies ceased publication. By 1963, however, it appeared that the Neo-Destour daily press, supplemented by a new French language paper, *L'Action,* edited by an able young Neo-Destourian,[32] might play a more positive role in the shaping of critical, well-informed public opinion.

Freedom of association, like that of the press, was at best a limited right. Trade unions and professional associations were guaranteed by the law of January 10, 1959, which debarred them from politics and excluded all non-Tunisian (European settler) leadership. All other associations had to reapply to the Department of the Interior for permission to continue to exist.[33] In this way a number of European religious and philanthropic associations were arbitrarily dissolved. Tunisian Scouting groups, too, were merged under a single organization controlled by the Neo-Destour. The remnants of the European settler population were not the only group discriminated against: the fellow travelers and Communists who had set up a Tunisia-USSR Cultural Association in 1956 also discovered that their group had been outlawed.[34] The authorities instead recognized another group of the same name, hastily formed for the occasion. The latter was, of course, led by trusted Neo-Destour members.

The constitution called for an Economic and Social Council. Though the UGTT had originally hoped that the government would be constitutionally obliged to consult it on all economic and social policy, the latter sidestepped this demand. The Council was eventually formed in the spring of 1961 and consulted in 1962 on the government's Three-Year Plan, but consultation had already occurred mainly in govern-

[30]As the result of an editorial on October 7, 1961, which dealt harshly with domestic politics (see below, pp. 99-100), *Afrique-Action* was compelled to change its name to *Jeune-Afrique.* However, it continued publication under the same direction.

[31]In the tense political atmosphere that followed the discovery of a plot to assassinate Bourguiba in December, 1962, the *Tribune du Progrès* was suppressed, along with *At-Talia,* the official monthly Arabic newspaper of the Tunisian Communist Party.

[32]Mohammed Sayah, once a leader of the leftist student opposition to the party, had served ably as general secretary of UGET, 1960-1962 (see below, p. 177).

[33]By the law of November 7, 1959, their statutes were to be deposited with the authorities by June 30, 1960; if no answer was received within four months, an association could consider itself abolished.

[34]See *Tribune du Progrès,* No. 3 (February, 1961) and No. 5 (April, 1961).

ment commisions. The chambers of commerce and agriculture and mining, important economic pressure groups during the Protectorate, were with one exception abolished by presidential decree on October 10, 1957. The government claimed that international law does not recognize political rights for the foreigners who had played a preponderant role in these organizations.[35]

A Council of State was to play a crucial role in limiting the executive branch.[36] But three years after the constitution had taken effect there was still no immediate prospect of implementing legislation.[37] Tunisian citizens had no tribunal of appeal to check administrative abuses, unless they enjoyed good personal relations with higher civil servants or could catch the ear of the Neo-Destour or the president's private secretary.

The constitution provided for an independent judiciary, but judicial processes in Tunisia were sometimes arbitrary, as the Khallady affair illustrated. Chadly Khallady was a distinguished French-educated lawyer, an active nationalist who had been a member of the old Destour until 1948. A contemporary of Bourguiba, he was voted president of the Tunisian bar association in June, 1958, when the bar was reorganized to exclude a number of European lawyers. Although politically independent, he was supported by the Neo-Destour lawyers because he had the confidence of the newly integrated traditionally minded *mouhami* (who constituted a majority) as well as the French-educated lawyers. In September, 1961, he was defending a European whose lease on a Tunis nightclub had been abruptly canceled by the municipality in the wake of the Bizerte crisis. The municipality had impounded thousands of dollars worth of alcoholic beverages that belonged to the former manager. Khallady was suddenly arrested for having made a comment while leaving the courtroom about the municipality's *"spoliation."* Bourguiba was furious that the man he had

[35]*Le Petit Matin,* October 11, 1957. Actually, even in 1955 the mixed chambers had sometimes come under the strong influence of the Neo-Destour. In Sousse a Neo-Destour businessman became president of the mixed chamber of commerce by a series of astute political maneuvers. Under the October, 1957, law the Tunis chamber of commerce was permitted to continue its activities, because the Neo-Destour controlled it. In 1958, chambers of commerce were reëstablished in Sousse and Sfax under the supervision of the Neo-Destour and UTAC.
[36]It was to be divided into two judicial bodies, an administrative body dealing with disputes between individuals and the administration, and an auditing office to verify state accounts. The former body would deal "with those cases where the Administration is accused of exceeding its authority" (Art. 57).
[37]In the autumn of 1961 a government commission was established to examine the problem.

had elected to the bar dared to criticize an aspect of his government.[38] After weeks of official silence Khallady was tried and sentenced to three months of farm-prison. In stormy sessions the Tunis bar association was taken over by the Neo-Destour lawyers, and those who were brave enough to support Khallady were suspended from the bar. In early 1962, however, Bourguiba was solemnly proclaiming the independence of the judiciary.[39]

As the constitution took effect, it was clear that the regime under Bourguiba had become a very personal one. Composed almost exclusively of Neo-Destour militants subject to party discipline, the National Assembly of 1959 was to be even more of a rubber stamp for government policy than its predecessors in constitutional matters had been. Most debate took place inside the standing commissions away from the public eye. The president of the Assembly, the member of the Political Bureau who had also managed the Constituent Assembly, considered it to be his role, in cases of disagreement between the commissions and the government, to try to reconcile the differences. He maintained that, as a member of the Political Bureau, he had the final word because he was able to explain Bourguiba's and the party's real intentions on any troublesome legislation.[40] Bourguiba's speeches before the Assembly were designed to publicize decisions he had already made rather than to defend a point of view.

Indeed, presidential rule encouraged the emergence of a new personal style of leadership: Bourguiba had displaced the Bey to become Tunisia's new monarch. As Head of State, he not only inherited the Bey's old palaces[41] but proceeded to embroider upon the pageantry traditionally associated with the office. His daily arrivals and departures were celebrated by the martial music and sworded salutes of the former Beylical Guard. On religious holidays he played the Bey's old role, though with far greater éclat: the Bey's annual tour of the Tunis medina on the Night of Destiny (27 Ramadan) became an annual demonstration of political loyalty to Bourguiba, as the populace greeted him to the ritual chant of "Yahia Bourguiba!" ("Long live Bourguiba!") He seemed to enjoy playing the role expected of a good

[38]Possibly Bourguiba was using the incident to punish Khallady for a far graver offense: his bar association had omitted to take a strongly nationalistic stance on the Bizerte affair.

[39]La Presse, February 2, 1962.

[40]Interview, October 19, 1960.

[41]Bourguiba built or restored at least two presidential palaces. One palace, described by Jeune-Afrique (June 4, 1962) in an ironical tone that apparently went unremarked, had gilded bath faucets, a huge cupola hand-worked for three years, and a private theater overlooking the sea near Carthage.

traditional monarch. With regal largesse, he often distributed sums from his personal budget to needy municipalities[42] or charities—and to the needy bedouin woman who might accost him on the street. Reminiscent of the early Arab caliphs, he was accessible to everyone so far as time permitted. People would wait for hours outside his office to gain a sympathetic ear. Yet Bourguiba also lived in the age of mass media: the personality cult was reflected in the pictures of the Supreme Combatant in every office and shop. The newspapers and radio reported every detail of his official life: the news that President Bourguiba had received a note of thanks for his birthday message of congratulation to some African Head of State took precedence over the latest world happenings. In technicolor the newsreels reported the "brilliant" or "sumptuous" diplomatic receptions given in one of Bourguiba's new palaces. His ostentatious displays (probably modest by African standards) perhaps impressed the Tunisian masses if not the educated elite; Bourguiba's avowed purpose was to foster a habit of respect not for his person but for the new state that it embodied. Pomp and circumstance, both traditional and modern, were thus designed to further the process of national integration.

Bourguiba and His Lieutenants

Buttressing the constitutional edifice, Bourguiba employed brilliant tactical skill in establishing presidential monarchy. In the first three years of independence he adroitly eliminated all sources of opposition, both outside and within the Neo-Destour Party. Even more astonishing was the ease with which he subsequently brought back most of his humbled lieutenants into the official hierarchy. He remained in full control by the simple expedient of shuffling them about in different positions, thereby keeping factions to a minimum and consolidating his position as the arbiter above shifting cliques. Even those in temporary disgrace could usually depend upon the President for subsequent restoration.

The elimination of all potential centers of contending power was a gradual process, the result more of changing political circumstances than of any Machiavellian design. First the UGTT, which had demonstrated its power in supporting Bourguiba during the Youssefist crisis, was firmly subordinated to the party in 1956-57. Then, after the Bey was eliminated, wealthy leaders of the Protectorate regime were prose-

[42]By 1961 Bourguiba's government had, in addition, spent $12,000,000—one-eighth of Tunisia's regular annual budget—to make his home town of Monastir a summer capital and tourist center and, incidentally, to build his own mausoleum there.

cuted by means of retroactive laws. Simultaneously the Neo-Destour's structure was overhauled to concentrate more power in the Political Bureau, and in the process two contending factions within the party were successively neutralized.

Ahmed Ben Salah

In 1956 the UGTT had reached peak strength. It claimed to have more than 150,000 members[43] and its nation-wide prestige rivaled that of the Neo-Destour. In the newspapers the declarations of its leader, Ahmed Ben Salah, were displayed almost as prominently as those of Bourguiba. The UGTT also had substantial patronage to dispense after April, when four of its leaders were appointed ministers in the new government.[44] The UGTT seemed to be reaping the rewards of loyalty to Bourguiba during the previous months of crisis.[45]

But the ambitious thirty-year-old trade-union leader soon alienated Bourguiba by his brash tactics. In April, Ben Salah angered Bourguiba by refusing a minor ministerial post,[46] and his efforts to expand the political role of the Constituent Assembly undoubtedly displeased the prime minister. The issue at stake, however, was not constitutional democracy but Ben Salah's socialist ideology. The trade-union leader was instilling the UGTT with an economic "faith" derived from the rigid *progressiste* ideas of a French economics professor.[47] Elaborated in an extensive UGTT document, the new doctrine was both a blueprint for social revolution and an implicit critique of Bourguiba's methods:

[43]In September the UGTT's pathetically weak Communist rival voluntarily disbanded its remaining few thousand adherents and suggested that they coöperate with the UGTT.

[44]Members of the UGTT's Administrative Council, they were, respectively, ministers for agriculture (Filali), education (Chabbi), communications (Khiari), and public works (Abassi); the latter two departments employed many clerks and workers.

[45]Fostering national union, Ben Salah had accompanied Bourguiba into the mining areas around Gafsa, where Youssefists allied with Algerians threatened public order. In the March elections Ben Salah was persuaded to head the list of the National Front in the most difficult constituency, that of the extreme south where military operations were going on.

[46]Bourguiba had wanted to neutralize Ben Salah by associating him with his government, but the latter demanded an economic superministry which Bourguiba, unprepared to launch a full-scale socialist policy of nationalization and economic planning, was unwilling to give him. Bourguiba, it was later reported (*L'Action,* September 24, 1956), was so infuriated that Ahmed Tlili, the only leading trade-unionist who also sat on the Political Bureau, had pleaded with him to avoid a rupture.

[47]The economist G. de Bernis seemed far to the non-Communist Christian Left in the French political spectrum.

There is no hope except in a continuous revolution sweeping aside all the obsolete structures that have weighed upon our social life for so long. The hope today is . . . to unify all productive forces, and to make of them a single economic force, working in enthusiasm and confidence for the realization of a social and economic plan unanimously accepted by the people. . . . And we think that it is an error to try to reform man and morality or society and its customs by exhortations, advice, and sermons. These are opiates unworthy of a people that lives. The individual or the citizen, like the collectivity or the people, can be reformed only in the framework of a profound revolution of the economic structures, because *it is upon these that the society rests* in the last analysis.[48]

As for concrete objectives, Ben Salah did not mince words: "Tomorrow we shall obtain the nationalization of all the companies, whatever their importance."[49] But Bourguiba could not advocate returning Tunisia's national fortune to Tunisian hands while he was still engaged in delicate negotiations with France to gain the substance of political independence. When Ben Salah argued that massive capital flights to France were undermining the Tunisian economy, Bourguiba rejected his argument before the Constituent Assembly.[50] Bourguiba retaliated by publicly questioning the right to strike—a right which the UGTT had been liberally exercising on the farms of large landowners during the summer. Then, amid rumors of an impending break between the UGTT and the government,[51] Ben Salah scored the inadequacy of the economic policy recommendations of a round table at which he had (reluctantly) sat. The Neo-Destour participants were infuriated at his repudiation of all the compromises so laboriously effected over the previous three months.

During the UGTT's sixth congress, in late September, Ben Salah held the spotlight as the delegates gave his economic report a virtual plebiscite and endorsed his strategy calling for "the organic participation of the UGTT with the action of the Neo-Destour on the basis of a truly democratic social and economic program."[52] Bourguiba, interrupting a vacation in the Alps to address the congress, had conveyed

[48]UGTT, *Economic Report,* Sixth Congress, September, 1956, pp. 5-6. The phrase that I have italicized was allegedly pointed out by some Tunisians to "prove" to Bourguiba that Ben Salah was a Marxist. Bourguiba, of course, had been relying upon the "opiates" of exhortations, advice, and sermons to reform man and society.
[49]*Le Petit Matin,* February 17, 1956.
[50]It later turned out that the French bank statistics given to Bourguiba had hidden capital transfers, but the fact that Ben Salah had been right did not improve his standing with Bourguiba.
[51]*Le Petit Matin,* August 28, 1956.
[52]See *ibid.,* September 25, 1956.

the impression that his truce with Ben Salah was precarious at best,[53] but the latter's shirtsleeve oratory overwhelmed a weak internal opposition.[54] Ben Salah appeared to be gathering the political momentum to launch a socialist mass movement based on his formula of "organic participation."[55] But his triumph was short-lived.

Ben Salah's position was vulnerable, for his meteoric rise to power had incurred the jealousy and distrust of many influential men.[56]

[53]Although there was no open dispute, Bourguiba elliptically attacked Ben Salah by criticizing any "'doctrine which falsely encloses moving reality." See *ibid.*, September 21, 1956.

[54]On September 17, three days before the opening of the congress, *L'Action* reported that Habib Achour, the veteran trade-union leader who had been Ferhat Hached's right-hand man in Sfax, was bitterly opposing Ben Salah. The regional unions of Sfax and Beja were accusing Ben Salah's central office of illegally discriminating against their regions by cutting down the number of delegates to the congress. *L'Action* ommitted to report, however, that the very small local unions (especially prevalent in Sfax) had previously been allowed a disproportionate number of delegates. It was presumably this inequality that the central office was rectifying. At the congress, Ben Salah accused *L'Action* of fomenting disunity within the UGTT. His solid support in the UGTT was confirmed by the congress' election of the Administrative Council. Two of the prime activists in Achour's camp, Mohammed El Ghoul and Mohammed Kraiem (who in 1953 briefly headed the UGTT), failed to get reëlected. Ben Salah received the most votes, 1,278 out of 1,599, whereas Achour and Abdelaziz Bouraoui, the most articulate member of the Sfax opposition, received respectively, only 537 and 573 votes. They were the sole minority members to gain seats on the 21-man body.

[55]The formula had ambiguous implications that the press exploited. In one paper banner headlines announced: "The Congress has laid the foundations for a Tunisian Labor Movement." However, it reported Ben Salah's words accurately: "This participation which lays the foundations for a Tunisian Labor Movement *and which nonetheless remains subordinated to the approbation of the Neo-Destour*, rests on a truly democratic and social program . . . which has captivated public opinion. . . ." (*Le Petit Matin*, September 25, 1956; italics mine). *L'Action*, without drawing any clear comparisons, featured an article on the British labor movement which added to the confusion. Two weeks later Ben Salah publicly denied any intention of creating a UGTT-based Labor Party. (See *Le Petit Matin*, October 7, 1956).

[56]Hardly a typical trade-unionist, Ben Salah's political background resembled that of the two other leading Neo-Destourians of his political generation, Taieb Mehiri and Mohammed Masmoudi. All three had attended Sadiki at about the same time and had then enrolled in university at Paris, where Ben Salah became general secretary of the Neo-Destour student branch. In 1946 Fares gave him the job of making contact with Moncef Bey, whom the French had exiled to Pau. By 1948, when Ben Salah received a *license* in Arabic literature, he already had the reputation within the party of being an *enfant terrible*. He became a lycée professor in Sousse, joined the UGTT's Federation of Civil Servants, and headed the party in his nearby home town of Moknine. Ben Youssef, who was then in charge of the party's apparatus, stripped him of party office after a dispute in 1949. Concentrating his energies on the UGTT, Ben Salah rose so rapidly that Hached may have been happy to send him to Brussels in 1951 to work for the ICFTU. Meanwhile Mehiri had returned from Paris to become a leading figure under Mongi Slim in the party apparatus; Masmoudi remained abroad as Bour-

After the congress many of the party faithful considered him not only to be in disagreement with the Supreme Combatant but also to threaten the hegemony of the Neo-Destour. Presumably those who with Taieb Mehiri controlled the party apparatus would lose some of their power in the event of a merger between the UGTT and the Neo-Destour.

Informed Tunisians consider Mohammed Masmoudi to have been the cause of Ben Salah's demise. Masmoudi, too, was ambitious and had risen to be a member of the Political Bureau and minister of state, through close friendship with Bourguiba rather than through party ties. It is not known to what extent he was influencing Bourguiba rather than acting under his instructions, but it is generally agreed that Masmoudi, who controlled *L'Action,* was Habib Achour's political adviser. Since 1955, when he had served as minister of the national economy, Masmoudi had formed ties with some of the business interests which Ben Salah threatened.

A few weeks after the UGTT congress, Habib Achour, a rugged and outspoken trade-unionist who had been one of the UGTT's heroes since 1947,[57] withdrew his regional union from the UGTT to set up a rival national organization, the Union des Travailleurs Tunisiens (UTT). Centered mainly in Sfax and Beja, the UTT subsequently claimed 50,000 members, not including civil servants.[58] Its manifesto strongly attacked the UGTT for sacrificing the workers' interests to politics. "Real trade-union action has given way to demagogy and verbal extremism. . . . The UTT denounces ideological subversion founded upon imagination and utopia and vigorously condemns the idea of a labor movement built on sand."[59] Its actual policies, which included rigorous planning in all sectors of the economy, did not differ greatly from those of the UGTT, but the UTT violently objected to the

---

guiba's envoy. After Hached's assassination in December, 1952, the UGTT drifted, for its other two capable leaders, Habib Achour and Ahmed Tlili, were under arrest. Into the vacuum Ben Salah returned in 1954 from Brussels to prepare a congress and get himself elected general secretary. The Neo-Destour had misgivings, but did not try to push other available but less competent candidates. Ben Salah was accepted as a reliable party veteran; his relationship with ICFTU, too, could serve the Neo-Destour's efforts to gain an international audience. At the congress it was a Neo-Destour man who made the speech nominating Ben Salah.

[57]See note 54, above. Habib Achour had received only a modest education in a technical secondary school. As a municipality worker in Sfax, he had helped Ferhat Hached to organize the UGTT. A member of the Neo-Destour, he was also the chief organizer and almost a martyr of the UGTT's general strike in Sfax on August 5, 1947.

[58]*L'Action,* December 24, 1956.

[59]*Le Petit Matin,* November 10, 1956.

participation of trade-unionists in the government and promised that, though it might support popular governments in the national interest, it would never join one. Habib Achour in mid-December framed his conditions for trade-union unity: (1) UGTT ministers would have to choose between government and trade union responsibilities; (2) Ben Salah the demagogue had to go; and (3) a unity congress would be arranged by an equal number of officers from both unions.[60]

Ben Salah, probably thinking of Mohammed Masmoudi, attributed scission to the "barely disguised will of certain people to divide the ranks of the nationalist movement in the Neo-Destour as well as in the UGTT."[61] He stressed his loyalty to Bourguiba and called upon the President to use his prestige to reestablish labor unity. Bourguiba, however, had received an official UTT delegation soon after its creation.[62] In mid-December, members of his Political Bureau[63] encouraged reunification of the labor movement on the basis of Achour's recommendations. While Ben Salah was away in Morocco, the Administrative Council of the UGTT made Ahmed Tlili general secretary; with the ground well prepared, Bourguiba unleashed a violent attack on Ben Salah just before the latter's return. In the presence of Tlili and Achour, Bourguiba declared, with obvious reference to Ben Salah: "We must avoid generating resentment, sowing seeds of division under cover of foreign doctrines and principles which we would be poorly advised to want to apply to our country." Recalling that national unity prevailed and indeed had been strengthened after the departure of Salah Ben Youssef, Bourguiba continued:

The same goes for trade-union unity. It has been compromised these last weeks; leaders of the labor movement have found themselves in the logical necessity of getting rid of elements which, within the world of labor, were at the origins of the difficulty. To block the road to erroneous orientations, the leaders of the labor movement themselves have had to take measures necessary for preserving the interests of workers and to be able to rediscover trade-union unity, which will soon flower anew, I hope, in the framework of National Unity.[64]

[60] L'Action, December 24, 1956.
[61] Le Petit Matin, October 17, 1956. Le Monde noted the heterogeneity of the UTT's support: disappointed Youssefists, landowners, commercial interests, ministers worried about losing their jobs, and trade-unionists reproaching Ben Salah's conformity to Bourguiba policies. Le Petit Matin, October 20.
[62] Le Petit Matin, October 27, 1956.
[63] According to Ahmed Mestiri, who was subsequently appointed to the Political Bureau, it had not been officially consulted about the UGTT crisis in the autumn of 1956, and some of its members had quietly disapproved of the organization of the UTT (interview, Cairo, March 13, 1962).
[64] Speech, December 27, 1956.

Not wishing to follow in Ben Youssef's footsteps, Ben Salah had no choice but to return to Tunisia, resign from the UGTT, and retire to the political wilderness. Under Tlili's skillful leadership, the trade-union scission was rapidly mended, and a UGTT congress reincorporating the UTT was held the following September. In effect the party had reasserted control over the UGTT, for Ahmed Tlili, though a veteran trade-unionist, had been a member of the Political Bureau since 1955; for his good services, Habib Achour was coöpted to it in April, 1957. Bourguiba had one less autonomous center of power with which to contend.

Mohammed Masmoudi and Taieb Mehiri

It had seemed that Ben Salah's downfall would profit two rival Neo-Destour groups of successful young politicians: the group associated with Taieb Mehiri, the minister of the interior, that was asserting its control over the party apparatus, and the more loosely knit group asso ciated with Mohammed Masmoudi, consisting of students, university graduates in the administration, and ambitious young businessmen. (The political attitudes of this group were expressed in the quasi-official party weekly, L'Action.)

After leashing the UGTT, however, Bourguiba found it necessary to curb the pretensions, in turn, of each of the rivals. The grounds were in neither case strictly ideological, although Mehiri and Masmoudi could be seen as standing for political alternatives that might become incompatible with presidential monarchy. Mehiri's avenue to power, the central party apparatus, could not be permitted to undermine the authority of Bourguiba's ministers and administrators who were outside the Mehiri clan. One-party government, however, could not be continuously subjected to the harassing criticisms of a newspaper which enjoyed the prestige of the Neo-Destour while evading party discipline.

Soon after the Bey was deposed—at a time when Algerian border incidents and the French severance of economic aid to Tunisia had put severe strains on Franco-Tunisian relations—Neo-Destour nationalism took a militant turn. The law of ill-gotten gains (August 13, 1957), followed by the law of national indignity (November 19, 1957), provided an arsenal of legislation against former Tunisian collaborators of the Protectorate regime.[65] Bourguiba's only public explanation of his

[65]These "traitors" were defined very loosely: the first law was to apply to civil servants who had acquired fortunes in office, to Tunisians who had been candidates in the municipal elections of 1953, to members of the Beylical family, to ministers in the Baccouche (1942-53) and Mzali (1953-54) governments, and to anyone who had had dealings with them. Regional commissions under the Neo-Destour governors were given wide powers and could sequestrate the property of

abrupt shift from a policy of national reconciliation[66] was that these collaborators "are found in diplomatic and other receptions. Their luxury and their arrogance are shocking. This situation is an insult to our dead; it wounds our conception of human justice."[67] It would seem, however, that Bourguiba was placating an increasingly powerful party apparatus and providing its militants with a welcome distraction[68] as he made preparations to overhaul it.

The legislation was applied by the *Haute Cour*, a revolutionary tribunal originally set up in 1956 for six months to condemn Youssefists. Its judges for the most part had no legal experience—one was illiterate —but all were veteran party militants. Legal arguments of the defense made little impression; the court "brushed aside . . . legalisms. It had exclusive jurisdiction over political crimes and there was no appeal from its judgments."[69]

The court's sentences were generally as severe[70] as its procedures were irregular. The first victims, in the spring and early summer of 1958, were mostly former members of the qaidal corps who had "repressed" the Neo-Destour. They were usually accused of being corrupt

---

virtually any wealthy person. By virtue of the law of national indignity a man could be sentenced to prison for life and/or "degraded" and stripped of his civic rights. This law was to apply to anyone who had worked in the Protectorate's security, press, or information services, members of the Grand Conseil, regional and municipal councils, participants in artistic or economic manifestations favoring colonization, and anyone who had aided the Protectorate authorities "directly or indirectly." Bourguiba subsequently amended the law to apply only to activities during the 1952-1954 period.

[66]On August 1, 1957, commenting on becoming President of the Republic, Bourguiba had said: "I have become the father not only of Destourians but of all Tunisians." *Le Petit Matin*, August 2, 1957.

[67]*L'Action*, December 2, 1957, quoted by Keith Callard, "The Republic of Bourguiba," *International Journal*, 1961, p. 27.

[68]Following Bourguiba's lead, *El 'Amal*, the party's official organ, was in a rage about the "traitors who must be brought to justice, these traitors who have exploited circumstances, who have sold their consciences as one sells animals, who have stepped on their consciences with their shoes . . . [and who] do not deserve to be let alone without accounts being demanded of them." *Le Petit Matin*, December 7, 1957.

[69]Callard, *op. cit.*, pp. 28-29.

[70]Baccouche, a former qaid who was seventy-five years old, was sentenced to ten years of forced labor. In the Mzali trials several veteran nationalists who had once closely collaborated with the Neo-Destour were condemned. Tahar Lakhdar had been a regular columnist for the Neo-Destour's *Mission* (1947-1951) and had participated on a provisional Political Bureau in 1935-36. Noureddine Zaouche had presided over a Political Bureau in 1935. They had been willing, however, to participate in a moderate government to apply limited reforms that Bourguiba in prison had rejected.

as well as traitors to the national cause.[71] As the trials wore on—they lasted through February, 1959—people were convicted who had not closely collaborated with the French, and personal quarrels twenty years old were dragged into court.[72]

Eventually even Tahar Ben Ammar was brought to trial. The transitional prime minister who had acted as the peacemaker between the French Government and the Neo-Destour was now, after having been made a deputy in the Constituent Assembly, to be sacrificed to the vindictive party. He was accused of not having paid back income taxes, although the regional commission on ill-gotten gains had found no fault with his accounts. He was also implicated in the case of the Bey's jewels, which Mme Ben Ammar, apparently without her husband's knowledge, had helped hide. His great political "crime" was in late 1955 to have forwarded to the French Government the Bey's request that France withhold its police services from the party. To *L'Action*, as to many Tunisians unrelated to the old elite, the trial was an undignified and petty display, amplified by the publicity that the government brought to bear. "Nasty little quarrels, pettiness on all sides, an absence of principles or perspective have been spread in the pages of our newspapers and on our radio waves, creating a general feeling of uneasiness and equivocation."[73]

L'Action's critique sealed its own doom and that of its patron, Masmoudi. Established in April, 1955, the newspaper had had a checkered history under the direction of Masmoudi's friend Bechir Ben Yahmed (who at twenty-seven had been the youngest minister, in charge of Information, in Bourguiba's first government).

Though Ben Yahmed was of Djerban origin, his paper had taken a strongly anti-Youssefist line. In 1956 it had been accused of dividing the UGTT. In January, 1957, however, it had incurred Bourguiba's wrath by publishing a balance sheet of government promises and their fulfillment—"on many points the government . . . has not realized what

[71]But a man like Aziz Sakka (condemned to twenty years of national indignity and a \$100,000 fine) made a strong defense. Formerly one of the most competent qaids, Sakka had never been a stooge of the French administration. At his trial he convincingly claimed to have upheld the rights of the poor against prosperous landowning families that had sometimes collaborated with the Neo-Destour! *Le Petit Matin*, February 5, 1958.

[72]Mohammed Attia, former director of Sadiki and Tunisia's first *agrégé* of Arabic literature, was sentenced to five years in prison, ten years of national indignity, and confiscation of his property. He was condemned mainly for having combated a Neo-Destour Scout movement in the early 1930's and for having removed Fares and Belhaouane from their teaching positions in 1938.

[73]*L'Action*, September 8, 1958.

it promised"[74]—and by broaching the subject of ministerial reshuffles.[75] Bourguiba had then criticized "storytellers harbored by friendly papers" and journalists who "sow trouble in people's minds" by talk of ministerial changes,[76] and *L'Action* had ceased publication for a week.[77]

After denouncing the Constituent Assembly, *L'Action* conducted a poll on popular attitudes toward the government: 44 per cent considered it had made mistakes, while only 43 per cent thought it had made no mistakes.[78] Then it discussed the Neo-Destour youth organization as a "pretty clumsy parody of Scouting."[79] Later it attacked Haute Cour trials: "This measure of public housecleaning was necessary," but it "would have gained by being commenced earlier and now should be terminated rapidly and clearly according to the rules."[80] As the summer trials dragged on, *L'Action's* tone became more vehement, questioning the mission of the Haute Cour, attacking the pettiness of the Tahar Ben Ammar trial, and recalling that the secretary of foreign affairs had once criticized *L'Action* for having attacked Ben Ammar's government.

The Political Bureau reacted on September 8 with the following communique:

The Political Bureau of the Neo-Destour . . . has examined the situation created by the editorials of the weekly *Action* . . . which aimed at confusing the public by systematically denigrating the policy of President Bourguiba's Government and attacking the fundamental institutions [the *Haute Cour?*] of the Republican regime.

The equivocation stemming from this paper's use of the prestigious name of the paper founded by the President of the Party for the national struggle for independence has permitted the former to wage its insidious campaign of confusion. Considering that these attacks against the Government and national institutions constitute an enterprise destructive of the efforts of the People and the Government . . . the Political Bureau withdraws all confidence and all support from the present management of the paper. . . . It

[74]Such as municipal elections, promised for October, 1956, the liquidation of public domains, and administrative recruitment by merit—"all this is important in the measure that it is the little nothings which spoil great things." *Ibid.*, January 7, 1957.
[75]*Ibid.*, January 14, 1957.
[76]*Le Petit Matin*, January 20, 1957.
[77]The following week it explained, while praising Bourguiba, that it was "up against the hostility and intolerance of all those—powerful and numerous—who conceive of liberty only as a one-way street" (i.e., the Mehiri clique). *L'Action*, February 4, 1957.
[78]*Ibid.*, May 26, 1958.
[79]*Ibid.*, July 9, 1958.
[80]*Ibid.*, July 7, 1958.

has also decided measures to clarify the relationship between this paper and the Party.[81]

Although Ben Yahmed was not brought before the Haute Cour, Mohammed Masmoudi was removed five days later from the Political Bureau for "serious indiscipline."[82] Ben Salah's rival would now also have to face the political wilderness.

But Mehiri, who quietly retained all his positions as secretary of the interior, member of the Political Bureau, and assistant general secretary of the Neo-Destour, could hardly be deemed the winner. In the late autumn of 1957, while the crusade against the "traitors" gathered momentum, the party was experiencing a severe internal crisis. Rumors were rife in mid-December that the party apparatus would soon be overhauled. Abdelmajid Chaker, director of the party and therefore formally in charge of its administration, publicly admitted, "We do in fact have the problem of adapting the structure of the party to its mission today."[83] It was thought that the party's federations would be suppressed, and Bourguiba's announcement was expected on December 30.[84] But, perhaps in the face of opposition and confusion within the party, he delayed announcing what would amount to a radical housecleaning and the subordination of the party apparatus to presidential government until October 2, 1958.[85]

Meanwhile, steps were taken to neutralize the growing influence of the Mehiri clique. Three high-ranking Neo-Destour officials, caught misusing governmental positions to further personal interests of some of their friends,[86] were suspended from the party; a fourth, Azouz Rebai, lost his job as secretary of state for youth and sports. These men were all from the party's Tunis federation, Mehiri's main power base. Another of his close collaborators was shifted at this time from the sensitive post as director of regional and local administration in the Department of the Interior to the innocuous position of secretary general in the Department of Agriculture. The director of the party, who was less closely associated with Mehiri, was sent off to the Middle East on a long tour. Bourguiba subsequently took care that Mehiri did not

[81] *Le Petit Matin,* September 9, 1957.
[82] *Ibid.,* September 13, 1958.
[83] *Ibid.,* December 18, 1957.
[84] *L'Action,* December 30, 1957.
[85] For analysis of the party reorganization and its significance, see below, Chap. IV.
[86] Bourguiba referred to the case of Tawfiq Ben Brahim in his speech of December 5, 1957: "It was reported to me recently that a miscarriage of justice was committed as the result of an intervention made under the cover of the Neo-Destour. I declare that this sort of thing is inadmissible." Bourguiba went on to castigate much of the administration, including the governors and the police.

rebuild an administrative empire escaping the president's control. Occasional purges of his friends served as a warning.[87]

But just as Mehiri could remain in office because he ceased to be a potential threat, Ben Salah and Masmoudi, sufficiently chastened, could be returned to power. Less than four months after having him expelled, Bourguiba reintegrated Masmoudi in the Political Bureau and gave him a cabinet post.[88] A few months after Ben Salah's downfall, Bourguiba brought him out of political retirement to be secretary of health, a harmless post where his ambitions might serve the regime. To test his loyalty further, Bourguiba later added social affairs to his responsibilities; so Ben Salah, ironically, became the government official in charge of bargaining with the UGTT. In 1961 Bourguiba appointed him secretary of finances and planning, a new economic super-ministry, to carry out many of the policies of economic planning that he had advocated in 1956. Bourguiba had made a right-hand man out of a potential adversary; his tactics served to keep most of the capable members of the political elite inside his own political system.

All the King's Men

By the early 'sixties the political process in Tunisia seemed increasingly centered on the presidential monarch. Around Bourguiba had gathered an entourage of courtiers, some of them virtually unknown to the public and unpopular in party circles. The President apparently did much of his work at the breakfast table with private advisers before conferring with his official cabinet. A favorite at court might exercise more influence than a lesser cabinet member who had access to Bourguiba perhaps once a fortnight. The President's private secretary had become a key power in the realm.[89] The Ben Ammar family was also noteworthy.[90] It included in 1962 the secretary of health and

[87]In 1960, while Mehiri was vacationing abroad, the commandant of the National Guard was removed from office on charges of corruption. The commandant had been considered by informed Tunisians to be especially close to Mehiri.
[88]Le Petit Matin, December 28, 1958.
[89]In late 1961 Bourguiba fired one of Tunisia's most competent governors simply because the latter had questioned the authority of the President's private secretary. The story well illustrates court politics in Tunisia. Sympathetic to the plight of a jilted mistress, the secretary told the governor to jail the unfaithful lover. The governor refused because he saw no legal ground for such action. Though the secretary of the interior sided with the governor, Bourguiba supported his secretary, summoned the governor, confiscated his official car, and fired him for not obeying presidential orders. Bourguiba somewhat atoned for his arbitrary behavior —which had shocked all Tunisian officialdom—by appointing the former governor a few weeks later to another important administrative position.
[90]But Tahar Ben Ammar, the former Tunisian prime minister, prosecuted in 1958, came from a different family.

social affairs, the effective head (under Bahi Ladgham) of the defense establishment, the general secretary of the Neo-Destour Youth, and the president of the National Union of Tunisian Women (UNFT).

But as an arbiter above the shifting political cliques, Bourguiba continued to control his political lieutenants. As President of the Republic he enjoyed the constitutional right to make all important governmental and administrative appointments—a right he exercised with great skill. By constant cabinet shuffles, he weakened the Political Bureau, the composition of which he could not control so easily. Bureau members who did not receive high-ranking government appointments became less politically influential; those who were more fortunate were not allowed to take their positions for granted. Kept in a state of insecurity, the political lieutenants had to struggle for presidential favor, but those who played the game could feel confident—was this not the lesson of the Ben Salah story?—that they would not be permanent losers.

Being President of the Neo-Destour Party also helped Bourguiba to dominate his lieutenants. The Political Bureau, composed of only five members in 1934, was steadily expanded to include fifteen by 1957. Of the original members, only Bourguiba remained on the Bureau.[91] An increased and younger membership served to diminish its importance as the party's top executive organ. This trend became even more marked after 1964, when membership was expanded to fifty, with a new presidium of fifteen members (appointed by the President) replacing it as the real executive authority.[92]

[91]Of the original members of the Political Bureau, Bourguiba's older brother Mohammed deserted the party in order to be released from jail in 1935. Mahmoud Materi, Bahri Guiga, and Tahar Sfar all disagreed with Bourguiba's intransigence in 1938 and ceased their political activities. In 1937 Bourguiba added Salah Ben Youssef and Slimane Ben Slimane to the Bureau. In 1949, however, Ben Slimane was expelled from the party as a leftist deviationist; he was discrediting the party by his activities with Communist front organizations. Ben Youssef was eliminated in 1955. Of the three new leaders coöpted in 1945, Mongi Slim and Hedi Nouira remain important members of the Bureau; Ali Belhaouane, who had stood by Bourguiba in the Youssefist crisis, died in 1958. Of the four elected in Bourguiba's absence in 1948, only Fares remained on the Bureau. At the Sfax congress six of the eleven elected to the Political Bureau were newcomers: Ladgham, Mehiri, Tlili, Mokaddem, Masmoudi, and Farhat. In 1956 Bourguiba coöpted Abdelmajid Chaker on to the Bureau and put him in charge of the party's machinery. His only political experience had been with UGET. A younger minister, Ahmed Mestiri, and Ferdjani Bel Hadj Ammar and Habib Achour, leaders, respectively, of UTAC and UGTT, were coöpted in 1957. Rachid Driss and Taieb Slim, Mongi's brother, were elected in 1959 in place of Belhaouane and Farhat, the only Bureau member ever to run and fail to be reëlected at a party congress. In 1961 Ben Salah replaced Masmoudi.
[92]Habib Bourguiba, Jr., and Messadi, Mzali, and Sayah joined eleven incumbents of the Political Bureau as members of the new presidium. Omitted from the latter were Ammar, Fares, Driss, and T. Slim.

Periodic cabinet reshuffles since independence kept most of Bour-guiba's lieutenants from becoming entrenched in their positions. The 1956 government was overhauled in July, 1957, when all the ministers resigned with the change of regime. At the end of 1958 Bourguiba reshuffled his secretaries of state. No formal *remaniement* took place during the next three and a half years, but the elevation of Ben Salah to head the new planning department in early 1961 constituted a key government change.

By 1963 there had been an almost complete turnover in the members of the government. Of the original eighteen, only Bourguiba, Lad-gham, and Mehiri had retained their positions. Mehiri's situation had sometimes been precarious, whereas Bahi Ladgham, a generally re-spected and uncontroversial figure, seemed content to serve as Bour-guiba's chief administrative coordinator rather than to build up a per-sonal following. Mongi Slim, who next to Bourguiba was the elder statesman of the party, was sent off as ambassador to the United States and the United Nations in 1956, not only because an experienced diplomat was needed but because his identification with the 1955 Conventions had made him unpopular within the party. At the 1959 party congress, however, after three years of successes abroad, he seemed to be the most popular of Bourguiba's lieutenants, and after many delays was appointed foreign minister in 1962.

The eight newcomers to the government since 1957 were, in order of seniority, Rachid Driss, Ahmed Ben Salah, Mahmoud Messadi, Ahmed Noureddine, Hedi Khefacha, Monthar Ben Ammar, Chadly Klibi, and Abdelmajid Chaker. Only three of the eight belonged to the Poli-tical Bureau, and these had been coöpted or elected only since the Sfax congress. Eight of the eleven-man Political Bureau elected at Sfax had been in the 1956 government; in 1962 a rather different seven of the Bureau's fifteen members were in the government. Bourguiba had allowed only two men to hold positions combining party and govern-mental authority.

In the absence of open policy discussions and press reports, it was not always easy to interpret particular shifts, nor did Bourguiba desire public speculation.[93] Ministers or secretaries of state were not to

---

[93]Some shifts simply reflected merely personal preferences. Hedi Nouira left the Department of Finances of his own accord to become governor of the Central Bank which he had largely created. Others lost their cabinet positions because of ailing health or through sheer incompetence. Some cabinet shuffles, however, had clear political grounds, as did those of Ahmed Ben Salah and Mohammed Mas-moudi. The moves of Filali, Khiari, and Driss in 1957 also reflected political realities. A Ben Salah supporter fortunate to have other ties—he and the director of the presidential cabinet had married sisters—Mustapha Filali was ousted from agriculture, where his talk of socialist coöperatives shocked Neo-Destour farmers,

symbolize policies generally; rather, they were to be interchangeable parts, agents for implementing Bourguiba's policies. Since 1956 Bourguiba's choices had tended away from men having a distinguished past as militants in the party toward those who owed their career personally to presidential favor. Most of the 1956 ministers, even those who were not on the Political Bureau, were political figures elected to high office in the party or national organizations. None of the newcomers, except Chaker and Driss, had earned ministerial rank by their political activities, and Chaker owed his political career to his party appointment by Bourguiba in 1956. Driss had been an active party militant since before the Second World War, had worked in the party's central office since 1955, but was elected to the Political Bureau after becoming minister. Ben Salah, his personal political power shattered, was coöpted to the Political Bureau after his government appointment. Messadi had been active in the UGTT until 1952, but he was appointed to the government only for his ideas and willingness to implement Bourguiba's controversial educational reform. The other four secretaries of state were technicians without a political past. Klibi perhaps owed his rise in part to close friendship with Ben Salah, whom Bourguiba wished strongly to support (while downgrading Masmoudi).

Those who were discarded from the cabinet or other high positions usually managed to remain in the system. The National Assembly was one of Bourguiba's favorite pastures for gracefully retiring those who were no longer needed. Although ousted from the cabinet and distrusted as a demagogue by those close to the President, Azouz Rebai was encouraged to play an active role in the Assembly and maintain a law practice.[94] Erstwhile Political Bureau associates like Bahri Guiga —even though he had been accused of Youssefism in 1955—were given high administrative positions. Even Slimane Ben Slimane, the fellow traveler expelled from the Political Bureau in 1949, was permitted for two years to publish a monthly newspaper that was highly critical of the regime; he too in a sense remained a member of the family.

---

and was given a less controversial cabinet post. Khiari was removed from the PTT because of his ties with the Ben Salah wing of the UGTT; he later achieved international fame as a United Nations administrator in the Congo. Driss replaced him and removed trade-unionists from high posts in the department—to the satisfaction of civil service technicians. His method was use of a law, extended for a year, whereby French civil servants had been removed without recourse to an administrative tribunal. The downfall of Azouz Rebai was also political, relating to the internal party crisis of 1957.

[94] In the summer 1962, however, he lost all his positions and faced the prospect of a jail sentence for having criticized police interrogation methods used on clients he was defending.

Those condemned by the *Haute Cour* to long prison terms were usually pardoned after a year or two. Except for Ben Youssef, with whom reconciliation was impossible after the virtual civil war—and a few of his hired killers, who were hanged—the hundreds of imprisoned Youssefists were released long before serving their time. Some of the political leaders were then appointed to key positions. In 1961 Bourguiba placed a former Youssefist leader of UGAT—an implacable foe of Ben Salah in 1955, when the UGTT was mobilizing agricultural workers—in charge of the State Domains Office, to carry out reforms under Ben Salah's plan. In 1962 Tahar Amira, a popular trade-unionist sentenced as a Youssefist in 1958 to twenty years of forced labor, walked out of prison to the board of directors of Tunisia's new quasi-governmental steel company.

The king's men, in short, could feel relatively secure even in the occasional hours of adversity when the royal favor was withdrawn. For Bourguiba seemed to manage Tunisia's political sweepstakes in a way that ensured that there be no permanent losers among those willing to compete on his terms.

Bourguiba and the Political System

Had Bourguiba's authority rested solely upon personal prestige or even upon his constitutional powers as President of the Republic, it would probably have become increasingly tenuous and unstable in the absence of real *charisma* or a constitutional tradition. To bolster his position would have required constant propaganda triumphs and a more adventurous, anti-Western foreign policy,[95] and controversial domestic reforms would probably not have been possible. Bourguibist methods of persuasion could hardly have been applied to Tunisia's

[95]Bourguiba once painted a brilliant portrait of countries in the forefront of the "struggle against neo-colonialism": "In many underdeveloped countries, you know, the leaders prudishly veil their internal political problems. They are constantly searching for distractions to channel popular passions. . . . Those who excite the crowd, by radio and other propaganda means, as an instrument of power, must always be denouncing enemies. The most fashionable enemy is colonialism. But no matter. Aided by the resources of imagination, one decries *neo-colonialism*. . . . One doesn't try sanely to study the [real] problems. . . . No, one eludes them. All pretexts are good. If there's no progress, it's because colonialism is still there . . . so that one can justify all failures. With this psychosis, the people remain in a permanent state of mobilization. They think they're fighting enemies. One leaves them no respite. . . . The leaders repeat to those who want to listen that they don't have time to worry about the price of bread. . . . Colonialism [is] holding them by the throat. Sad alibi! Convenient scapegoat! . . . Everyone abandons work to demonstrate against . . . colonialism, or rather against neo-colonialism. . . . Beside the mystique of endless struggle against enemies more or less real, there is the mystique of victories unceasingly accumulated so much that one can ask why they continue to fight after so many victories. . . ." Speech of January 12, 1961.

internal problems, for Bourguiba risked unpopularity that a more fragile leader could have ill-afforded.

The secret of Bourguiba's effectiveness lay as much in his political instruments as in his personal appeal. At the twenty-fifth anniversary of the Neo-Destour, he analyzed the three conditions that had brought independence:

1. A minority of trained and dedicated shock troops supported by the active sympathy of the people.
2. Total confidence in the leader, entailing strict discipline and allowing the leader large room for maneuver with the assurance of always being understood and obeyed.
3. A well-planned strategy permitting intelligent use of the first two assets.

Bourguiba was underlining the role of the party and the need for discipline within its ranks. "It is a fact that the call to arms, to holy war, doesn't raise objections. But as soon as one speaks of 'respecting the acquired rights' of Frenchmen, for example, or returning the arms of fellagha to French military authorities, there is the risk of a negative reaction from the militants, especially if it is enticed by the demagoguery of a rival party crying treason."[96] When favorable compromises with France were possible, Bourguiba had needed a mechanism "to silence the demagogues and be obeyed and understood by the rank and file." The Neo-Destour had served the purpose and thus made possible the cleverly oscillating tactics of Bourguibism. Despite Youssefism and internal difficulties in the party after independence, Bourguiba preserved and reënforced the apparatus, coördinated it with the new administration, and maintained the tradition of discipline. It was his skill as a political manipulator and conciliator of interests as much as the forcefulness of his personality which provided a relatively stable basis for his authority. While his influence permeated the political system, Bourguiba on most occasions had to act within the context of the system, with the support or at least the acquiescence of Neo-Destour politicians inside and outside the government.

Long after Bourguiba had consolidated power in his new regime, the Bizerte crisis highlighted the importance of the party apparatus. Without it, Bourguiba would surely have experienced far greater difficulties in withstanding the events of July, 1961—if, indeed, he could have survived without the full support of the party.[97] For once, Bour-

[96]Speech of March 2, 1959.
[97]For a fuller treatment of the Bizerte crisis and the general Tunisian political situation in 1961, see my article, " 'Bourguibism' in Tunisia," *Current History*, January, 1963, pp. 34-40.

guiba's boast proved empty that "Bourguibism accepts battle when forced to do so and is always victorious." He tried to pressure de Gaulle into negotiating the evacuation of the French naval base by organizing demonstrations and blockading its various (separated) installations. When the French retaliated by sending paratroopers to break up the poorly manned barricades, the Tunisian (largely civilian) casualties of the four-day battle—the official estimate of 1,365 killed was probably conservative—surpassed that of all previous martyrs to the national cause. A Tunisian "victory" at the United Nations failed to budge France from Bizerte, and Bourguiba's Western friends, taken aback by his sudden shift from gradualist tactics, did not give Tunisia the support it requested. He was therefore forced to seek the support of the Afro-Asian bloc, thereby apparently justifying the Pan-Arab slogans that Ben Youssef had stood for. His abrupt intransigence hardly endeared him even to the Algerians (though they offered him military support!); they were seeking an accommodation with France and resented his simultaneous claims to part of the Algerian Sahara. When, on August 12, Salah Ben Youssef was assassinated in Germany,[98] many Tunisians wondered whether men close to Bourguiba were responsible. After Bourguiba on September 8 optimistically interpreted de Gaulle's uncompromising comments on Bizerte and offered a peace settlement on the latter's terms, Tunisians who had been enthusiastic about national sacrifice, rapprochement with Egypt, and Bourguiba's participation at the Belgrade Conference joined more moderate Tunisian nationalists in questioning Bourguiba's judgment.

But the party held firm throughout the crisis, thus belying the only public criticism of its leader. An editorial in *Afrique-Action,* the weekly supported by Mohammed Masmoudi,[99] denounced the "personal power" exercised by leaders of single-party states like Tunisia: "Because it develops pride and disdain in him who possesses it, and docility and servility in others, it is in itself a menace to the moral health of a

[98]According to press reports, Ben Youssef was assassinated in his Frankfurt hotel room by visitors whom he had journeyed to Frankfurt to meet. The crime as of this writing remains officially unsolved. In view of the rapprochement at this time between Egypt and Tunisia, some Tunisians thought that Egyptians might have been involved. But this seems unlikely in view of the subsequent decision of Mme. Ben Youssef (who had traveled with her husband to Frankfurt and presumably knew who the visitors were) to maintain residence in Cairo.
[99]Masmoudi, who had just returned from Cairo, pointedly praised Nasser's austere way of life and thus tacitly criticized Bourguiba's palaces.

country."[100] However, Bourguiba's "personal power" was fully supported by the party apparatus, as his devastating response to Masmoudi's challenge indicated. He went ahead with his long-expected cabinet shift, replacing Masmoudi with a Ben Salah supporter, and the former declined the humiliating offer to become ambassador to an African country.

Three weeks later, the Neo-Destour organ, *Al 'Amal*, printed a series of editorials vigorously defending Bourguiba and the Neo-Destour veteran activists ("who often felt shunted aside by 'technicians' [like some of Masmoudi's associates] who arrived just after Independence to occupy government positions").[101] A polemic ensued: *Afrique-Action* elliptically recalled the party editor's Youssefist past, while militants at party cadre conferences questioned the "aggressive attitude of *Afrique-Action.*" The hitherto quiescent National Assembly received prominence as meetings between deputies and their constituents were arranged (for the first time since the 1959 elections). The stage set, the Political Bureau formally expelled Masmoudi and coöpted his rival Ben Salah to take his place. Bourguiba publicly tongue-lashed

[100]*Afrique-Action*, October 7, 1961. The editorial deserves to be quoted at length, for it accurately communicated the flavor of politics under Bourguiba: "Today he wields more legal and real power than did the Bey and Resident General combined. . . . Personal power is conquered in high struggle but in a very short time: on the basis of moral prestige patiently acquired outside power—during a liberation struggle, for example—and which serves as a cover, one gains in a few months or years . . . absolute supremacy in the country and power in its entirety.

"All rival forces are then dislocated, subjugated, or eliminated: the judiciary, a deliberative assembly, trade unions, or political parties, and the press continue to exist, but their liberty of action no longer exists. Their prestige and their authority declines to nothing. They constitute nothing more than supporting instruments of the power, which addresses itself without an intermediary to the people. Everything converges toward the holder of power, who, alone, exists, decides, and in expressing himself expresses the country and incarnates it.

"In the orbit of power others can benefit from a certain consideration or play a role. Outside there is no possibility.

"The police is not all-powerful, but it is omnipresent. Imprisonment without trial exists, but is used more as a means of intimidation. Anyone can be arrested, but the prisons are not full. That is to say, personal power is not a dictatorship. . . ."

[101]For a translation of the editorials, see *Le Petit Matin*, November 1-5, 1961. The series gave, by Neo-Destour press standards, an extraordinarily frank analysis of the political scene. Obviously having conferred with Bourguiba first, the editor admitted that the country was experiencing three types of anxiety: (1) political: the French were not evacuating Bizerte; (2) technical: many Tunisians were uneasy about the impact of Ben Salah's plan and Neo-Destour socialism; and (3) psychological: police abuses were committed. In public places people had become reticent for fear of police surveillance. However, the editor argued, there was nothing fundamentally wrong with the form of government. "He [Bourguiba] is not a Machiavelli because he is too sentimental for that. He is authoritarian but not dictatorial, for he would suffer if he felt himself to be disliked."

Masmoudi and relegated him to the political wilderness. In the municipal elections of 1963 he was not even allowed to run for rëlection as mayor of his home town of Mahdia.

In retrospect, the tragedy of Bizerte did not lead to utter catastrophe, primarily because the party supported Bourguiba when he was most in need of help. In October, agreement was reached with France for the return to Tunisia of thousands of desperately needed French schoolteachers. Economic disasters were avoided as trade relations between the two countries were informally resumed. With no real choice in light of overwhelming French military superiority, the Tunisians nonetheless displayed great moderation in postponing demands for a calendar of evacuation for the base. Their patience was rewarded when, after two years, the French completed a phased withdrawal in agreement with the Tunisians. Meanwhile, as if in recognition of the party's services, Bourguiba emphasized its importance in 1963 by supervising a reorganization of its structures that might in the long run give it a much greater collective voice in policy-making.

After independence Bourguiba remained President of the Neo-Destour. He continued to keep in close touch with ranking party cadres, and used the party to sustain mass support for himself. Its "orientation" (propaganda) service in theory provided a commentary on every Bourguiba speech. Whenever he made one of his frequent visits to the countryside, the party cadres organized mass demonstrations of welcome; in Tunis it was the party's responsibility to transport the hundreds, often thousands, of unemployed to the big rally and to orchestrate the chants of "Long live Bourguiba!" The cult of Bourguiba permeated every facet of party activity; at local meetings the mention of his name was the signal for prolonged applause. His preponderant role in government, his personal power, was somehow legitimate by virtue of direct democracy, shown by his massive popular support. Tunisia's leader received a plebiscite every day. Without the party apparatus, however, it is doubtful that the intense rhythm of national solidarity focused on his person could be sustained. Daily plebiscites require organization which only a centralized and well-organized party can provide. Bourguiba needed the party as much as it needed its volatile and inspirational leader to supercharge its élan after the objective of decolonization was achieved.

However tenuous the limits that a consensus within the party might impose on Bourguiba's power, he seemed to know how to listen to advice and profit from it. As he once said, probably in all sincerity:

The fact that I now have more authority than I had before is for the good of this people. I listen to advice, I discuss, I change when I am mistaken, for, like everyone, I can make mistakes and do not feel immune from error. I remain open to all confrontations. Aside from the respect due to my position and my past, I enjoy the affection of the men about me. This is a considerable privilege.[102]

Bourguiba apparently enjoyed good arguments—in private to be sure—criticizing his policies. Frank and straightforward himself, he appreciated this quality in his subordinates, though he was often disappointed by their servility. He always consulted the members of his cabinet and the Political Bureau before making important policy decisions. During the Bizerte crisis he was in frequent sessions with both bodies for days before the shooting started.[103] His ideas were far from rigid, and developed under the impact of other people and circumstances. To crush Ben Salah and fulminate against his doctrinaire socialist ideas and then five years later to promote him to carry them out is ample testimony to Bourguiba's willingness to experiment. As a politician one of his greatest talents, unseen by the public but corroborated by leading Tunisian officials, was "to coöperate with others and make them coöperate with each other and with him" behind the scenes.[104]

By frequent personal consultation as much as by party or police reports, Bourguiba kept in touch with political currents below him. Governors, Neo-Destour political commissioners, local political leaders,

[102]Speech, August 8, 1957.

[103]In an interview with the author on November 11, 1961 (a few days before Masmoudi was expelled from the Political Bureau), Bourguiba insisted that he had even consulted Masmoudi during the crisis while the latter was abroad. It is less certain, however, that Bourguiba consulted anyone before his spectacular about-face on September 8; Al 'Amal changed tune one day late.

[104]As Bourguiba described the requirements of leadership in a letter to a favorite subordinate in 1952 (La Tunisie et la France, pp. 375-378). "It is the difficult role of the leader to see farther ahead than the militants, to have a true scale of values, to sacrifice what is secondary to what is primary, to sacrifice even his preferences or personal jealousies in order to assure the durability, strength, and especially the efficiency of the whole . . . [in cases of disagreement] I have never despaired . . . of bringing a patriot [back into the fold]—as long as he be honest and sincere. . . . I have always tried—and often succeeded—to dominate clans, especially those which claimed to be mine, to control susceptibilities, jealousies, or individual antipathies in order to pull the whole into a solid and coherent bundle. . . . Sometimes a kind word or a smile is enough to conquer a heart and make a valuable addition to our grand 'Army.' . . .

"In this work of conciliation I have often run into resistance and reticence from the best militants—especially the tough ones, and the tough are the best. But each time that I was able to make them hear reason—unfortunately not always—I never regretted it. I had to deal with the failings of a people that during decades was a dust heap of individuals where the anarchic individualism flourished that was the prime cause of our decadence and impotence. I had to use all my prestige to maintain this essentially unstable equilibrium which characterizes the existence of a big party."

the national organizations, and many personal friends had formal and informal access to the President. His frequent trips about the country served to keep up his friendships as well as to maintain his public image. Bourguiba escaped bureaucratic routine, which was handled by Ladgham, the government's coördinator.

Although he had the powers of a modern dictator—powers extended and made legitimate by virtually automatic mass support—Bourguiba did not rule like a dictator. His speeches were factual analyses of current developments, not exercises in ideology or propaganda, which kept the public informed of policies and the reasoning behind them. Unlike an American president at a press conference, Bourguiba was not challenged by questions, but he probably reached a larger proportion of the people.

Bourguiba's important decisions were rarely made in haste. He first tested the reactions of others to his ideas, which then rapidly made the rounds of Tunisian political circles. Ben Salah's appointment to the Plan was being discussed confidentially more than four months before he was actually named. Rumors were sometimes official: that of the impending reorganization of the party in 1957 was published ten months before the decision was announced. From the idea to the decision, more than a year elapsed in the case of economic planning. More than three months of rumors preceded the Bey's deposition. When important decisions could not wait, as after the bombardment of Sakiet or the French devaluation, Bourguiba consulted his Political Bureau.

As with all transitional political systems, where new institutions are not effectively planned for the control and organization of political power, boundaries were unfixed and actors unpredictable. Bourguiba's decisions were always a gamble, not so much because the unpopularity of any one measure would mean the downfall of his regime, but because too many political mistakes might produce dangerous cumulative resentment. During the Bizerte crisis, Bourguiba was under pressure both because of the catastrophe and because the religious issue was a potential danger. Prior consultation gave him the needed protection. Generally Bourguiba felt obliged to use his prestige sparingly. He gave Ben Salah his unstinting public support for the Plan only when it became necessary to stop the rumors of Ben Salah's adversaries about the weakness of the latter's political position. Even then, it was to be the party's as well as Bourguiba's Plan.[105] However, Bourguiba was sufficiently strong-willed and powerful to take daring initiatives when

[105]The National Council of the Neo-Destour was specially convened in March, 1962, to pass judgment on the Three-Year Plan.

the Political Bureau was divided, as over the Ramadan issue. Even here the law of anticipated reaction possibly served as a limit upon Bourguiba's power.

In the last analysis Bourguiba's leadership was unique. It was not charismatic in the sense of resting upon some inspiration. It was not traditional in the sense that Tunisia's absolute monarchy used to be. It was not democratic in the sense of being limited by the institutional devices of modern constitutional governments. Yet all three elements were included in the man's personal synthesis. Instead of *charisma*, Bourguiba had political genius and the prestige of having successfully led his country to independence. As Head of State, there was much of the monarch in Bourguiba. "Le système? C'est moi le système." Yet his political success depended upon his ability to persuade rather than force people to accept his point of view. The democratic basis of his authority remained the Neo-Destour Party and the national organizations, for they were his mass instruments of persuasion. Just as Bourguiba needed a mass party to convince France of the reality of Tunisian nationhood, he needed it to maintain the cohesion of the nation and to elaborate a modernist consensus. The need to rekindle the vitality and ensure the approval of these political organizations posed a vaguely defined limit to Bourguiba's personal power. Although the limits cannot be accurately gauged by an outside observer, the functioning of the organizations and their relationships with the government can shed further light on the system and put Bourguiba's role in perspective.

IV PARTY AND GOVERNMENT

By VIRTUE of its mass organization, the Neo-Destour provided Bourguiba with the popular support that made his rule legitimate by modern standards. By virtue of its history, too, the party gave the regime a certain legitimacy. On the first anniversary of the founding of the Republic, Bourguiba declared "By its very essence the republican regime gives the whole of the people—leaders, cadres, and masses—responsibility for its destiny. . . . In reality the people were aware for more than twenty-five years that it had taken over its rule, and handed it to the guides it chose. . . . The men invested by its confidence, who oriented it from the depths of prison or exile, were found again at its head."[1] The only difference between the heroic period of opposition and the post-independence days, Bourguiba went on to say, was that now "the directives emanate from the presidency."

In a single-party regime, it is perilous to draw rigid distinctions between party and government. In Tunisia one existed in symbiosis with the other. Both were bureaucracies with overlapping staffs, vaguely differentiated functions, and parallel structures. To many Tunisians the party was the government, although it was not clear whether the party actually determined the policy of the government or merely served as its instrument of mass support. The party was supposed to represent the people, but the government was also supposed to be an emanation of the general will. The ambiguous relationships between party and government were reflected at all levels of authority. Whatever its representative character, the party also appeared to be a ruling institution, the government's alter ego.

Such ambiguity was probably necessary if the Neo-Destour was to play both an integrating and a representative role. It could mobilize popular support for government policies while representing (to a degree) the interests and aspirations of the rank and file. For the former task an efficient and disciplined apparatus was required; for the latter, a measure of internal discussion, compromise, and conciliation. Internal democracy, however limited by traditions of party discipline, would hardly seem possible in a single-party system if the party determined government policy. The risks of genuine dialogue within

[1]Speech of July 25, 1958.

the party would be too great. In Tunisia the symbiotic relationship between party and government permitted a more flexible party structure. The Neo-Destour's word was not law, whatever its influence upon the government. Although the party's mission might, as Bourguiba suggested, be "permanent," the Neo-Destour did not become a cult or an end in itself.

The party apparatus was played down after independence. In Tunisia there were really two Neo-Destours, the historic myth and the bureaucratic reality. Unlike political parties, whether fascist, communist, Catholic, or socialist, which rely upon a specific philosophy of life and society for their sustenance, the Neo-Destour relied mainly upon its past. A *mystique* of shared experience in the struggles for independence gave it a substitute for ideology. In the myth the party was identical with the nation because nationhood was the sense of solidarity which party agitation and propaganda had fostered in each Tunisian. The highpoints of the struggle became national holidays, annually celebrated by the party and recollected by Bourguiba in his speeches. More than concepts, the concrete historical events were the symbols of the nationalism that the Neo-Destour stood for.[2]

The party, like the Radical Party in France,[3] had an ideology of sorts that distinguished it from other parties. Its modernist outlook was in strong contrast to the old Destour's fainthearted reformism. But Bourguibism meant an outlook and political style fundamentally opposed to doctrine; indeed the very elasticity of the party's principles is what distinguished it from the Communist Party. No "scientific" laws predetermined the strategy and tactics of Bourguibism even after

[2]In the attenuated sense in which Bourguiba could be considered a "charismatic" leader (see above, Chap. II), the party could also be deemed charismatic, by virtue of its prestige and the *mystique* associated with it in the minds of most Tunisians. This line of analysis, suggested by W. G. Runciman in connection with the Ghanaian CPP, seems even more relevant to the older and more solidly implanted Neo-Destour. See his article, "Charismatic Legitimacy and One-Party Rule in Ghana," *Archives Européennes de Sociologie,* IV (1963), pp. 148-165, esp. 159 ff. In Runciman's terms, "It is in the separation of the party as the source of authority from the government as its agent and in the institutionalization in this sense of the party's necessary charisma that I have tried to suggest that Weber's discussion [of *charisma* and legitimacy] is most relevant. . . ." (pp. 164-165). (Runciman would not carry his analysis further, because he recognizes the ambiguities inherent in Weber's notion of the "routinization of *charisma*.") Similarly, with regard to Tunisia one can only say that the party's *mystique* (or *charisma*) is relatively well protected, in that the party directly exercises little authority—"*le parti règne mais il ne gouverne pas.*"
[3]See Francis de Tarr, *The French Radical Party* (Oxford University Press, 1961), pp. 1-13. In some respects this ideology bears a striking resemblance to Bourguibism; both stress the role of reason in politics and maintain a cautious faith in progress achieved in gradual stages, and both are opposed to doctrinaire ideologies.

he launched "Neo-Destour socialism" in 1961. Thus the regime of single-party government did not become a doctrine in which all must believe. Members of the party could have diverse views, for its authority did not rest on a dogma which demanded conformity. Whatever the nature of the myth holding it together, the party did not demand total intellectual commitment from its members. Although the struggle for independence demanded the devotion and unquestioned discipline of the activists, the myth of past sacrifices ought not be mistaken for the post-independence reality.

The party was reorganized in 1958 to give Neo-Destour leaders in the government greater control over the party apparatus. Two years after independence it seemed that the party was to become a subservient instrument of the state it had created. It was unthinkable that the party might, as in Guinea or Communist countries, become the ruling apparatus giving political directives to government technicians. Bourguiba remained president of the party, but his position as Head of State—and hence as the father not only of the militants but of all Tunisians—was emphasized.

In 1963-64 the party was again reorganized, but this time the purpose was to stimulate popular participation by democratizing its structures and extending its influence upon the government. Even then, however, neither the new socialist ideology nor organizational changes sufficed to give the party decisive jurisdiction over government policies. There was a sense, however, in which the party had always dominated the political process: its *mystique* and a sense of party loyalty pervaded the organs of state that its leaders had captured or created. To understand the party's role in contemporary Tunisia, one can examine formal changes in party structure, but without losing sight of the loose structures of influence cemented by a history of shared memories.

The Party Before Independence

The Neo-Destour was originally organized as a democratic mass party modeled on those of the French Left. Intellectually, Bourguiba had not been impressed by socialism during his student days, but politicians of the Left were his natural allies at times during the independence struggle. Dr. Materi, the first president of the Neo-Destour, had been a member of the French Communist Party until 1924, when he was expelled for Trotskyist deviationism.[4] As Hedi Nouira, a member of the Political Bureau, wrote of the early leaders: "Trained in the

[4]Interview, June 23, 1961.

Western school, they borrowed from French political parties their tactics, their organization, and even their slogans."[5]

Long before independence, the Neo-Destour had an imposing structure, reflecting a modern revolutionary style. By 1937 the party claimed 100,000 members grouped in more than 400 local branches throughout the country.[6] Its highly articulated structure was codified by internal statutes passed by party congresses.[7] By 1937 the party consisted of the Political Bureau, National Council, congress, permanent commissions, federations, and branches. Any local branch of at least fifty members elected a delegate to the annual national congress, the supreme authority of the party.[8] The Political Bureau, elected by the congress, was responsible to it. At the regional level, branch delegates at annual congresses elected the bureau of their federation, an intermediary body designed as the link between the Political Bureau and the branches. Between congresses, at least every four months, the National Council was supposed to meet to supervise the work of the Political Bureau. The Council, with twenty-nine members in 1937, consisted of the federation presidents and twelve delegates elected directly by the congress. Formally the party appeared, with its many representative organs, to have a highly democratic structure.

The party at the same time had to be highly centralized in order to be an efficient instrument of emancipation. The Political Bureau was to execute congress policy directives, administer the party, handle its finances, maintain contact with "the people," and represent the party to the authorities and governments. The Political Bureau acted within the context of National Council and congress resolutions, but "the door is nevertheless open to initiative and personal effort bringing effective results and benefits to the National Cause."[9] For propaganda and agitation, the party developed a chain of command. The Political Bureau, aided by permanent commissions of appointed technicians, gave directions to the federations, transmitted in turn to the branches. Staffed by seasoned militants, the federations closely supervised the branches and investigated their activities every six months. The federations could institute disciplinary proceedings against branch members, but final decisions were made by a six-man commission drawn from the Political Bureau and the National Council.

[5]Hedi Nouira, "Le Néo-Destour," *Politique Etrangère*, June-July, 1954, p. 317.
[6]Henri de Montety's estimate of 28,000 active members in 432 cells is probably more accurate. He kindly lent me an unpublished essay on Tunisian nationalism.
[7]As the party grew, the original statutes of 1934 were modified in 1937, 1948, and 1956.
[8]Only the congress could modify the internal statutes of the party and, with a three-quarters majority, change the general policies of the party.
[9]*Les Congrès du Néo-Destour* (1959), p. 102.

Hedi Nouira's estimate of the party before independence seems fair:

It is far from being a confessional or totalitarian party. If it is clearly hier-archical, its doctrine and tactics are not the exclusive possession of a minor-ity of leaders, but the expression of a collegial will, be it the Congress or National Council. Thus the Neo-Destour militant is attached to his party because in his eyes it represents an instrument of emancipation and because he has the clear feeling of contributing either directly or through his dele-gates to the elaboration of its doctrine and the definition of its tactics.[10]

In practice, however, the impressive democratic structure existed mostly on paper. The leaders of the Political Bureau do not appear de-liberately to have ignored the statutes they drafted, but the exigencies of the nationalist struggle did not permit the regular consultations and democratic controls outlined above. From September, 1934, until May, 1936, the party's top leadership was incarcerated by the Protectorate authorities. Even during the party's experiment of coöperation with the French Popular Front governments, from May, 1936, until January, 1938, the party was tolerated but had no legal existence. From April, 1938, until early 1943 its leaders were in prison and its political activi-ties were clandestine. Until 1949 it operated in a precarious context that did not permit public meetings. The party was again forced under-ground in 1952, when its leaders were once more arrested; overt politic-al activities were tolerated only after Mendès-France's visit. Even during the periods of relative toleration by the Protectorate authorities, the party's democratic institutions were rarely in use. The Neo-Destour was usually engaged in delicate Franco-Tunisian negotiations requir-ing discretion and rapid decisions. It was not surprising that, in the political flux of negotiations and repression, congresses and national councils met irregularly.

These bodies met either to display national solidarity to the Pro-tectorate authorities or to justify a tactical shift that Bourguiba had decided. Apart from the Ksar-Hellal meeting in 1934, the party held only four national congresses before independence.[11] Only in 1937 and 1955 did the congresses, organized under relatively normal conditions, permit a real discussion of issues. At the 1937 congress a temporary compromise was reached between the moderates who wished to pur-sue the experiment of conciliation with the Popular Front and the

10Nouira, op. cit.
11These met in 1937, 1948, 1952, and 1955. The meetings of 1948 and 1952 were hardly congresses in any regular sense. That of 1948 was a clandestine meeting at Mongi Slim's house; that of 1952 was an emergency session that took place after the arrest of leading members of the Political Bureau.

more extreme leaders who were discouraged by the meager results. In 1955 the congress decided, after strong and persuasive intervention by Bourguiba, to support the policies of the Political Bureau and to reject Ben Youssef's appeals.

Before independence the National Council often in practice fulfilled the policy-making functions of a congress. In 1938 the Council decided to cease coöperation with France and to withdraw the party's "favorable prejudice" toward the French Resident. Bourguiba was then outmaneuvering some of his moderate associates on the Political Bureau. In 1950 the National Council accepted the party's participation in a transitional government, and in 1954 it similarly decided for negotiations with France. Before independence, however, political conditions did not allow the National Council to meet regularly, except in the years 1937-38, 1950-51, and 1954-55.

Whenever the party was forced underground, the formal structure of branches and federations virtually disappeared. Mass membership melted, and the party became a hard core of activists distributing political tracts and, on occasion, sabotaging public installations.[12] During the clandestine periods, elected members of the Political Bureau were either in jail, in exile, or under house arrest. In the interim, friends of the imprisoned leaders took charge of party activities. From 1938 to 1942 a string of provisional political bureaus replaced successively arrested leaders.[13] The clandestine political bureaus were an important source of new party leadership,[14] and succeeded, often at great odds,[15] in holding the party together.

[12]In 1939, according to one of the clandestine leaders, the party consisted of only two thousand activists. In 1943, however, amid the confusion of the Axis occupation, the party was intervening in much of the country's local administration through the Red Crescent, a relief organization it infiltrated, and various youth organizations.

[13]The succeeding Bureau was always coöpted in advance, its members being told to take charge of the party when they read in the newspapers of the arrest of their predecessors (interview with Taieb Slim, January 3, 1962).

[14]Ahmed Mestiri, after being a clandestine member of all the successive bureaus from 1952 to 1954, became a minister in 1956 and a member of the Political Bureau in 1957. Though Bahi Ladgham became general secretary of the party without any previous formal position on the Political Bureau, he was recognized as one of the party's senior leaders: in 1938-39 he had been the animator of a clandestine Political Bureau. Rachid Driss and Taieb Slim had similar experience in that area. Mehiri owed his rise in large part to clandestine activities, as did Ahmed Tlili.

[15]Until 1955 Tunisia remained technically under a prewar state of siege that gave the French Resident General virtually unlimited rights to repress nationalist activity. See Victor Silvera, "Les libertés publiques en Tunisie," Revue Juridique et Politique de l'Union Française, IX (1955), 291-316.

Perhaps the most spectacular evidence of their effectiveness was Tunisia's 2,500-man Liberation Army which, in the spring of 1954, made daring raids on colon farms, post offices, and even trains.[16] The so-called fellagha reduced their operations after July 31, when Mendès-France promised Tunisian home rule, but controlling them was a serious problem for the Neo-Destour when negotiations with France became possible.

The most important fellagha leaders had worked closely with the Political Bureau.[17] Available evidence suggests that the Neo-Destour had deliberately and systematically organized the fellagha bands, and that they were dependent upon the party for money and arms.[18] The party probably had conceived of the idea of a mass rural uprising as early as 1950.[19] Violence, however, was for Bourguiba only a means to stimulate political negotiations. It was therefore crucial that the Political Bureau maintain its control over the armed bands it had unleashed. It is a tribute to the party's organization that control remained possible, even while Bourguiba and other top leaders remained in

[16]The 15,000-man French Army was ill equipped to conquer the guerrillas, whose potiential threat was illustrated by Dien Bien Phu. The *Times* (July 26, 1954) reported that between March 19 and June 23 the Tunisians had killed 74 civilians and 21 policemen or soldiers and had wounded, respectively, 87 and 57, while losing only 60 men. See Cora Bell (ed.), *Survey of International Affairs, 1954* (1957), pp. 229 ff.

[17]Tahar Lassaoued, who enlisted tribesmen in the Gabes area, was the first militant to take up arms. Hassen Ben Abdelaziz came from the village of Ouardanine and was on good terms with his fellow villager Abdallah Farhat, who in 1955 became a member of the Political Bureau. Mahjoub Ben Ali was the most important fellagha leader in the area north of Tunis. A disciplined Neo-Destour militant, he refused to accept funds from any source other than the Political Bureau, and later integrated his forces with the new Tunisian state. In the mining centers of Gafsa, Lazhar Chraiti was the leader, and he coöperated with Gafsa's Neo-Destour leader, Ahmed Tlili, who like Farhat in 1955 became a member of the Political Bureau. In the mountains of Kasserine and Le Kef, Sassi Lassaoued (No relation to Tahar) also acted under party orders.

[18]Most of the real activists were Neo-Destour militants acting under party discipline. Although the Political Bureau's original leaders were all arrested at one time or another in 1952 and 1953, the Bureau maintained itself underground by prearranged recruiting of new members. A key man during the period was Ahmed Mestiri, who like Slim was a lawyer who came from a baldi family. Since he had never been engaged in overt political activity with the Neo-Destour, he was not suspected by the police. The Political Bureau continued its contacts with the fellagha through Mestiri, whose main tasks were to raise money to support the terrorist groups, care for needy families of Neo-Destour prisoners, and supply party delegations abroad with funds to carry on international propaganda. Thus the Political Bureau controlled the Neo-Destour's use of agitation and violence even when its leaders were in jail.

[19]Close associates of Bourguiba intimate that he had no real expectation that the Chenik government, which the Neo-Destour had supported in 1950-51, could peaceably obtain the internal autonomy that it sought.

prison or abroad. Eventually each rebel band was contacted by a mixed team representing both the French authorities and the Tunisian government. The safety of the fellagha was guaranteed, in accordance with an official Neo-Destour resolution, in return for their arms. This compromise, worked out by the French authorities and the Neo-Destour, could hardly be interpreted as a surrender to the French Army, for the Tunisian emissaries were themselves party militants. The fellagha leaders responded to the party order to "lay down your arms for Bourguiba."[20] The guerrilla army in Tunisia, in contrast to Morocco, was disbanded before developing a nation-wide terrorist potential that might have seriously endangered Franco-Tunisian negotiations and Neo-Destour unity.[21]

The disciplined, clandestine network established during the "trials of strength" with France was as basic to the evolution of the Neo-Destour as the democratic structure copied from French parties during periods of negotiation and peace. If the latter nurtured democratic discussion, debate, and voting, the former demanded self-sacrifice and unquestioning obedience.

The Deliberative Organs of the Party

The party's procedures after independence continued to fall short of its democratic norms. One explanation was the severe shortage of responsible local leadership in the early independence period. With victory in sight by late 1954, the party was swamped with new recruits. From a membership estimated at 106,000 before July, 1954,[22] the Neo-Destour had roughly 325,000 adherents represented at the

[20]By December 10, 1954, 2,514 fellagha had laid down their arms. The party also deviously procured extra safe-conduct cards for the return of some of its exiled militants (interview with Ahmed Mestiri, March 12, 1962).

[21]Though the more intransigent activists of the party argued—and could not be publicly contradicted by their leaders in 1954—that their violence rather than political bargaining had led to French concessions, Tunisia experienced relatively little violence. The potential danger of the fellagha bands to party unity, however, was illustrated by the career of the notorious leader Tahar Lassaoued. When the French and Tunisian emissaries came to parley with him, he shot them both, thinking that the Tunisian Neo-Destour cell leader was a French spy. Bourguiba's son and Azouz Rebai, an influential and militant youth organizer, tried to persuade Lassaoued to lay down his arms for the sake of Bourguiba and the success of the negotiations, but he refused. Taieb Mehiri, the chief party organizer of the fellagha, was able to convince Lassaoued to stop fighting only when the French Army was threatening his group with extinction. Lassaoued later broke with the party and joined Ben Youssef.

[22]Documentation Tunisienne, *Tunisie 1958*, p. 22, quoted by Keith Callard, "The Republic of Bourguiba," *International Journal*, 1961, p. 34.

Sfax congress in November, 1955,[23] and supposedly 600,000[24] in 1957. Some of the new arrivals, especially the educated sympathizers, did not take to party discipline; others, local notables who had not aided the party during the fight for independence, lacked mass support.[25] Many of the new recruits were loyal to Bourguiba without feeling loyalty to the party. Meanwhile, with independence the people were demanding more of the party apparatus, yet the best party cadres were needed in the new administration. Branches multiplied but lacked competent leadership, and many tried to use the party as a stepping-stone to a good government position. The party's public image naturally suffered.

On October 2, 1958, Bourguiba launched an extensive reform of the party's structure. The federations, whose officers had been elected by the branch leaders, were abolished and replaced by regional offices, one in each governorate, headed by a commissioner appointed by the Political Bureau. The party's 1,800 branches were reduced to 1,000, or one per *sheikhat*, the lowest administrative division. Thus, under the tight control of the Political Bureau, the party structure was made to parallel the government's regional and local administration. The commissioners were given more authority over the branches than the federations had enjoyed, to compensate for the relative immaturity of the branch cadres.

Bourguiba went to great lengths to justify the changes, which seemed a blow to democracy within the party. He recalled that the federations had only been instituted in 1937, three years after the party was founded. Decentralization had been necessary during years of French repression of the Neo-Destour, when the leaders of the Political Bureau were in prison. Though originally founded to carry out the latter's directives, the federations had acquired autonomy when the Political Bureau was crippled. But the federations, largely a function of the "personal radiation of certain militants," were no longer needed after independence. What was now needed, Bourguiba continued,

[is] a strong power which does not dissipate in multiple ramifications. We need cohesion and discipline to increase efficiency. . . . It is indispensable that the Party adapt its organization to the administrative armature of the country, so that the two structures support one another and progress in perfect harmony. . . . The new organization is called to liberate us from innumerable difficulties which, until now, have taken up a large part of our

[23]*National Congress of Sfax* (1956), p. 58.
[24]Callard, *op. cit.,* p. 34.
[25]According to one Neo-Destour official, whose article appeared in *L'Action,* January 13, 1958.

time, hindered our action, and paralyzed the activity of the Governors and their Delegates. The reform in reality is not doing anything more than reducing the evils of the inflation of cadres. Some leaders, especially those who claim a glorious past of struggles and sacrifice, have paralyzed the activity of the administration by their constant interventions. . . . We cannot permit anyone to paralyze the State apparatus. Those who, by lack of consideration, are tempted to do so will be treated as enemies. . . . I will never be able to compromise, for whatever motive, on the necessity of ensuring the reputation of the State and its prestige.[26]

The ten months he had taken to arrive at his decision emphasized the significance of Bourguiba's reform. He deliberately chose to maximize the importance of the government administration, at the expense, if need be, of democratic discussion within the party. The risk was that the party would lose contact with the masses, but perhaps after independence bureaucratization had become inevitable. The bureaucracy had to be centralized in capable hands, since the party's role as anticolonialist agitator had given way to the more routine functions of supporting a newly independent government.

Other formal, structural changes also limited democracy within the party. It was decided in 1956 to hold the national congress only once every two years instead of annually, and in 1959 the interval was extended to three years. In practice the party from 1956 to 1964 held only one congress, in Sousse, March 2-5, 1959. Two years after the Sfax congress (November 15-18, 1955), when the congress should have been held, the time was inopportune. In late 1957 a party reorganization was already being planned, and the Political Bureau evidently decided that it would be safer to suppress the federations and institute the new system before convening a congress. In March, 1962, when in theory a congress should again have been held, the Political Bureau hastily called a National Council meeting to discuss the Plan. A congress had to be avoided because of the critical economic situation after poor harvests in 1961 and because no permanent solution to the Bizerte crisis had been achieved.[27]

The National Council also suffered a decline. After the Sfax congress it met only three times, January 21-23 and June 23, 1956, and April 11-12, 1957. It was not consulted in 1958 about the party reorganization. Yet in 1959 the new party statutes called for a National Council to meet every six months, "to assist the Political Bureau in framing positions within the context of congress resolutions."[28] To com-

[26]Speech, October 2, 1958.
[27]The congress was not held until 1964, a year after the French evacuation of Bizerte.
[28]Article 17.

pensate for the suppression of the federations, with their annual congress of branch delegates, the National Council was to be composed mostly of delegates elected by the branch committees rather than by the congress. The director of the party suggested that the party would thereby maintain its democratic character. But the branch delegates were not elected nor was the National Council convened until March, 1962, when such a meeting could give the Political Bureau an excuse for not convening a congress. Its discussion was limited strictly to the theme of Ben Salah's plan.

The vague resolutions passed by the party's representative organs hardly constituted guidelines for government policy.[29] When the National Assembly was formed, the National Council no longer acted as a parliament, made specific recommendations, or discussed government activities in detail.[30] In April, 1957, the National Council provided the setting for a weekly Bourguiba speech.[31] The concluding resolution read like a message of congratulation to the government: "The National Council is convinced that the steps taken because of the wise policy of establishing greater national cohesion to disengage Tunisian sovereignty from the vestiges of the colonial regime and of consolidating the basis of internal and external sovereignty constitute decisive

[29] The only exception was the National Council that met in January, 1956, before independence. During three days of discussion the Neo-Destour ministers explained and defended the policies of their government departments. The Council called upon the government and the Political Bureau to Tunisify the administration rapidly, to hasten the creation of the organized armed force promised at the Sfax congress, and to implement the social and economic policies of the congress by specific measures such as an agricultural workers' statute. Like the Sfax congress, the Council put pressure on the transitional government to attain independence rapidly. The method of selecting National Front candidates for the Constituent Assembly was discussed at length before the Council mandated the Political Bureau to draw up the lists. Bourguiba promised that the composition of the Assembly "will not differ much from that of our present reunion. It will also be able to discuss as we are doing." *Le Petit Matin*, January 24, 1956.

[30] Its brief meeting in June, 1956, passed almost unnoticed by the press because it conflicted with a meeting of the Council of Ministers. Only Mongi Slim and Ali Belhaouane of the Political Bureau attended the National Council in the afternoon, while the party's statutes were revised and youth activities were discussed. In the evening Bourguiba and Ladgham appeared with a general report on government activities, but no resolutions seem to have been voted.

[31] The Council also listened to Ladgham's report on party activities and discussed the imminent municipal elections. It decided that, except in Tunis, where the Political Bureau would fix the list, local branches would draft their own electoral lists, subject to the approval of the federation. Government policies seem to have been discussed in the vaguest of terms. In a resolution the Council praised the government's judicial and administrative reforms and approved of Bourguiba's demands for the French evacuation of Tunisian territory, the strengthening of the Tunisian Army, the revision of Tunisia's Saharan frontier, and economic and technical assistance without political strings.

steps that should be pursued with firmness and vigilance to achieve the effective attributes of sovereignty and territorial integrity. . . ."[32]

The same vagueness characterized the resolutions of the Sousse congress in 1959: "The Party has not only achieved but gone beyond the objectives assigned it by the Sfax congress and subsequent National Council meetings." Admiration was expressed for the draft constitution, "defining a regime of true democracy, founded on the principles of popular sovercignty and separation of powers."[33] Agrarian reform was to be pursued by the distribution of unoccupied lands and by the recovery of colon lands.[34] The goals of economic growth and social justice expressed by the congress were aspirations rather than concrete demands or recommendations to the government, although economic planning was mentioned.

Votes on resolutions were usually unanimous at congresses and National Council meetings. At the April, 1957, meeting the general resolution, rather than being laboriously drafted in a commission, was simply read amid general applause by a council member who was on Bourguiba's presidential staff. Yet these meetings were not solely displays of solidarity orchestrated from above. Discussions at the Sousse congress and the 1962 National Council each took four days. The six-hour report that Ladgham delivered to the Sousse congress was greeted with discussion and criticism that lasted into the night and continued during the following morning and afternoon sessions, before the report was unanimously adopted by the congress. During the full day of debate, six ministerial members of the Political Bureau answered batteries of questions from the delegates. Debate covered all important government policies and many specific questions. The congress afterward more rapidly accepted the party director's explanation of the controversial reorganization of the party that the Political Bureau had already executed. But on the following day the new statutes reflecting these changes were passed only after "laborious" discussion.[35]

[32]Le Petit Matin, April 13, 1957.
[33]Ibid., March 8, 1959.
[34]Apart from a phrase about "individual or collective property," however, the congress seemed to advocate conservative economic policies, such as state aid to private and mixed enterprises, a stable currency, and possible ties with the European Common Market.
[35]Le Petit Matin, March 4-5, 1959. Party finances, in contrast, were barely touched at the Sousse congress. The financial commission of the Sfax congress had complained of the insufficient information provided by the Political Bureau (National Congress of Sfax, p. 58). Therefore at Sousse the party's finances were discussed on the first day, just after protocol speeches of welcome. The treasurer's report was quickly passed while the congress was preoccupied with the anticipation of more exciting business (Le Petit Matin, March 3, 1959).

Political discussions could be lengthy and penetrating, but they were not focused on clear-cut alternatives on which delegates could vote. They simply asked questions or made particular criticisms of the Political Bureau. There were no clearly defined factions with competing leadership and policy alternatives. The one obvious faction inside the party, with a policy and dynamic leadership, had been the UGTT. It was an important force at the Sfax congress, but after the scission and the demise of Ben Salah it lost its identity.

Considered a danger by Bourguiba, factions inside the party were discouraged by his tendency to shift political lieutenants around, disgrace them, and bring them back to favor. Obviously, too, the fact that the party's representative organs seldom met discouraged political ties among delegates. At Sfax and Sousse they numbered more than a thousand. The suppression of the federations may have prevented the formation of factions, for branch delegates could no longer look to their provincial leaders for guidance in national forums.

Voting procedure at the congress also discouraged factional alignments. Rather than making up competing lists, candidates for the Political Bureau were placed on a single ballot. Delegates then voted for as many candidates as there were places to fill, and those receiving the most votes were elected. This procedure recorded the popularity of individuals rather than the strength of any underlying factions. Conceivably the congress could display its lack of confidence in a particular minister's policy by not reelecting him to the Political Bureau, but the situation did not arise.

The Sousse congress emphasized Bourguiba's primacy by directly electing the president of the party. (But he turned down the suggestion that he be made president for life.) The general secretary, the assistant general secretary, the treasurer, and the director were chosen by the Political Bureau from among its members. Congresses in practice did not even have sole responsibility for electing the members of the Political Bureau. On April 12, 1957, at the request of the Political Bureau, the National Council coöpted four new members; one of them, Abdelmajid Chaker, had been appointed director of the party the previous year and was thus already one of the more important members of the Political Bureau. In November, 1961, the Political Bureau coöpted Ahmed Ben Salah without any reference to a National Council or congress. Bourguiba's unorthodox explanation was that the expulsion of Masmoudi had created a vacancy on the Political Bureau that had to be filled and that Ben Salah was entitled to it for having received the most votes among the unsuccessful candidates at the Sousse congress.

Congress votes for Political Bureau candidates did have some significance. The accompanying tabulation lists the candidates with the votes they received at the Sfax and Sousse congresses.

1955		*1959*	
Bahi Ladgham	1,158	Mongi Slim	944
Djalouli Fares	1,110	Djalouli Fares	905
Sadok Mokaddem	1,095	Sadok Mokaddem	901
Mongi Slim	1,088	Bahi Ladgham	894
Hedi Nouira	984	Taieb Mehiri	878
Ali Belhaouane	978	Hedi Nouira	798
Taieb Mehiri	970		
		Abdelmajid Chaker	797
Ahmed Tlili	941	Ahmed Mestiri	785
Mohammed Masmoudi	886	Ahmed Tlili	777
Abdallah Farhat	468	Rachid Driss	740
		Taieb Slim	692
		Mohammed Masmoudi	608
		Ferdjani Bel Hadj Ammar	594
		Habib Achour	379

Unsuccessful candidates

Taieb Slim	433	Ahmed Ben Salah	(figures not
Rachid Driss	423	Mustapha Filali	given)
Ahmed Mestiri	228	Abdallah Farhat	
Bergaoui	109	Ben Sassi	
		Azouz Rebai	

In both elections the same people gained the top six places, if one discounts Ali Belhaouane, who died in 1958 (and was not replaced at the time). Masmoudi and Farhat lost much popularity, while Taieb Slim, Driss, and Mestiri greatly gained. The votes in 1959 for Chaker, Mestiri, Ferdjani, and Achour were probably due in part to their having already been coöpted to the Political Bureau. Tunisians, like militants in most parties, tend to vote for the man who is already in office. But Driss and Taieb Slim had not been coöpted, and yet they obtained more votes than Masmoudi, the well-known secretary of information. More surprising, the once-powerful Ben Salah, who had since become a respected minister, was beaten by his old trade union rival, Habib Achour. Yet it was generally known that Bourguiba had personally encouraged Ben Salah to throw his hat into the ring.

Candidates' ministerial records seem to have had little bearing on the electoral outcomes. Ladgham and Mongi Slim, admittedly in the public eye because of his important work in the United Nations, exchanged places in the popularity contest. Slim, indeed, enjoyed a personal triumph at the Sousse congress; he was elected by acclamation as president of the congress. His popularity perhaps helped his brother, Taieb. The ministerial work of Ben Salah was not an issue that might have cost him votes at the congress.

The elections suggested a number of hypotheses. Those who were least identified with the regime's day-to-day internal administration got the most votes: Slim, Fares, and Mokaddem, the secretary for foreign affairs. Bourguiba preferred to remain above the fray rather than engage his prestige in the electoral outcome. Therefore Farhat and Ben Salah lost. Farhat lost because he was a leading member of Bourguiba's personal entourage and, sensing Ben Salah's rise to power, had supported him. Ben Salah's defeat showed that, regardless of Bourguiba, he had many influential enemies within the party. Obviously there were implied limits to Bourguiba's presidential power.

The real victors in 1959 were the junior collaborators of Slim and Mehiri: Mestiri, Driss, and Taieb Slim. Replacing Belhaouane and Farhat on the Political Bureau, Driss and Taieb Slim were newcomers who altered the balance slightly in favor of Mongi Slim. As a result of his personal triumph at the congress, Mongi Slim was considered to be Bourguiba's heir apparent.

The election results had no apparent impact, however, upon the composition of the government. Ben Salah continued his rise to power. Mongi Slim was not appointed to foreign affairs for another three years. Mestiri lost his ministerial post and became an ambassador in August, 1960. Driss was almost sent away from his ministry to become ambassador to Turkey,[36] and Taieb Slim remained an ambassador. The top party offices remained in the hands of Ladgham, Mehiri, Tlili, and Chaker; a second assistant general secretary was not appointed to succeed Ali Belhaouane.

In the last analysis the role of the party's representative organs seemed primarily symbolic. The discussion and debates injected a democratic atmosphere into the party's otherwise bureaucratic structure, and the unanimity and applause gave living evidence of national solidarity. The Sousse congress was timed to coincide with the twenty-fifth anniversary of the founding of the party, and the delegates made a commemorative pilgrimage to Ksar-Hellal. The very theme of the congress, victory, emphasized past achievements rather than current

[36] *Afrique-Action*, October 7, 1961.

issues. Although issues were debated, the debates did not seem to terminate in any specific conclusions. By being able to ask questions of ministers, however, the delegates were given a feeling a participation in national politics. The fraternal atmosphere perhaps served to increase their devotion to Bourguiba's regime, so far as the congress substantiated the regime's myth that perfect harmony prevailed between a truly democratic party and a popular government.

The myth was essential to Tunisia's political stability. That Bourguiba and his lieutenants took seriously the need for the delegates' approval was shown by their caution in convening congresses and National Council meetings. These bodies also served another very practical purpose of informing the country's leadership of public opinion and its grievances. In free discussion, the comradely militant ethos of the party was resurrected. Harassing a Neo-Destour minister with penetrating questions was permitted in the family reunions, as long as the prestige of the father figure was not questioned.

Although congresses and National Council meetings were important political spectacles, the local branch leaders had other means of expressing themselves on national questions. Often the political commissioner assembled them in informal party cadre conferences. These consultations somewhat took the place of the annual federal congresses. A visiting member of the Political Bureau would address the meeting and be questioned by the cadres. Instead of a resolution, the conference usually ended with the political commissioner, amid general applause, reading a telegram to President Bourguiba supporting "all your enlightened foreign and domestic policies."

In Tunisia's more backward provinces, these conferences were little more than attempts of the Political Bureau politically to educate the cadres, so that they could explain policies at local propaganda meetings. A former political commissioner at Gabes recalled that he had encouraged the timid local leaders to ask critical questions, and was happy when one branch leader asked, "What business is it of the party to try to abolish Ramadan?" Such questions revealed the problems of greatest concern to the rank and file, and showed the party where to concentrate its propaganda.

In the politically more sophisticated areas, as in Sousse and especially Tunis, the cadre conferences became representative institutions that the Political Bureau took seriously. Held three or four times a year, the conferences obtained added prestige and public notice in November, 1961, when National Assembly deputies attended them to develop contact with their constituencies. For the first time the Tunis meeting was recorded in full in one of the Arabic dailies.[37] Taieb Mehiri presided at the conference, which lasted from 9:30 A.M. to 2:30 the following morning. According to the political commissioner, the purposes of the meeting were to allow the cadres to express citizens' views, to clear up administrative problems, and to resolve any doubts about government policies. Some of the "questions" of the cadres are worth recording:

"We are surprised by the aggressive attitude of *Afrique-Action*. We respect Mohammed Masmoudi, member of the Political Bureau and one of *Afrique-Action's* leaders . . . [but] we ask the Government clearly to explain its attitude."

"We propose the creation in each governorate of an office to inform citizens of employment opportunities, because citizens often go to the governorate and then to the administrative delegation. Each passes the buck to the other."

"During Bourguiba's trip to the United States, Kennedy made a pleasing declaration about modern Tunisia, but his B-26's bombed Bizerte."

"In the Ten-Year Perspective we see that the work sites for the unemployed are to diminish. How is this when we are working for maximum employment? We want the Government to explain the socialist policy it wants to follow."

"The number of prostitutes and licentious youths is increasing. There is a need for serious penalties because the man has been severely punished for such infractions, but the woman, at the origin of all the evil a man can make, is condemned to a maximum of fifteen days in prison. We're practicing austerity today? But each day before the administrations I see more luxurious cars. Wives and children drive about in cars with official license plates. And the citizen can't get anywhere with the administration unless he happens to know someone in it. . . ."

"National Assembly deputies, who do nothing, should work in the administration without salary."

"The party should organize elections for the new National Council mentioned in the statutes. Though there was a law creating the Economic and Social Council and its members were appointed, it has not met. In this new difficult economic period, it should meet. A Council of State should also be created in accordance with the Constitution."

The comments of the cadres did not seem to be prepared in advance by higher party authorities. Even the question about Masmoudi and *Afrique-Action*, which jibed so well with the decision three days later to expel Masmoudi, seemed spontaneous. The branch leader who raised the issue subsequently explained that he had read the editorial

[37]*Es-Sabah*, November 15, 1961.

about personal power, felt perplexed that a member of the Political Bureau should implicitly compare Bourguiba with former King Farouk, and discussed the problem with his branch before attending the cadre conference.

The conferences may have affected the actions of the Political Bureau. It organized the meeting in 1962 of the National Council at least in part because a number of militants had raised the issue in conferences. Ministers listened carefully to the militants and sometimes used their comments in support of their own ideas. Ben Salah argued privately to the author and probably also to members of the Political Bureau and the cabinet that militants in one rich farming area formerly owned by Europeans wanted agricultural coöperatives rather than see the vacant lands rented to private entrepreneurs. (But Ben Salah was temporarily defeated on this issue.)

The cadre conferences were purely consultative channels for informing party leadership of rank-and-file opinion. Some were huge meetings including all the branch officers of a governorate. Others consisted only of the presidents and general secretaries of the branches. The political commissioner could invite well-known party veterans who had no official position. When the focus was on regional problems, the governor and government technicians were invited. As in the party's more formal assemblies, there was no structured debate on issues. But shifts of opinion, such as neutralist and anti-Western sentiment after the Bizerte crisis, were discernible to party leaders, even though they were not codified in votes or resolutions that could be binding upon either the Political Bureau or the government.

On March 2, 1963, Bourguiba announced a fundamental recasting of the party's structure to promote more institutionalized forms of consultation within the party. A specially convened National Council agreed after three days of discussion: (1) to impose more rigorous conditions of active membership in the party, (2) to abolish the office of political commissioner in favor of regional committees of coördination directly elected by the branches, (3) to expand the Political Bureau from fifteen to forty or fifty elected members, and (4) to institute a new executive body, a presidium of five or six members selected by Bourguiba.[38]

These innovations would not be official until ratified in 1964 by a full party congress, but the implications were clear. Bourguiba was regularizing and stimulating a deliberative process within the party. In place of the cadre conferences at the regional level, the committees of coördination, together with regional representatives of the national

[38]See *Jeune-Afrique,* March 11-18, 1963.

organizations and the democratically elected heads of the municipalities, would constitute a Governorate Council with consultative powers.[39] At the national level, the expanded Political Bureau, a body which Bourguiba would presumably have to consult regularly, would in effect supplement the National Council and the congress.

The fact that the new presidium would be appointed rather than elected was not of great significance; rather, the innovation in a sense ratified existing practice and underscored limitations of the old Political Bureau as a policy-making body.

The Political Bureau

The Political Bureau, consisting since 1957 of fifteen members, was not a form of collective leadership. Despite the principle that "every party committee is collectively responsible" (Art. 17), Bourguiba, elected directly since 1955 by the congress, was obviously more than a first among equals. On paper, however, the fifteen-man body was the supreme executive power, and implicitly made party policy.

The Political Bureau was responsible for the administration, direction, and finances of the party and for the application of party statutes and congress decisions. It reported to the congress and the National Council, and was empowered to call special sessions of these bodies. It managed technical central services for youth, orientation, and social development. It determined the number of branches and delimited their territorial competence. Its chain of command to the branches was direct, through the political commissioner it appointed to each of Tunisia's thirteen governorates.[40]

Within the Political Bureau the chain of command reflected presidential government under Bourguiba. The president of the party "watch[ed] over the activities of all party organs, orient[ed] its policy in accordance with the decisions of the congress, preside[d] over meetings of the Political Bureau, and . . . assure[d] the vitality of the party" (Art. 13). The general secretary, Bahi Ladgham, "coördinate[d] all the activities and executive decisions of the Political Bureau" (Art. 13), just as he served as Bourguiba's superminister in charge of coördinating the various departments. The assistant general secretary was the secretary of the interior; the treasurer, Ahmed Tlili, was also the general secretary of the UGTT.[41] Hedi Nouira might be

[39]Bourguiba inaugurated the first of these councils in March, 1964, at Le Kef. See New York *Times,* March 15, 1964, p. 20.
[40]Until 1963 the commissioner " supervise[d] the branches and watch[ed] over the application of the decisions of the Political Bureau" (Art. 9).
[41]But under Bourguiba every lieutenant is expendable. Tlili lost his position in the UGTT in 1963 (see Chap. VIII).

added to this list of influential leaders. The governor of the Central Bank, a member of the Political Bureau since 1948,[42] he was once the party's leading intellectual, and even after Ben Salah's rise probably had Bourguiba's full confidence on economic matters. Older than Mehiri, Masmoudi, and Ben Salah, he was above their rivalries.

Including Ladgham and Mehiri, the Political Bureau consisted of six ministers in 1963. The others were Mongi Slim, Driss, Chaker, and Ben Salah. Since the only cabinet members not included on the Bureau were technical ministers—for education, health and social affairs, information and culture, and public works and housing—discussion could range over governmental as well as party matters.

The Political Bureau, however, carried real weight only on paper. Its other members either were absent from the country or lacked the necessary prestige or political experience. Even Mongi Slim, in Washington and New York until 1962, rarely attended Political Bureau meetings and, despite his popularity, seemed to exercise little domestic influence. His brother Taieb and Ahmed Mestiri were also ambassadors away from home. Three other members of the Bureau were figureheads at best. As president of the National Assembly, Fares was only as important as the latter, mainly ceremonial body. A politician and educator with a distinguished past, he had little day-to-day contact with Bourguiba or the party apparatus. Ferdjani Bel Hadj Ammar and Habib Achour were on the Political Bureau simply because of their positions in UTIC and UGTT. Marginally elected at the Sousse congress, neither was a leading personality. Respectively a former café waiter and a municipality worker, their political horizons were limited. The former had failed as a minister.

In theory, according to a Political Bureau member, the body met weekly around Bourguiba's dinner table. But actually the President convened it as he pleased. Only on rare occasions, such as Bourguiba's trip to Rambouillet in February, 1961, did it meet without Bourguiba. Its deliberations were secret and informal, but sometimes, to underline the importance of a decision, the meeting concluded with a formal communiqué. On these occasions the Political Bureau seemed to take the place of the party's more representative organs that had fallen into disuse. Rarely, in times of crisis, the Political Bureau met formally before Bourguiba assembled his ministers in a Cabinet Council meet-

[42]Until 1954, when he resigned to signal his disapproval of the party's fellagha campaign, Nouira was assistant general secretary of the Neo-Destour. He returned to the Political Bureau in 1955, but as the architect of Tunisia's stable financial and monetary policies he was no longer active as a political organizer. His brother Mohsen Nouira had held the rank of governor since 1956. Like Bourguiba, they come from Monastir.

ing. Only then did it appear that the party (rather than Bourguiba or his ministers) made the political decisions—as in Guinea or Mali—which the government was to execute.

The leading members of the Political Bureau were in constant contact with the President. There was no distinction, however, between these meetings and Bourguiba's consultations with his more important ministers (Ben Salah was secretary for plan and finances for almost a year before the Bureau coöpted him). In the web of party and government decision-making, the Political Bureau as an entity had reduced significance. The key figures had dual roles difficult in practice to compartmentalize; matters directly touching on party administration rested with Bourguiba, Ladgham, Mehiri, Tlili, and Chaker—when Bourguiba did not by-pass them.[43]

But to the extent that any formal body decided policy in Tunisia, the elected Political Bureau seemed to have precedence over the appointed Cabinet Council. Members of the two executive organs privately observed that the discussions of the former were more heated, touching on controversial issues, whereas formal cabinet meetings dealt primarily with administrative detail.

One example cited by Ahmed Mestiri concerned economic negotiations with France in early 1959. The French decision to devalue the franc had caught the Tunisians—in the midst of a government reshuffle affecting finances—by surprise; although their monetary policy was controlled through the newly created Central Bank, the Tunisian dinar was pegged to the French franc. On December 30, after Ladgham had met with his ministers, Bourguiba decided not to devalue the dinar. After a week of negotiations with the French, the new Tunisian finance minister, Mestiri, wanted to break them off. The French were balking on maintaining supporting prices for wine and wheat and on freeing the Tunisian foreign exchange account held in Paris. On January 4 the Political Bureau met at Monastir, where Bourguiba was vacationing. Mestiri persuaded most of the Bureau members to accept his point of view. Bourguiba cut short the discussion—there is never formal voting—and backed Mestiri. On January 6, 9, and 11, the Cabinet Council discussed what Mestiri described as "technical implementation" of the decision of the Political Bureau. On January 11, Tunisia suspended all transfers to the franc zone.

[43]When Mohammed Ben Amara (for details of his career, see Chap. V, p. 157) in the wake of the Bizerte crisis was appointed assistant director of the party, the director felt it necessary publicly to deny "tendentious rumors by malevolent people" about the creation of this new party post. See *La Presse*, October 17, 1961.

Bourguiba's decisions were of two types: general options, such as economic planning or breaking the Franco-Tunisian customs union; and administrative decisions relating to personnel. Members of the Political Bureau could have their say and might even persuade Bourguiba to accept new ideas. But Bourguiba had the last word. On the question of Ramadan he rejected the cautious advice of his collaborators. Six weeks after the Bizerte crisis he suddenly moderated his intransigence without consulting anyone. In regard to appointments, Bourguiba as President of the Republic made his own decisions. He might ask individuals for their opinions, but the Political Bureau as such was not consulted. Even the coöptation of a new member to the Political Bureau seemed to have become a personal decision; it is doubtful, if put to a formal secret vote, whether Ben Salah would have been admitted.

Yet Bourguiba did rule by persuasion, and the Political Bureau was not a rubber stamp. It was important that Bureau members support his decision to put Ben Salah in charge of the planning superministry. When Mestiri in April, 1961, returned briefly on leave from his Moscow Embassy, he conferred with his successor, found himself largely in agreement, and claims to have tried to convince other Bureau members of the wisdom of Ben Salah's approach to the problems of planning. His efforts to persuade these members to Bourguiba's new way of thinking suggested the importance of agreement—which was not automatic—inside the Political Bureau. In the aftermath of the Bizerte crisis, too, it was hardly a coincidence that the Political Bureau received more publicity than usual. Without its support Bourguiba might not have weathered the autumn of 1961. It was perhaps with this in mind that he called for an increase in its membership in 1963.

Governors and Commissioners

At the regional level, relations between party and government were much improved as a result of the decision in 1958 to replace the party's forty-one federations with fourteen political commissioners whose jurisdiction corresponded with that of the governorates. Even so, relations between government and party remained ambiguous, and clashes between governors and commissioners could not always be avoided.

The governor in Tunisia was a political as well as an administrative figure. Appointed directly by the president, he was considered to represent the entire Cabinet Council in his governorate.[44] Administratively he reported to the director of regional and local administration in the Department of the Interior, but he had his own provincial budget and directed the officials working for other ministries in his province. As the on-the-spot decision-maker, he sometimes overruled a technical minister.[45] Directly responsible for public order (except in the city of Tunis), the governor had the police, National Guard, and Army at his disposal, though they were directed from Tunis. Until October, 1961, when the State Domains Office was created, the governor (with mixed results) managed all former colon lands on an *ad hoc* basis. He headed the regional commissions concerned with distributing the vast private habous lands between heirs and tenants. He was also directly responsible for the functioning of work sites for the unemployed, grouping as many as 30,000 workers in a given province. In his province the governor was supreme, and few decisions were taken in Tunis without consulting him.

On the party's side the political commissioner, though without a popular electoral mandate, controlled the grass-roots party apparatus and, enjoying the confidence of the Political Bureau, was an important political figure in the province. As the Bureau's envoy, he could claim to represent the regime.

In April, 1959, soon before the first serious clash between a governor and a political commissioner, Bourguiba tried to define their roles to Neo-Destour cadres and leaders:

Their activities should not clash but rather should be coördinated. The Political Commissioner should capture the attention of the party militant and make the party remain above all a school of education for the people. . . . This work of education has as its aims to facilitate the projects and achievements of the government and to make the people ready to understand them. . . . The activities of the Governor and the Political Commissioner must be harmonized so that, on the one hand, the Governor, the executive agent of the government, does not undertake projects that the citizens will not understand until they have been prepared; on the other hand, the

[44]Formerly, under the Protectorate, Tunisia had been divided into French administrative regions (*contrôles civils*) and thirty-six native qaidats. In June, 1956, the newly independent government abolished the system of qaidats and redistricted the country into fourteen governorates. That of Tozeur was subsequently eliminated. Only two of the new governors had served in the qaidal corps before 1955. Actually, under the new system of decentralization, the governors were granted more power than that of the *contrôleurs civils* and qaids combined.
[45]The governor of Gabes disagreed with the minister of public housing on the location of the site for a new village. His political reasons were considered to outweigh the technical considerations of the ministry.

Political Commissioner, having been told of these projects, must work to prepare the ground. . . .[46]

Bourguiba concluded the decisive argument for harmony: "'The Governor and the Political Commissioner are an emanation of my person.'"

Thus the commissioner was supposed to mobilize mass support for projects decided by the governor. Or, as Mehiri's *chef de cabinet* explained, the governor was to personify the regime while the political commisioner supported it by his administration of the party apparatus. Yet in the same breath it was suggested that the political commissioner had a policy-making function. In contact with the people, he was to be the diagnostician, and the governor was to provide the remedies.

Governors and political commissioners were for the most part drawn from the party's old federations and the UGTT, as were the more than a hundred governors' delegates in charge of the delegations into which the governorates are subdivided. Only one of the governors in 1962 was a professional administrator from the old qaidal corps. The others, including two trade-unionists, had been party federation leaders. All the political commissioners were likewise veterans of the party. They had little formal education.[47]

As if to emphasize administrative cohesion, governors, delegates, and commissioners were almost interchangeable in the new bureaucracies. Former governors were sometimes appointed political commissioners, as were at least nine former delegates. Conversely, commissioners were sometimes made delegates, and at least two former delegates and one former commissioner were governors in 1962.

In their new roles as administrators rather than representative party cadres, they were periodically shifted from one province to another. Rarely did a governor remain in the same place for more than two or three years. Amor Chechia was the only governor appointed in 1956 who remained in 1964.[48] Like the governors, political commissioners rarely had home ties to the region where they were posted. The only enduring exceptions were Taieb Tekeya (Bizerte) and Dr. Razgallah (Sousse); generally the commissioners were shifted almost once a year, and few of the old federation leaders survived long as commissioners in their old regions.

[46]*Le Petit Matin*, April 10, 1959.
[47]Of the six governors in 1961 who had been granted a *brevet*, only two had gone as far as the baccalaureate; two had a Zitouna education. The education of the commissioners was comparable; one especially astute boss from the Sahel was illiterate.
[48]After the Kairouan riots of January 17, 1961, Chechia had to stay there for the sake of the regime's prestige.

Continuity was generally greater among the governors than among the commissioners, for nine of the original fourteen governors remained in office (elsewhere) in 1962. In the conflicts between governor and commissioner, however, the former did not always have his way. The latter, as the "diagnostician" from the Political Bureau in direct contact with the branches, acted as a check upon the governor's otherwise virtually unlimited power in his province.

In Tozeur a clash occurred when the governor, considering himself to be the dominant political authority, tried to control the party branches and infringe upon the domain of the commissioner. Two weeks after Bourguiba's speech about their respective roles, Ladgham visited Tozeur, and within two months it was decided to place the area under neighboring governorates. The governor was retired; a few months later he became a deputy in the National Assembly. The commissioner was shifted to Gabes and later removed for incompetence.

In Le Kef a similar problem developed. The governor, one of the most competent of the group, wanted to discipline a branch president whom the commissioner defended. The latter then discovered mismanagement of some of the lands that were the governor's responsibility. Amid rumors of corruption, the governor was shifted to a different governorate. But in order that commissioners not acquire the reputation of being able to undermine governors, the party leader was also shifted to a different governorate.

Sometimes, as in Kairouan, the governor deliberately tried to have a weak commissioner appointed. Some commissioners were politically more active and capable than the governors. Their functions seemed poorly differentiated and required close coöperation between the two officials. In early 1958 important patronage was given to the governor in the form of transport and café licenses. Yet in late 1960 Bourguiba was asking Chaker, the director of the party, to reëxamine and revise transport licenses.[49] Clearly the party needed to keep tight control on patronage, yet the governor was to have the last word on this matter.

In cases of disagreement, the commissioner reported in theory to the party director and the governor reported to the secretary of the interior. If Chaker and Mehiri could not agree, the problem would go to Bourguiba. In practice Ladgham and Bourguiba were kept informed of problems in the provinces, though Chaker and especially Mehiri were more directly responsible for the smooth functioning of the party-government apparatus.

Regional conflicts between party and government could be managed from above, but the system had obvious shortcomings. In 1964,

[49] *Le Petit Matin,* December 10, 1960.

after the elimination of the political commissioners, it was too early to see how the new pattern of consultation between the governors and the more representative governorate councils would work in practice. One auspicious sign during the summer was the appointment of a number of new governors who had recently completed university studies.

The Virtues of Symbiosis

There was no clear cut functional separation between party and government. Overlapping membership and diffuse functions are found at all levels of the instruments of power. The flexible symbiosis of party and government reflected Bourguiba's art of minimizing factions and keeping them in a fluid state. The virtues of the system—or the lack of system—are suggested by a look at the only real alternative.

The alternative would have been to maintain the supremacy of the party and to respect to the letter the grass-roots representation implicit in its statutes before 1959. The government would then have been the servant of the party; moreover, Bourguiba would probably not have been able to avoid the crystallization of cliques. It seems clear that one very powerful clique would have developed—that of Mehiri. Bourguiba would not have had leeway to tolerate the criticisms of the rival "liberals" under Masmoudi, nor could he have elevated the "socialist" Ben Salah, Mehiri's other rival. Despite a more formally democratic structure, the party under the "iron law of oligarchy" would have been even less of a vehicle for the rise of new men and ideas. Instead, Mehiri's veteran activists would have blocked newcomers, probably in the administration as well as in the party apparatus.

Bourguiba's formula of symbiosis was better suited for handling the main problem of party-government relations, that of resolving tensions between veteran politicians and the young "technicians" in *both* bureaucracies. By the latter is meant those who were students in French universities after the Second World War. (The group included Mehiri as well as Masmoudi and Ben Salah, but the former was politically identified with the veterans of the party apparatus.) As a group, the technicians stood to loose in a single-party system that provided prestige and power on a seniority basis. Most of them had not actively fought the struggle for independence. Finding jobs in the administration on the basis of merit after independence, they were the object of the less-educated party veterans' jealousy. Symbiosis allowed the technicians to enter party as well as government despite such jealousy, while giving more competent politicians a chance to serve in the administration. By preventing the formation of a strong clique of party veterans, Bourguiba stimulated internal mobility—at the paradoxical cost of less formal democracy inside the party. While making the party an effective educator and integrator under his personal rule, Bourguiba perhaps also made it a more truly representative body, as subsequent chapters will indicate.

If all internal cliques were neutralized, was the party a political force distinct from its leader? Did it have the power to reflect anything but the leader's wishes? Formally, perhaps not: after all, Bourguiba and selected associates, rather than the Political Bureau, controlled the political apparatus. Yet it would be a mistake to underestimate the party as a national symbol. The crisis provoked by Ben Youssef showed the collective importance of the Political Bureau, which subsequently represented the main trends within the party and symbolized its authority.[50] As long as Bourguiba retained his vitality and avoided compounding disastrous errors like Bizerte, the party and its father were scarcely separable; Bourguiba gave the party its living image. But the dominant party that brought independence had a *mystique* of its own apart from Bourguiba's personal magnetism. Long years of service in the party were a necessary credential for any political leader. In the event of a succession, the party's voice would be decisive, and the man to succeed Bourguiba would need the support of the party's representative organs. Below the surface a muted battle for the succession was perhaps already under way. Meanwhile, if Bourguiba was the unchallenged leader, it is partly because he remained sensitive to opinion channeled through the party.

[50]Here again the Bureau remained representative partly because Bourguiba had the power to promote people who had support *outside* the party structure. Ben Salah was a good example.

V PATTERNS OF LOCAL POLITICS

NATIONAL UNITY and the new consensus for economic and social development would have little meaning or effect unless they were shared by an open elite and filtered down to the Tunisian masses. Popular sovereignty and solidarity, the founding principles of Bourguiba's nation, required that the people participate in political life. The regime would lose its legitimacy if Bourguiba's role marked simply the substitution of a native oligarchy for colonial rulers. Paternalism could be justified, however, so far as it narrowed the gap between the ideals of modern Tunisia and the realities of the transitional society.

Patterns of local politics varied according to the population's educational attainments, economic activities, traditions, and social development. The activities of the fifty-odd party branches in the city of Tunis, with distinctive problems and experienced cadres, hardly compared with those of rural branches in the disinherited Center and South. The same local institutions, however, flourished throughout the country, and everywhere fostered participation in as well as support for party activities.

The Neo-Destour branch served as the local organ of social integration by combining diverse factions and clans and filling the vacuum left by the decay of traditional structures. The branch also played a representative role in transmitting the demands and grievances of the people to the party apparatus, and stimulated participation in local self-government. The branch was a prime instrument of political recruitment. Its membership until 1963 was open to all. The branch was also an instrument of education. It mobilized the people in support of government projects by explaining their significance, and trained party cadres for further political responsibilities.

The Branch and Local Society

The Neo-Destour branch seemed to fill a social vacuum. As traditional ties of family, brotherhood, or tribe weakened, the modern voluntary organization replaced them as a structure of social integration easing the transition toward a modern society. Many of the party's thousand branches, in addition to their prestige as instruments of national emanicipation, inherited the prestige of traditional structures. The branch often replaced the local chapter of a religious brotherhood.

132

Using the latter's zawiya as a meeting place before independence, the Neo-Destour activists capitalized on its appeal to the supersititious masses (and clothed politics in a religious garb that the French authorities dared not disrobe).[1] In Le Kef the party's key organizer—whom the Political Bureau subsequently awarded a seat in the Constituent Assembly—had been a leader of the Rahmaniya order, one of the most important religious brotherhoods in North Africa. Even in the Tunis of the 1960's, some Neo-Destour branches were housed in the (abandoned?) tombs of marabouts, the founder-"saints" of the orders.

After independence, the party continued to respect local traditions, despite Bourguiba's repeated exhortations for rapid social change. Thus there was a paradoxical gap in attitudes and values between the modern urban elite and the common man (in cities as well as countryside). To the elite, the religious orders, connoting "superstition" and "backwardness," no longer existed; yet at a branch assembly in the relatively sophisticated Sahel, the party official representing the political commissioner did not wish to appear disrespectful to the memory of the local marabout: in the zawiya where the meeting was held, he did not light a cigarette until the local party leaders, sensing his hesitation, gave him permission.

The Ramadan issue was even more revealing. Although Bourguiba could make the gesture of drinking orange juice at a party rally,[2] the party officials in contact with the branches had to observe the fast in public—whatever their personal convictions—to maintain the respect of the rank and file, even in the city of Sousse. The issue had disturbed many national and regional party officials; the most they could accept was that fasting was a matter of personal choice that ought not be collectively enforced. Clearly the party could not actively proselytize for Bourguiba's convictions. Nor was this Bourguiba's intention, for the party's task was not to remake human souls but rather to provide the political conditions for gradual social progress.

[1] In Hammam-Sousse, a village intensively studied by the author, the Neo-Destour branch, founded in 1934, had outdistanced the old Destour by 1938. It held clandestine meetings in the village zawiya to escape detection by the French authorities. In 1945 it supported the efforts of a Zitouna-trained schoolteacher to build a private Quranic school just opposite the zawiya. These schools taught a modern curriculum and an orthodox Islam at variance with the zawiya type of instruction. In 1960, when the sheikh of the zawiya died, the building was remodeled to house the town council and the Neo-Destour branch office. The tomb of the marabout was removed. Yet the party was not so much following a conscious policy of social revolution as reflecting the social evolution of the villagers. For further details see my article, "Politics in a Tunisian Village," *Middle East Journal*, late autumn, 1963, pp. 527-540.
[2] *Jeune-Afrique*, February 3-9, 1964.

At the grass roots the party was not the vanguard after independence of "permanent revolution" but a vehicle for social integration. Its task was that of conciliation, bringing into its organizational framework the disparate elements of local society. By independence the branches, being open to all but the most notorious collaborators of the *ancien régime*, attained social respectability—at the price of revolutionary fervor. Even so, there were many obstacles. Since, in most Sahel villages, a small number of extended families had competed for generations for political and economic power and social prestige, it was difficult for the branches to avoid being based on one "family" faction at war with others that had enjoyed links with the Protectorate administration or the old Destour. In some villages, too, the party had several branches before the reorganization of the party in 1958. In the Sahel they were geographic, but based on the extended family that inhabited a particular section of the village. In Tunis, colonies of immigrants from southern Tunisia were organized along ethnic lines. After independence they maintained their close ethnic ties, often reënforced by the pursuit of a common occupation.[3] The Metouia, the most important and militant of the minorities, were in large part longshoremen living in a certain area of Tunis. After many decades they still enjoyed strong home ties: at their branch assembly in 1961 they were discussing the land problems of their native oasis with the political commissioner from Gabes.

Rivalries between adjacent villages, too, were traditions that did not disappear, even in the Sahel. Ksar-Hellal and Moknine had always feuded with one another, although barely a mile separated them. In 1947 their quarrels within the Neo-Destour led to the creation of two federations, one for Ksar-Hellal and one for Moknine. In 1956 the two were merged, but, to avoid all jealousy, both federations were abolished and integrated into the new federation of Monastir. In 1962 it was vaguely planned that a common administrative center would be built halfway between the two villages, and that they would become an important economic center of 40,000 inhabitants. But separate markets were constructed after independence.

Another rivalry concerned Djemmal and Monastir. It was ironic in the 1956 elections that Bourguiba's constituency included Djemmal as well as Monastir, while the party's federations overlapped with other areas. Djemmal's inhabitants had always looked upon their traditional Monastiri governors as exploiters who stole their land. But Bourguiba

---

[3]Those from Douiret worked in the central market. The Chenini from Tatouine sold newspapers. The Omrassen from Matmata sold pastry on the streets, while the Oudref specialized in roadbuilding.

ran in Djemmal because its leading "family" (numbering in the thousands)—which had acquired its olive-tree fortune by despoiling the Monastiri intruders a century earlier—would not have voted for any local Neo-Destour candidate. The party federation had systematically discriminated against the leading family because some of its members were notorious collaborators of the old regime.

In Tunisia's seminomadic regions of the Center and South, where the Neo-Destour was not so solidly implanted as in the Sahel, the problems of party organization were complicated by tribalism. In the mining areas the UGTT sometimes played a more important role in social integration. In Mdilla, a small mining town near Gafsa, the Neo-Destour was divided into five branches grouping the diverse tribes that constituted the mining population. The UGTT, in contrast, had a single local union with a decade of political experience behind it. It had supplied the party with cadres. When in 1958 the branches were regrouped in a single unit, the UGTT was able to guide the provincial party officials and effect compromises between the tribal factions, so that acceptable branch officers could be elected. In another mining center, however, the majority tribe controlled the party branch in 1961 to the dissatisfaction of minorities in the UGTT. Elsewhere in the South, where village life barely existed and no disciplined workers' force had upset local habits, the party had no choice but to work with the tribes and try to mediate between them. In the extreme south (Gabes, Mednine), which had been under French military control during the Protectorate, the party was able to organize only after the Youssefist disorders had pitted tribe against tribe. Bourguiba made a speech forbidding the victorious Bourguibist tribes from annihilating the defeated Youssefist tribes, and the governors and political commissioners tried to maintain a balance between the two.

The Branch and the Commissioner

From 1958 until 1963 the political commissioner exercised vast powers over the branches, and presumably the democratically elected secretary of the regional coördinating committee that replaced him would retain many of his powers. For it was primarily through tutelage from above that the branches could perform their local integrating roles.

The commissioner closely supervised each branch.[4] He could, with

[4]He was aided by one or two assistants, who like himself were not necessarily from the region, and by a coördinating committee of a dozen or so branch officers that he selected with the consent of the Political Bureau. His office was in contact with the central office of the Political Bureau and its youth, propaganda, financial, and social development services.

the approval of the Political Bureau, take disciplinary measures against any branch officer or member, although members theoretically had the right to appeal to the national congress. Infractions were vaguely defined in the party statutes.[5] One branch president in Tunis thought that the then defunct National Council had been transformed into a secret service to keep the party cadres under observation! Actually, disciplinary cases—less than a dozen a year reported—were either infrequent or were not always announced in the party's newspaper.

Although the branches' executive committees were in theory freely elected at the annual branch assemblies,[6] the political commissioner could screen out any doubtful candidates. He had access to police reports and confidential party sources. In fact, a candidate who was eliminated, unless he was befriended by a higher official, had little recourse, and usually feared to exercise his right, at the branch assembly, of challenging the judgment of the commissioner. Elections, however, were relatively free in that the commissioner did not often use his wide powers; also, there were almost invariably more candidates than positions to fill.[7]

To the branch membership — usually numbering 50-400, though branches in Tunis from 1955 to 1958 sometimes included thousands— the candidates were usually well known, and the tendency was to re-elect the same officers. There seemed to be no systematic effort of members close to the commissioner to elect a fixed slate. The converse was not tolerated either, and a political commissioner once annulled an election because the rivals of some incumbent branch officials had

[5](1) Infractions consisted of: prejudicing party interests and departing from its political principles; (2) actions that might endanger the party or give aid to one of its enemies; (3) breaking the party covenant or internal statutes, or lowering the dignity of the party; (4) public expression of hostility toward the party or its organs.

[6]All party members who had paid their annual dues of $3 were entitled to vote at the Assembly meeting. Actually, members in the poorer villages of the Sahel were allowed to vote if they had paid dues for even four months. To be a member of the party—at least until 1963, when the conditions were to become more stringent— required little commitment. One had to "respect the principles of the party," "execute its decision," and pay (some) dues. The traditional oath of allegiance was abolished in 1959. In Tunis the candidate for membership had to be sponsored by two party members; it was up to the executive committee of the branch to accept or reject the application.

[7]Voting procedure was similar to that of the Political Bureau elections at the National Congress. On a single secret ballot the voters marked as many names as there were places to fill. The elected committee then allotted the various offices among its members, usually in consultation with the commissioner or his representative who presided over the Assembly. Outside the cities most of the voters were illiterate, but the secret ballot was individually administered by disinterested party officials from other branches.

used their village sport organization as a voting bloc at the branch assembly. Voting patterns in the elections, however, were usually irregular (though the fifty women belonging to a branch in Sousse once voted as a bloc and swung the balance to the established officers!).

The commissioner was empowered to dissolve an entire branch executive committee and replace it by his own appointees (though in theory he had to arrange new elections within six months).[8] He could also dissolve and regroup existing branches or create new ones. Because of the shortage of trained leaders, the number of branches was reduced in 1958, but in 1961 the Political Bureau encouraged a moderate expansion of branches, especially in the Center and South, where recently trained cadres were available. After the Kairouan incidents of January 17, 1961, the number of branches in the city was increased to thirteen,[9] an astonishingly large number for a relatively small population.[10] The expansion was presumably designed to keep closer watch on the population and possibly to downgrade branches infected by the seditious feelings of the old families.

Commissioners made full use of their power to dissolve branch committees, in order to maintain local harmony.[11] After the reduction of branches in 1958, the single village branch was plagued by internal dissensions based on long-standing family rivalries. In the more dynamic villages, where commerce, small industry, and education had challenged traditional peasant life, new rival cliques based on modern interests emerged.[12] Another cause for intervention from above was

[8]Before 1959 the legal time limit was two weeks, but even the six-month deadline was not always respected.

[9]El 'Amal, March 5, 1961.

[10]According to the 1956 census, Kairouan had a Tunisian Muslim population of 33,062; the respective figures for Tunis and Sousse were 272,000 and 37,888. In 1961 there were about 45 neighborhood (nonprofessional) party branches in Tunis, while the number in Sousse had been reduced from 10 to 3. Even discounting the increase in population since independence, when many Tunisians supplanted the departing Europeans in Tunis, the new proportion of branches to urban population seemed exceptionally high in Kairouan after the riots.

[11]Out of 120 branches committees in the Sahel, six were dissolved in 1960 alone. The proportion was probably higher in the politically backward country areas.

[12]The branch in Ksar-Hellal, the seat of the party's first congress in 1934, was plagued with dissension and had to be dissolved in 1960. The old political boss, an illiterate but shrewd former fellagha leader, had lost local favor in 1958—for a time it was not safe for him to walk in the village streets—after Bourguiba's nephew-in-law was elected mayor on the Neo-Destour list. The latter, originally from Ksar-Hellal, had been a businessman in Tunis for many years, and had not been identified with the former's severe treatment after independence of nonparty villagers. The businessman had a commercial rival, the president of the Sousse chamber of commerce, who was also from Ksar-Hellal and had risen with the

the complacency of old militants no longer interested in party activities after winning independence and acquiring patronage jobs.[13]

Branches, however, had more autonomy than the hierarchical structure of the party suggested. Especially in the Sahel, where branch leaders often had connections with ranking national politicians, the political commissioner had to exercise diplomacy and restraint. In some villages, too, important national leaders were active locally.[14]

At least one political commissioner was eliminated because of pressure exerted by the rank and file upon the Political Bureau. According to a young bilingual schoolteacher from Gafsa who was on the commissioner's coördinating committee[15] and the leader of a local

---

help and guidance of the political boss. It would have been natural in 1958 for the political boss to turn to his old protégé for political support, but, thinking he had been betrayed, he turned to the mayor, who was eager to isolate his commercial rival politically. However, the old boss's fortunes had a turn for the better, and he was successively a member of the Haute Cour, a deputy in the National Assembly (along with the two rivals), and a political commissioner. Thus all three cliques had to be represented on the branch committee. In 1961, as a compromise, a fourth man, a former general secretary of UGET recruited into the party's central office, was elected branch president of his home town. Exposed to modern politics over two generations, Ksar-Hellal was transcending a politics based on family for one based upon interest and involving national politicians.

[13]Ouardanine, one of the most famous centers of the fellagha movement in the Sahel, under Hassen Ben Abdelaziz, had provided Neo-Destour shock troops under Sadok Hamida, one of Bourguiba's most useful early collaborators, in the 1937 campaigns against the old Destour. Since independence, two of its native sons were governor's delegates, and Abdallah and Mohammed Farhat, the president's cabinet director and state prosecutor, respectively, were born in Ouardanine. But in 1961 the branch executive was suspended for lack of activity, and in the town council elections of 1960 a relative outsider, a schoolteacher born in Ouardanine who had spent most of his life in Sousse, was selected mayor for lack of a competent local candidate. The old resistants like Sadok Hamida and Hassen Ben Abdelaziz were preoccupied with private business and had no interest in providing leadership, and the successful politicians had made their reputations elsewhere. To complicate matters, the village was divided into two main cliques of large families. One was led by two old militants who had married into the Farhat family and for whom Abdallah Farhat had garnered a number of business concessions. They headed the branch until 1961, but proved incompetent and did little for the village. The leader of the other clique had been mayor until 1960, but Abdallah Farhat had not provided him with government support for the town council's projects. Paradoxically, Farhat had owed his meteoric rise in the party in part to the prestige of Hassen Ben Abdelaziz, a supporter of the second clique. In 1961 the only active community leader seemed to be the schoolteacher from Sousse, who was not identified with either clique but enjoyed Abdallah Farhat's respect.

[14]Ahmed Ben Salah was mayor of Moknine and president of the party's branch. Taieb Mehiri was mayor of La Marsa, a fashionable Tunis suburb. Ahmed Noureddine, public works minister, was mayor of Sousse. Mohammed Masmoudi until 1963 was mayor of Mahdia. Bourguiba himself was mayor of Monastir until 1963, when he passed the office on to his son.

[15]See note 4, above.

branch,[16] tension had developed from the outset between the comissioner and the coördinating committee. A veteran from the Sahel, the commissioner arrived in Gafsa in January, 1960. He told his local collaborators that he did not wish to organize party activities during the (cold) winter. By springtime some of the young activists on the coördinating committee were insisting that mass rallies should be held to keep in contact with the population. The commissioner opposed this idea because there were no government achievements in the area to report. The schoolteacher and his friends thought that their chief was lazy. During the summer the director of the party invited the leaders, including the schoolteacher, to Tunis to clear up their disputes. When Mehiri visited Gafsa in December, he was said to have made the commissioner promise the impatient activists a freer hand. On Independence Day, March 20, 1961, however, the commissioner refused to march in a parade organized by the coördinating committee. The schoolteacher enlisted Tlili on his side, and in June the commissioner was suspended from all party activities.[17] Some months later he was appointed a governor's delegate in Kairouan, while the schoolteacher, perhaps considered to be overly enterprising, was transferred by the Ministry of Education to a small town away from the political center of Gafsa.

There was obvious resentment in Gafsa of rule by militants from the the Sahel.[18] The conflict, too, probably reflected local tensions between the party and the UGTT.[19] Normally, coördinating committees did not play an independent role, but the Gafsa committee seems to have been very jealous of its autonomy. In most governorates the coördinating committees had little initiative and differed greatly in composition from the elected federal executives they had replaced. In Souk El Arba not one former federation chief was included on the new committee. The four chief leaders had been quietly removed in 1958; two were schoolteachers shifted away by the Ministry of Education. In Sousse the coördinating committee, though consisting mainly

[16]He had been a delegate to the 1959 party congress, and his brother, as general secretary of the regional UGTT committee, was a protégé of Ahmed Tlili, Gafsa's leading national politician.
[17]El 'Amal, June 14, 1961.
[18]The governor, the political commissioner, and a number of governor' delegates were from the Sahel.
[19]In his previous job as governor's delegate in Matmata, the commissioner with the help of Chaker and Mehiri had blocked the nomination of Khiari, the old UGTT leader, to the party's list for the 1959 National Assembly elections. Abdelaziz Bouraoui, a trade-union leader, had been much more successful as political commissioner in Gafsa, where the UGTT was important locally.

of former federation leaders, was for the most part inactive, and the commissioner had coöpted younger party activists as working aides.

Guided Democracy

Despite the commissioner's vast reserve powers, the branches exercised real representative and governing functions. In the summer of 1961, a fortnight after the fighting had erupted in Bizerte, the author was touring some villages of the Sahel with British and American guests. After stopping for a swim on a deserted beach, the group returned to their car to discover that all their passports—required at each of the many roadblocks the Tunisian National Guard had set up during the crisis—had been stolen. The nearest village, a famed center of fellagha seven years previously, was a mile away. When they reached it and asked for the police, they were escorted instead to the local party headquarters. The branch president, a courteous young man, seemed embarrassed that a misfortune should have befallen foreign visitors in his home community. But he refused to call the police. Instead, he persuaded the group to drive him back to the scene of the theft. Within two hours, after quietly conferring with villagers who lived in the area, he had recovered all the passports! Only then did he call the police—to have the three schoolchildren who had stolen the documents put into jail briefly as a lesson.

The branches had wide scope for initiative, especially when (as in this case) the local president was held in high esteem by the commissioner. Branches represented the interests of the constituency to higher party and governmental authorities and were also centers of limited local self-government.

The representative function, however, had few national political implications. At the assemblies, policy was rarely discussed, except as it was mentioned in ritual telegrams of total support to President Bourguiba. Instead, the party's orientation service propagated the news of government achievements to the branches, which relayed them to the people. Every branch sent at least one delegate to the national congress, but he was given no specific instructions. In the executive committee, national policy might be informally discussed, but the delegate was not to "represent" a clearly articulated point of view. Rather he was to be a sounding board for the higher authorities.

The branch represented primarily the local interests of the population, as expressed in annual assemblies and fortnightly meetings of the executive committee. Whoever wanted anything in Tunisia went to his local branch. The officer in charge of "social development"—before independence it was "defense of the interests of the population"—

would inform the Neo-Destour commissioner of specific local needs, such as schools, clinics, sewage, garbare collection, electricity, water, and roads.[20] He conferred regularly with the commissioner and his assistants for social development, who were in daily contact with the Political Bureau's central office. Roughly once a year the commissioner arranged meetings with the governor, his technical assistants from the various ministries, and the branch officers. Technical priorities were explained to the branches, but government action was sometimes modified in light of branch needs. The Neo-Destour persuaded the government to restore various mosques. In Tunis one branch got the better of the Tunis city council—the large administration of which is virtually a part of the government—as to whether a municipal swimming pool or a school should be constructed on an important piece of real estate owned by the council in the branch's district. The branch leadership successfully argued that a school would be more profitable to society than a swimming pool that earned money for the city council.

Outside the large towns the branch had access to the government through the local sheikh, who often was a former branch president. The governor's delegate also kept in constant touch with the branch leaders, though in theory the administrations of party and government converged only at the level of commissioner and governor. The delegate, usually a veteran party militant, needed the good will of the branch in order more effectively to carry out the government's projects; and the branch could informally present suggestions to the delegate as well as to the commissioner. Friends in high places, too, were perhaps more important than formal party channels. As one pragmatic branch official claimed when fellow villager Ahmed Ben Salah rose to power, "Now with him where he is, we're sitting near the faucet and when we're thirsty we can drink."

The branch used to be a local employment bureau. Immediately after independence anyone who wanted a job, whether as a street-cleaner or as director of a company, had to be a party member. The local branch usually knew about his political past, and the prime function of the federation was to find jobs for deserving militants.[21]

[20]One very democratically minded commissioner pointed out, regretfully, that to balance tribal fractions he had to decide upon the location of schools and wells without consultation, for discussion made everyone feel dissatisfied with the compromise decision.

[21]In Hammam-Sousse, with a population of eleven or twelve thousand, fifty members claimed to be active resistants, and many of them were unemployed. Some were hired by Mokhtar Latiri, a native of Hammam-Sousse who had become one of the chief engineers in public works. One of the village fellagha who used to be a fisherman prevailed upon the branch to persuade the federation president to intervene on his behalf. He wanted the job of pilot in the Sousse harbor. The

Old resistants were awarded pieces of land from the State Domain,[22] but in Sousse, at least, the commissioner claimed in 1961 that many deserving former militants had yet to be taken care of.

Between them the governor and the commissioner handled most patronage on the advice of trusted branch officers. However, key members of the Political Bureau were sometimes involved in particular cases. State land, the main lever of patronage, was closely guarded by Ladgham, and the personal entourage of Bourguiba also exerted important influence.[23]

With the installation of the commissioners, the party tried to diminish its patronage activities. The rank and file were told by Bourguiba that as good Destourians they had to set an example of self-sacrifice and dedication rather than to expect special favors,[24] and the commissioners were able to implement his advice more effectively than the federations. Henceforth patronage was no longer a serious local problem for the branches; special favors were bestowed almost exclusively upon educated younger relatives and friends of high officials in the central administration. As one ranking civil servant wrote of his colleagues:

[After 1958, with the massive departure of French personnel], the hunt for high level civil service jobs was open. Appetites, once satisfied, again grew. As soon as they were occupied, command positions in the administration were abandoned for more lucrative jobs in the rapidly expanding public and semipublic sector, and also in the private sector being rapidly Tunisified. . . . Most directors' positions are occupied by young cadres with subordinates who graduated from the same schools with the same diplomas. . . .[25]

Commissioners discouraged requests for employment by party members, or referred them to their local branch, the facilities of which were very limited. Pre-independence shock troops, however, were well cared

---

president in turn got Ladgham to request the relevant minister to hire him. The case became a scandal when the minister, Abassi of the UGTT, hired a UGTT man who had had previous experience as a pilot but a questionable political past. The latter is reported to have told the fisherman, "I am the UGTT and have my job; go look for your Bourguiba!" and to have slugged him. But the party was usually successful, especially after the UGTT was brought to heel.

[22]Between 1956 and 1961 about 150,000 ha. of land, 500,000 olive trees, and 100,000 date trees were disposed of by the state to particulars, and it can be presumed that much of it, like 150,000 olive trees in Sousse, was disposed of as patronage in the form of grants or at nominal prices.

[23]Abdallah Farhat's intervention helped Hassen Ben Abdelaziz to acquire thousands of hectares near Kairouan. See above, note 9 to Chap. II.

[24]Speech, August 1, 1957.

[25]Mustapha Zanouni, "Le rôle de l'administration dans l'exécution du Plan," *Aspects et Perspectives de l'Economie Tunisienne,* March-April, 1962, p. 61.

for. Even in Tunis, where they could not be given land, an assured job in public works provided more than thrice the salary they could earn on a government work site for the unemployed.

Although they were not supposed to discriminate against nonparty applicants, the branches continued to dispense some patronage. They handed out cards to the needy to certify their poverty qualifying them for public benefits. The branch could keep nonparty children out of the school canteens and even out of the few primary schools built exclusively by its labor and fund-raising activities, much to the embarrassment of the Department of Education, which could only tell aggrieved parents to send their children to a neighboring school built by government funds. The commissioner exerted a balancing influence, and his power to decide between conflicting demands was an important lever for eliciting efficiency and harmony from branch committees that would otherwise be bickering among themselves.

With independent Tunisia's first municipal elections, held on May 5, 1957, many branches acquired an additional channel of influence in local affairs. Bourguiba had intended that the elections be a "real apprenticeship in democracy and proof of the vitality and maturity of the Tunisian people."[26] Independent lists and cross-voting (panachage) were allowed. It was hoped that new blood—including nonparty members—would be injected into local politics to liberalize single-party rule. Old militants incapable of adapting to the new order would be displaced.

The branches drew up the Neo-Destour lists subject to the approval of the party federations.[27] These lists were victorious in 88 of the 94 towns and villages where municipal councils were elected. Independents were, however, given a fair chance. Three out of sixteen Independent lists won, and five additional Independents in three towns won seats by panachage. But subsequently the experiment in local democracy ran into trouble and further confused the hierarchies within the party and the government. Within a few months the municipalities controlled by the Independents were dissolved by governmental decree. Bourguiba had stated that he did not wish the councils to be merely extensions of the branch executive committees, but it appeared that any alternative would lead to bitter conflict reflecting the latent antagonisms of local cliques.

[26]Bourguiba's speech to the National Council; see Le Petit Matin, April 13, 1957.
[27]Apparently the federations gave the branches a relatively free hand. In cities where more than one branch was affected the federations had a greater say. Tunis was a special case; although municipal councilors were elected, the president of the council, or mayor, was appointed by the government, in accordance with the decree of March 14, 1957.

Such, at least, was the situation in Hammam-Sousse, a village suburb of Sousse where a list of Independents won. The list was headed by a schoolteacher who, as president of the local sports association, was a popular and loyal citizen, though he had never served as an officer in the party branch. His running mates were two other schoolteachers, three functionaries, the most well-to-do village farmer, and a grocer. The party's list, including a prison guard, the village postman, and a former fellagha leader, comprised most of the branch leaders. The main electoral issue concerned the fellagha and his younger brother, who a year previously had killed an alleged Youssefist for ridiculing the fellagha "bandits." The Independents promised good local government purged of the clique of party leaders. They capitalized on the revulsion felt by many villagers toward the fellagha, who boasted of their heroic past, expected constant adulation, and offered few peacetime skills. The party candidates accused the Independents of being against the party that had brought independence; the latter protested their loyalty to the Neo-Destour and claimed they could better serve its true ends.

The electoral campaign, limited by law to the two weeks preceding the election, seemed uneventful. The Independents held only one small public meeting forty-eight hours before the election. The party held three public rallies, including one in which the president of the Sousse federation backed the local branch candidates. The Neo-Destour mobilized its militants and youth cadres to campaign individually in the village cafés. Tension mounted as the Independents, perhaps fearing reprisals from the party's youth squads if they held public meetings, discreetly canvassed and campaigned from house to house and exhorted the women to vote and to persuade their husbands to vote Independent. The Neo-Destour later accused the opposition of handing out candy to children in order to sway the mothers.

The Independents won the election by a two-to-one majority in a record turnout, of which one-third were women.[28] The villagers decisively demonstrated their impatience with the former fellagha, and the branch subsequently removed its controversial hero from the political scene. But the newly elected town council was active for only a few months. The branch executive accused the council leaders of attacking the party's prestige and smearing the reputation of a former local leader, who had become a governor's delegate and was sub-

[28]In 1957, out of 5,783 registered voters, 3,309 voted; the teacher won 2,215 votes, while the top Neo-Destour man received only 1,199. In 1960, out of 3,343 registered voters 2,362 voted, but there was only one list. Only 510 women voted, compared to 1,146 in 1957.

sequently made a governor. The branch then eliminated the council one evening by beating up the new mayor. The Department of Education transferred him to Tunis, and the governor of Sousse dissolved the town council and replaced it with a special delegation.[29] Ironically, even the special delegation proved a fiasco: the secretary in charge of administration embezzled funds and was eventually jailed.

In light of these unfortunate local experiences, subsequent municipal elections, held in 1960 and 1963, were uncontested. Although not illegal, nonparty lists were discouraged by the administration, for under the electoral law the withdrawal (under pressure) of one candidate entailed the elimination of the entire list.[30] Moreover, the branches were more effectively supervised in the drawing up of the lists. In the governorate of Sousse, the political commissioner in 1960 drew up all the lists himself in consultation only with trusted local collaborators. Thus the elections provided the party hierarchy with a very convenient means of enhancing the prestige of favored local leaders. In other areas, the governor and his delegates exercised more influence. In one instance the delegate and the village sheikh (the former's administrative subordinate) arranged the list and by-passed the branch.

Under these conditions of guided democracy, it was sometimes difficult for the voters to understand the point of the elections. One branch leader, in an effort to mobilize them in 1960, explained that they should vote *en masse* to display their satisfaction with Bourguiba's regime, in order to be able in the future, if the need arose, to express discontent by abstention. Women's registration was voluntary,[31] but all

[29]Articles 26 and 27 of the March 14, 1957 decree on town councils (*JOT,* March 15, pp. 296 ff.) allow for such a procedure, but the provision for new elections to be held within two months of the dissolution was not respected.
[30]The *Cour de Cassation* affirmed this interpretation in its ruling on the Sfax list of Independents in the National Assembly elections of 1959. See *Le Petit Matin,* November 3, 1959. The electoral law for the municipal elections has the same key provision as the national electoral law: "A list is considered invalid if it comprises more names than there are town councilors to elect. Incomplete lists are *ipso facto* invalid." See Article 23, Electoral Regime Decree for Municipal Councils, *Journal Officiel Tunisien,* March 15, 1957, p. 307.
[31]In light of the great Tunisian emphasis upon female emancipation, it is curious that women's registration was markedly lower in 1960 than in 1957, at least in the Sahel, where this author was able to discover the relevant statistics. Possibly this was related to the failure of Bourguiba's campaign against fasting during Ramadan, which took place two months before the elections. At any rate, the party's zeal in recruiting women voters seems to have declined. Of the sixteen towns in the Sahel holding municipal elections in 1957, only two, Sousse and Ksar-Hellal, showed an increase in female registration in 1960. The following statistics were reported in *Taqdim,* official bulletin of the Neo-Destour commissioner's office in Sousse, in April, 1960:

men from the age of twenty were automatically registered by the municipality. Generally the local branch exerted sufficient moral pressure on the population to ensure an adequate turnout, and men who failed to vote were sometimes reprimanded. In Hammam-Sousse, where this was not the case, participation was two-thirds what it had been in 1957; but in most of the other towns and villages where the elections of 1957 had been contested, participation was greater in 1960.

Since 1960, harmony was assured between branch and town council. The higher authorities could dissolve a council by presidential decree, and had to approve all council decisions concerning its budget, local taxes, management of communal property and public services, and even changes in the names of streets.[32] Financially, too, most of the town councils had inadequate resources for their ambitious plans and were dependent upon the largesse of higher authorities. The President of the Republic often gave personal grants as an encouragement to local democracy.

Town	Tunisian Muslim population (1956 census)	Registered women (1957)	Voting (1957)	Registered women (1960)
Msakken	26,107	3,854	135	393
Enfidaville	3,134	344	275	329
Sousse	37,888	3,810	1,930	5,171
Kalaa Sghira	7,872	1,000	531	710
Akouda	7,635	1,006	616	820
Ouardanine	5,860	1,266	765	506
Kalaa Kebira	16,700	1,500	1,112	563
Ksour Essaf	11,322	1,096	664	319
Moknine	17,648	541	141	110
Ksar-Hellal	12,195	1,491	1,397	2,589
Mahdia	10,314	2,369	1,571	1,842
Djem	6,673	1,575	1,387	159
Monastir	12,027	2,578	1,326	1,476
Zeramdine	6,005	1,216	412	432
Hammam-Sousse	9,419	1,981	1,146	510
Djemmal	11,158	2,027	166	895

Contrasting the numbers of women registered in 1960 with those actually voting in the 1957 elections, Hammam-Sousse marked the sharpest decline, owing, presumably, to the absence of opposition which had stimulated the women to vote in 1957. In other towns, with the exception of Kalaa Kebira, Ouardanine, Ksour Essaf, Moknine, and Djem, the numbers of women registered in 1960 still exceeded the numbers voting in 1957; and four of the five exceptions were, socially and economically, extremely "backward" in comparison with Sousse and Ksar-Hellal. Possibly, then, the party was merely being more "realistic" in 1960.

[32]Article 50 of the March 14, 1957, decree lists thirteen types of decision subject to approval by the governor.

Virtually every town in Tunisia had its plan for new construction and long-term development drawn up by its council aided by government experts. In theory, at least, it was the task of the branch to mobilize popular support for the council's projects. Plans usually called for modern buildings and facilities that the council budgets and the local economy could not support, but most councils managed to build an outdoor sports arena or a market center.

In Hammam-Sousse guided democracy seemed to be producing promising results. After completing his university studies in France, Hedi Baccouche returned during the summer of 1959. A native of Hammam-Sousse, he had been elected president of the Neo-Destour Federation of France and was one of the party's promising young leaders. He became assistant political commissioner of Sousse and in 1960 was the party's obvious choice to head the town council list. The commissioner and Baccouche wisely refused to allow the controversial former fellagha to be listed, though the branch clique wanted him. Baccouche listed four members of the branch executive and a businessman not identified with the clique, all of whom had been defeated in 1957.

The clique distrusted Baccouche, who by his very presence in the village intruded upon their hitherto untroubled reign. Since Baccouche was a higher party official, however, they had little choice but to obey him. Behind the scenes Sheikh Bahri, leader of the clique, spread rumors to discredit Baccouche. Bahri thought Baccouche had been responsible for keeping him off the 1957 list, though the latter denied the accusation. Since votes for each candidate were separately counted, Bahri hoped by his campaign to make Baccouche appear unpopular and receive noticeably fewer votes than the other candidates (results, Baccouche 2,267; others 2,322-2,305). After the election a demonstration was organized against Bahri by a village youth who typified the rising generation which had received some secondary education and was engaged in modern occupations in Sousse. This progressive element had felt itself a handicapped minority in local village life. The chief organizer argued that educated young men had systematically been frustrated by the clique until Baccouche's return.[33]

The Neo-Destour had performed its revolution almost too well. With little bloodshed over a thirty-year period, it had convinced the village that it belonged to a Tunisian nation; and it virtually dominated the social fabric of the village. The branch clique was headed by two

[33]The organizer's uncle had been a schoolteacher in charge of the village Scout group. The clique did not like him and spread rumors that he had a fondness for little boys. Like the former mayor, he had left Hammam-Sousse to find a teaching job elsewhere.

Zitouna-trained imams who had founded and taught in the village's modern Quranic school. They had joined the party not long before independence, and their authority in the village was needed by the party to attract the villagers to its slogans and ideas. In some respects Sheikh Bahri was a modernist; unlike conservative Muslims, he approved of birth control. But the two imam schoolteachers did not encourage the participation in village affairs of young villagers who might undermine their authority. Middle-aged and not attuned to the ideas of an open society, they wished to hold on to all the strings of village life.

Baccouche recognized the struggle between generations as a manageable political competition rather than a deep division between rival families or between traditionalists and modernists. He accordingly kept the clique in power, while moderating its conflict with the younger generation. In the 1961 branch assembly elections, the executive committee was reduced from eight to five members, in accord with the Sahel commissioner's policy of ridding the branches of dead wood. Requirements were made more flexible to give younger militants a better chance of election. In 1961 four of the clique's satellite executive members were not reëlected; and, because Baccouche wisely refused to run for office except as a supplementary honorary president, an educated young militant whom he actively supported was the fifth man elected to the committee. Guided democracy was resolving village tensions.

The Branch as Mass Mobilizer

The main task of the branches concerned political education. The commissioner curtailed the early excesses of irresponsible cadres, so that branch executive committees were no longer able to abuse their patronage powers, make excessive demands on overworked government technicians, or exercise unrestrained domination over populations that were apathetic during the independence struggle. The branches became training grounds for developing civic responsibility under the tutelage of the commissioner. To stimulate awareness of Tunisia's economic problems, the party congress of 1959 called upon all the branches to carry out local projects on their own initiative. By early 1961 there were 792 projects under way or completed.[34] The branches were setting up agricultural or industrial coöperative ventures, providing restaurants for needy children, and building classrooms, houses for teachers, or medical dispensaries, in conjunction with government efforts.

[34]*La Presse*, February 4, 1961.

In 1960 the Neo-Destour placed "animators" on the government work sites for the unemployed to encourage the workers to identify themselves with the nation's economic struggle. The animators were supposed to notice any bottlenecks in the work and try to increase productivity. When the workers had valid grievances, the animator intervened on their behalf. As the work sites became centers of civic training, featuring literacy campaigns and physical education, the animator was likely to have more duties. Through him the party tried to elicit the active consent of the brigades of unemployed who under other conditions might be a revolutionary force.[35]

In Tunis and its suburbs the branches played a key role in the government's efforts toward slum clearance. Tunis was overcrowded by tens of thousands of miserable tribesmen and peasants who were seeking a better life in the magic city. The Neo-Destour government's policy was to return those who were jobless, less than ten years in Tunis, and without property, to their place of origin. The slums inhabited by the remaining squatters were to be cleared, and new housing erected with generous government credit. The branches had to explain the government's policy and try to dispel rumors that the squatters were going to be kicked into the street. Branch presidents tried to convince the disinherited that it was in their interest to accept free government transportation back to their native provinces, where the governor would find them work. Often the unemployed preferred to work on government sites in Tunis, where their children at least could be educated. Some of those who were allowed to remain were expelled from their homes into tents, and their *gourbis* were demolished long before new housing could be erected. The branches, which claimed that they had persuaded many to accept free government transportation home, while organizing the homeless in new quarters, were clearly acting as instruments of the government administration for an unpopular program.[36] Thousands of squatters remained in the Tunis area, but the program was unobtrusively ended in 1961 for lack of funds and perhaps also because of its unpopularity. Periodic campaigns launched by the party against street beggars met with limited temporary success.

[35]During 1961 and 1962, a record annual average of 200,000 unemployed (actually many more on a seasonal basis) were working on government sites at an annual wage of $30,000,000. By early 1964, Tunisian officials claimed that 80,000 had been transferred to new agricultural coöperatives, established under Ben Salah's plan, thus alleviating the severe drain on the Tunisian budget. See New York *Times*, March 5, 1964.

[36]See P. Sebag, "La Bidonville de Borgel," *Cahiers de Tunisie*, No. 23-24 (1958), for an example of "degourbification."

In coöperation with the Ministry of Public Health, annual campaigns against trachoma, a common eye disease, were organized. During the month of June, 1962, the party launched a national hygiene campaign against flies and microbes.[37] The party's orientation service tried to keep the population informed of national political problems and goals. Tunisia's constitution was explained in detail at meetings and in a special party brochure. When the "struggle against underdevelopment" became the party's major theme, an annual Tree Day was organized to set the masses to work planting tens of thousands of trees. In the heat of the Bizerte crisis the branches held mass meetings almost every day, and in Tunis loudspeakers amplified the radio's news and martial music.

With Ben Salah's Plan, the Neo-Destour acquired a new focus for its educational activities. In June, 1961, a special "Week of the Plan" was proclaimed and, after the Bizerte crisis of July had subsided, the party concentrated on the plan. The branches discussed economic planning after Political Bureau members had given formal talks at cadres conferences in all provinces. Economic planners were called into Tunis branch meetings, and in October the branches were discussing Ben Salah's Ten-Year Perspective in detail.

Some branches had adult education programs, in coöperation with the Department of Education's anti-illiteracy campaign. Propaganda, too, was geared as much to educating the population as to eliciting enthusiasm, for the Neo-Destour has no serious worries about political stability at the grass roots. That it is possible to reason with people to gain their support was a faith shared with Bourguiba by many Neo-Destour officials. The party even hoped to build a popular university.

Neo-Destour activity obviously facilitated government projects by publicizing them to the local population and enlisting their coöperation. The farmer of a mountain slope was made to understand why the government had to plant trees on his property, and the cart-driver was told why he had to replace his metal with rubber wheels. The illiterate Tunisian peasant, at least along the extended Sahel, was not apathetic and unquestioning, although economically he was usually an inefficient producer. By virtue of the party's constant propaganda about the need for greater production, he was perhaps more willing to listen to the government's agricultural adviser. A genuine social consensus on the value of education, reënforced by the traditional Islamic respect for learning, favored government and party literacy campaigns. Moreover, the city dweller and the Sahel peasant, however poor, had been suf-

[37] *Jeune-Afrique*, June 11, 1962.

ficiently exposed to politics during the thirty-year history of the Neo-
Destour to require explanations of the current political situation.

Flagging attendance at branch assemblies, and declining membership in the party were indications of public apathy, but the party did
not admit any drastic decline in membership. Unofficially its central
administrators claimed between 250,000 and 300,00 members, while
the 65 delegates to the National Council in March, 1962, would indicate a membership of 325,000. Although 600,000 members were
claimed in 1957, the party's ranks were abnormally swollen after independence because branches could break the careers of those who did
not join. In November, 1955, according to the official report of the
Sfax congress, the party had 325,000 members; so it could be argued
that party membership had remained roughly constant.

Specific figures for Sousse, however, told a different story. On the
basis of the number of stamps sold by the Sahel federations in 1955,
what is now the province of Sousse had roughly 45,000 members.[38]
Party records in 1960, in a sample of 86 of the province's 122 branches,
indicated a total membership of roughly 22,000—half of the membership five years previously. Even so, about one man in five belonged
to the party. Party officials claimed, too, that great inroads were made
in the Center and South, the politically underdeveloped regions, since
the installation of the party commissioners. No reliable statistics were
available; but informal claims by party officials that more than half
the (adult male) population in most areas belonged to the party seem
unfounded, as did the party director's unofficial assurances to some of
his cadres in 1961 that the party had increased its total membership
since the Sfax congress.

In times of crisis, such as Bizerte, the masses were easily aroused,
but routine rallies needed careful organization from the commissioner's
office to be successful. The unemployed would be transported in trucks
loaned to the party, and the applause and chants of "Yahia Bourguiba"
were orchestrated by party organizers. At one branch assembly in 1961,
only a few members came out to listen to a lecture by the editor of
the party newspaper. At the assembly itself—the branch was one of the
oldest in Tunis and famed for its active women's section—a maximum
of 150 persons, including 30 women, turned up. At another Tunis assembly in 1961, that of the famed Metouia militants, barely 150 of a
membership of 500 appeared. Out of the 280 members of another
branch, barely 80 showed up. In the Sahel villages where there was
little else to do in the evening, attendance was slightly better. In Hammam-Sousse, only 104 out of 230 members voted at the 1961 assembly,

[38]*National Congress of Sfax* (1956), pp. 57-58.

though at least 220 were entitled to vote. At four other branch assemblies, however, the official quorum of half the membership was achieved.

Before the Bizerte crisis the party seemed to be losing momentum as an instrument of mass mobilization. The Kairouan riots painfully brought this home to Bourguiba, who immediately urged party leaders to revitalize the apparatus. To the man in the street, however, party and government were the same thing, run like a bureaucracy by a relatively small group of men. Structurally, indeed, the party was a bureaucracy, and the powers of the commissioners over the branches made the latter, though freely elected, an instrument of the former. The local party apparatus seemed no longer capable of instilling the mass loyalties it had aroused during the independence struggle.

Recruiting and Educating the Cadres

By their limited exercise of political power, the party cadres on the branch executive committees—roughly ten thousand Tunisians—were acquiring the arts of leadership and were learning new skills. The more promising cadres, simply on the basis of native ability and enthusiasm, would acquire the confidence of the commissioner. For instance, one of the Tunis commissioner's right-hand men, a young branch president with little formal education beyond primary school, was put in charge of a glass factory, the branch project decided upon after the Sousse congress.

The ten thousand cadres were a very mixed group, reflecting the population at large. The product of varying social environments and local political histories, their quality was considered best in the cities and in the provinces bordering the eastern coastline, especially around Tunis and Sousse.

In the province of Sousse statistics were obtained from party records about the cadres of three-quarters of the region's 122 branches in 1960. Apparently many cadres had been party members for years, although their claims were sometimes exaggerated. One-quarter claimed to have joined the party before 1942, and only a slightly greater number were youths or opportunists who had joined since 1954. The cadres did not seem to constitute an educated or professional elite. One-twelfth were schoolteachers, while less than 2 per cent were high-school teachers, doctors, important government officials, or deputies. One-twelfth worked for the government as petty bureaucrats, hospital orderlies, or post-office clerks. More than one-quarter held such village occupations as clockmaker, café waiter, imam, and forest watcher,

Party Cadres in the Sousse Governorate

Date of entry into Neo-Destour	Sahel/ Sousse City	Rest of Sousse governorate[a]	Totals[b]
1920-1941	161/10	41	202
1942-1948	114/7	31	145
1949-1953	87/1	126	213
1954-	165/16	87	252
Totals	527/34	285	812
Occupation			
Liberal professions	11/3	2	13
Schoolteachers	53/4	4	57
Government employees	49/8	10	59
Farmers	242/ -	241	483
Miscellaneous	202/19	38	240
Totals	557/34	295	852
Educational attainment			
Illiterate	39/ -	41	80
Can read, write (self-taught)	133/2	124	257
Primary schooling	113/14	30	143
Secondary schooling	64/9	15	79
Baccalaureate	7/ -	-	7
French university degree	7/3	2	9
Zitouna schooling	57/ -	12	69
Zitouna university degree	15/3	1	16
Did not say[c]	143/3	71	214
Totals	578/34	296	874

[a] The rest of the Sousse governorate is composed of the delegations of Enfida, El Djem, and Chorbane-Souassi, areas on the fringes of the Sahel that are less socially developed and produce fewer olive trees.
[b] Discrepancies in the totals are due to the fact that some cadres omitted to declare their date of entry into the party or occupation.
[c] We may assume that most cadres who did not declare their level of education were either illiterate or could (barely) read and write.

while more than half were farmers, usually traditional Sahel peasants of very modest means.

The formal education of the cadres was much better in the city of Sousse than in the province as a whole. But the level was generally low[39]—and possibly inadequate for a party engaged in educating and

[39] One-quarter left a blank space on their party data cards, suggesting no education and perhaps shame. Of those answering, almost one-tenth admitted total illiteracy; two-fifths claimed only that they could read and write; more than one-fifth claimed a little primary school education; one-seventh claimed some modern secondary school education, but only 1 per cent had university degrees; another eighth had some formal traditional school, but only 2 per cent had diplomas from Zitouna University.

transforming a society rather than waging a nationalist struggle. In the Sahel many of the school teachers had traditional Zitouna rather than modern diplomas. Although the Sahel was vaunted for its many modern university students—perhaps one-third of Tunisia's total[40]— they did not work in the party organization. The dearth of educated cadres in the Sahel suggests that the problem was serious in other less educated areas of the country. Elsewhere, too, the cadres lacked the years of experience in the party that helped to train the Sahel cadres.

Since the cadres were close to the population and reflected its way of life, political communication was presumably more effective. Political experience was often a substitute for formal education. Seasoned cadres, while maintaining their local sources of authority, were attuned to modern ideas and social change. As in Hammam-Sousse, the word of the Zitouna-trained teachers of the former Quranic schools on such matters as birth control would probably carry more weight than that of a university-trained outsider.

In areas less politically developed than the Sahel, however, the branch cadres often came from the Sahel. In administrative centers, civil servants with experience as militants elsewhere were sometimes drawn into the town branch where they worked. Even the branch of Le Kram, a suburb of Tunis, had three Sahel militants, including the president and general secretary, on the ten-man executive committee.[41] In Souk El Arba the commissioner, hardpressed to find men with political experience, coöpted a public-works engineer from the Sahel to the coördinating committee to take charge of propaganda. Many of the key cadres who kept the local party apparatus functioning seemed to be petty officials or schoolteachers from the Sahel.

The ranks of the party elite were in theory open to anyone who could get elected to a branch committee. But in villages and in the old quarters of towns and cities, outsiders, even if they had worked in the area for a few years, usually could not be elected. Only in relatively new communities lacking corporate solidarity and traditional roots could the outside party organizer play a leading role in local politics without assistance from the central apparatus. The imported schoolteacher was often considered a foreigner by the local population, but he could hope to play a supporting role in the commissioner's office.

The better-organized branches in cities and large towns trained numbers of militants—especially the young and ambitious who wanted

[40]Of the 201 new scholarships awarded to university students in 1959-60, natives of the Sahel were given 68. See *L'Etudiant Tunisien*, April, 1960.
[41]The president had been a schoolteacher in the town since 1949, but his general secretary arrived as a post-office clerk only in 1957.

to compensate for their mediocre education—by coöpting them to the branch's committees for orientation, youth, social development, and finance. In a well-organized Tunis branch, roughly thirty militants on the various committees met regularly with the branch officer in charge of their sector. An additional thirty militants helped the orientation committee to organize demonstrations or to spread the party line on a given issue. For the urban youth who was unemployed or bored with a small clerical job, the party offered a more interesting career. A competent and loyal youth could be elected to the branch committee or given more important duties in the commissioner's office. To some dedicated individuals, too, the party was perhaps an emotional outlet.

To discover and train young cadres was a serious concern of the party's central office. Hundreds attended training seminars during the summers of 1956 and 1957, though out of the three hundred in 1957 only a third were considered to be qualified for the party's bureaucracy. In subsequent years the accent was on Neo-Destour youth cadres, but the seminars were not very successful, for the youths, having to work for a living, did not spend enough time on party activities. In 1961 a new program was under way to bring schoolteachers and graduating secondary school students to seminars during their vacations. The few who seemed promising were sent abroad to international work camps (in Yugoslavia) the following summer, and could then be recruited into the party bureaucracy, with a starting salary of $100 a month.

Unlike youth groups affiliated with democratic parties in the West, the Neo-Destour Youth had no autonomy and passed no resolutions. It was a division of the party bureaucracy administered by officials as a department of the Political Bureau, with a chain of command running through the commissioners to the branch committees. Before independence the youth kept public order at political rallies, and some of them formed sabotage networks. Although they continued to assist the police in keeping order at public ceremonies, the prime tasks of the organization were to train good citizens and recruit active party members. In theory, it was building a homogeneous new generation of forward-looking Tunisians.[42]

But in 1961 Bourguiba was in despair about the youth.[43] No more

[42]Other youth organizations, such as UGET, the Scouts, and associations for youth hostels and vacation colonies, also existed under the control of the party and government. The government's direction of youth and sports had an annual budget of more than 300,000 dinars (1960) and for the period 1962-1971 planned to invest more than 11,000,000 dinars in buildings and facilities. *Perspectives Decennales de Développement*, pp. 118-119.
[43]He made a speech on the youth situation on March 30, 1961.

than 100,000 out of 2,000,000 Tunisians under the age of twenty belonged to a Tunisian youth association. Organization was confined mostly to the larger cities, but even the Neo-Destour Youth failed to provide enough social outlets for the young urban masses. Those who were unable to finish their schooling or find a job were apathetic. In the countryside the youth were isolated from social change, whereas Bourguiba wanted Tunisia to become a vast school. In 1959 only 2,383 youths had taken part in specific programs of the Neo-Destour Youth,[44] though thousands more probably enjoyed some contact with their local branches.

After independence the Neo-Destour Youth suffered a steady decline, because it could no longer offer the excitement of political agitation or provide jobs for all the boys. In a relatively analytical article in the party's propagandistic youth magazine, a presidential aide who was also a part-time youth leader tried to explain the organization's difficulties.

We have seen the youths' ranks continuously renewed, but the motive of the new elements was finding work or advancement or prestige. Most of the time the youth enters the party to find work, and that is his last link with the party. . . .
Then there is another thing. . . . The educated youth and especially the well-heeled class within it has withdrawn from party activity. . . . While all our comrades used to be side by side in the days of struggle, we see them no more except in some café on a rare occasion. Has their mission in the party ended? . . . They will ask regretfully, "Where is the party?" and say that it . . . has become the property of others and that they are not responsible for the party's shortage of cadres. . . . Most of the time they disdain mixing at the branch office with the classes of little people thirsty for knowledge and orientation. . . .[45]

In 1961 the party was concentrating in each province on forming an elite of well-trained Neo-Destour youths. Each branch was to group ten promising ones in a cell, making a total of ten thousand who might, as an active, dedicated minority, set an example to the rest of Tunisia's youth and provide future party cadres. Many—at least 1,500, according to a reliable party official—died as "volunteers" in the Bizerte fighting.

[44]See *Bulletin Mensuel de Statistiques* (Republic of Tunisia, Direction du Plan), No. 72 (November, 1960), cited in Michel Lelong, "Les mouvements de jeunesse," *IBLA* (Tunis), No. 93 (1960, 1st trim.), 61-64. Membership in the Neo-Destour Youth was claimed to number 120,000 in 1958, but recent official figures indicate no more than 25,000, according to Douglas E. Ashford, *Second and Third Generation Elites in the Maghreb* (U.S. Department of State, Bureau of Intelligence and Research, 1964), p. 17. Even this figure would seem high, if the party's youth policy formulated in 1961 were being carried out consistently.
[45]Ahmed Chtourou, "Destourian Youth at the Crossroads," *Esh-Shebab*, May, 1961.

In more normal times, the party tried to reorganize work camps, discussion groups, lectures, and travel to stimulate the youth. A party student section was reorganized under a political commissioner who had once been elected president of the student Federation of France.

But the key problem remained of attracting the educated youth into the party. Many of those who terminated their studies abroad and returned to Tunisia soon became disillusioned with the paternalistic political structure. They stayed aloof from politics and did not need to be party members in order to find administrative positions. A handful of professional politicians entered the party apparatus from above, but the typical young educated Tunisian had no interest in becoming an active member of his local branch and mingling with the masses. The extent of his political participation would be informal conversations with friends. Among the students of Tunis, perhaps half were in the party, but, as the head of the student section admitted, they were neither disciplined nor dedicated activists.

Seven years after independence, it seemed that the party had developed solid local roots in the course of its thirty years of activity. The branch was a social institution, an organ of integration that had become a national habit. Under the tutelage of the commissioner the branch remained relatively open and was developing new leadership. Mobility and advancement were no longer what they had been in 1956, but leaders were trying to renew the ranks. The few talented militants could still rise high in Bourguiba's favor. Mohammed Ben Amara was perhaps the best example. An obscure veteran of a Tunis branch 1959, he caught Bourguiba's eye and was put in charge of the Neo-Destour Youth in Tunis. The self-educated schoolteacher (he had done much of his studying as a political prisoner before independence) was successful and was made commissioner in Gabes. Then in 1961 he was appointed assistant director of the party, and took charge of its internal administration in 1962.

But all was not well at the party's grass roots. Some militants complained of being stifled by the bureaucrats at the top. Apathy seemed not so much a product of the absence of ideology, for Neo-Destour socialism was filling the doctrinal vacuum. Rather, the old sense of mission was fading. Presumably this was due in part to the deterioration since independence of the party's deliberative organs. Cadre conferences were multiplied in 1962, but the cadres wondered whether their criticisms were really heard. Between the branches and the Political Bureau, more messages seemed to be relayed downward than were reaching upward. One sensitive young party leader thought that the 'sixties would be remembered as the years of confusion.

The party's mission was, in Bourguiba's words, to be "permanent," but how could its sense of mission be revitalized? The give and take of politics existed (barely) only at the local level. Above, the political process seemed hidden in bureaucratic channels, while the only outward manifestation was the cult of personality. The cadres had assimilated the Neo-Destour's democratic education, but then—with the honeymoon of independence ended—some were privately asking how it might better be implemented.[46]

In 1964, it was still too early to tell whether the reorganization of the party would resolve the problem by encouraging more internal democracy. At the local level much depended upon how the new regional coördinating committees would operate. Would they be more responsive to the branches that elected them than the commissioners they were replacing? A greater degree of internal democracy would conceivably be stimulated by the introduction, called for in the reorganization plan, of a distinction between active militants, members, and sympathizers. If the Neo-Destour were to become an elite party of cadres, the price of internal democracy might be a growing divorce between the elite and the mass of sympathizers—a divorce already intimated by the apathy the reform was designed to combat.

---

[46]Among local party officials, it was possible for the interviewer in 1962 to hear this reaction. Somewhat independent of the party and attempting to speak for the new student generation, Bechir Ben Yahmed, editor of *Jeune-Afrique,* praised Bourguiba's proposals for reforming the party structure in 1963 (though, in the editor's words, "It is always difficult to break out of a freeze, and the thaw is a slow process"; see *Jeune Afrique,* March 11-17, 1963). In the issue of January 13-19, 1964, he wrote an editorial attacking the concept of the single-party system as a permanent state of affairs: ". . . in the best of cases the single party and personal power can be advantageous only so far as they assure a transitional phase" toward a democratic multiparty system.

VI THE NATIONAL ORGANIZATIONS

WITHIN the consolidated single-party regime, the national organizations performed on a horizontal plane some of the functions carried out on a vertical plane by the party's branches. These associations articulated and represented the interests and aspirations of their members, but as "national" groupings they mobilized support for the regime and collaborated on specific projects with the government. Embracing politically significant sectors of the society—workers, businessmen, farmers, students, and women—they appeared to be well-disciplined appendages of the dominant party. Yet as pressure groups they required a measure of freedom to influence policy. Obviously they led an equivocal existence, being neither fully autonomous groups nor blind instruments of the party. So far as they subordinated professional interests to the national interest, they helped to maintain Tunisia's cohesion; but party control sapped their vitality and tended to divorce them from their members.

Patterns of Political Subordination

Before independence the national organizations made common cause with the party. UTAC was virtually a Neo-Destour creation. At the end of the Second World War the black market and various import restrictions gave artisans and shopkeepers serious grievances which the Tunisian Communist Party exploited through a front organization. Alarmed at its success, the Neo-Destour detailed Ferdjani Bel Hadj Ammar, a café proprietor and veteran militant, to infiltrate the Communist front. Within a year he created a split within the front between Europeans and Tunisian Muslims; by 1948 UTAC had come into being with a membership of 40,000; it articulated genuine professional grievances to the colonial authorities, and as its leader later admitted, invented grievances to instill the shopkeepers with nationalist fervor. UGAT, the farmers' organization, was created under similar circumstances in 1949, and UGET, the student group, was established at a clandestine congress supported by the party in 1953.

Tunisian trade-unionism, in contrast, had roots antedating the party. In 1924 Mohammed Ali had created the General Confederation of Tunisian Workers in opposition to the French-run CGT. In 1937 the union was resurrected, and the Neo-Destour tried through Hedi Nouira to control it, but that effort was short-lived. In 1944, however, Farhat Hached was able to organize the workers of Sfax into a more durable organization. A militant of the CGT, he had not taken part in the previous attempts to organize a national labor movement. But with the support of the Neo-Destour he succeeded in founding a second autonomous union in Tunis, and in January, 1946, the UGTT was born. A number of veteran party militants, like Habib Achour and Ahmed Tlili, assisted Hached, who collaborated closely with the Political Bureau. Although not originally a member of the party, Hached saw no conflict between nationalism and trade-unionism. National liberation was a prerequisite for the satisfaction of working-class claims, possible only under democratic conditions that were incompatible with colonial domination. In 1952, when the party was suppressed, Hached became one of the leading clandestine collaborators of the Political Bureau, until his assassination in December.

Historically, then, the national organizations all served as arms of the party for national liberation. Even the UNFT, created in 1958, was led by women who, at least in Tunisian national mythology, had previously played heroic political roles. The division of the Tunisian people into national organizations, Bourguiba explained, "was tactically necessary [before independence] to keep some elements outside the party and protect them from repression and the risks of overt political activity. Controlled by the party, these organizations were placed in the context of defending professional interests. . . ." Bourguiba after independence used this historical explanation as a justification "to warn these organizations and their leaders against excessive zeal in exclusively defending the interests which they represented and which threatened to divide the people into classes or cliques and to erect walls between the citizens of the same nation."[1]

Indeed, after independence the "national" organizations threatened to become free-wheeling pressure groups rivaling the supremacy of the party. The organized workers under Ben Salah might have accelerated nationalization and social revolution—or fought with a greater militancy for higher wages. The business interests, backed by the Masmoudi clan, might have blocked the party's acceptance of "socialism" and economic planning. The farmers, in theory representing three-quarters of the Tunisian population, might have teamed up with dissatisfied traditionalists to defend private property from public encroachment. Whatever Tunisia's "middle class" social outlook, political differences within the party and national organizations existed after independence.

[1]Speech, November 7, 1958.

Youssefism, however, emphasized the need for national unity. The fate of the farmers' organization demonstrated the need for conformity to Bourguiba's party. The leaders of the UGAT actively sympathized with Salah Ben Youssef, lent him their local offices as nuclei for his party branches, and refused at the Sfax congress to speak in support of Bourguiba.

By early November, 1955, before the congress, the Bourguibist press was already writing of the "break-up" of UGAT and the disaffiliation of its local branches.[2] It was explained that the local cadres of UGAT were small peasant Destourians dissatisfied with an intellectual leadership divorced from their problems. UGAT was accused of having come under the control of large landowners who thought that Ben Youssef would better serve their interests. The assistant general secretary of UGAT, a politically unknown technical-school teacher, challenged UGAT leadership by persuading the farmers of his native Sahel to disaffiliate. With the support of the Sahel, he held a rump congress in Kairouan in early December, where many farmers were already gathered on a religious pilgrimage. Dignified by Bourguiba's presence, the congress established a new national organization, Union Nationale des Agriculteurs Tunisiens (UNAT). UGAT was dissolved by government decree a few weeks later, and UNAT took over its local offices. The important precedent was established that national organizations were to remain politically in step with the Neo-Destour.

The case of the farmers seems not to have concerned professional interests as such. Although the leaders of UNAT were better prepared to compromise with Bourguiba over the subsequent promulgation of an agricultural workers' statute, the differences between UNAT and UGAT seem to have been mostly personal differences among the top leaders. Those of UGAT were loyal to Ben Youssef, while the new leaders were loyal to Bourguiba. The organizational change apparently had little effect upon the rank and file.[3]

The affair of the UGTT scission further helped to define and limit the role of the national organizations in independent Tunisia. Whatever the personal differences among trade-union leaders and other men

[2] L' Action, November 7, 1955.
[3] In Souk El Arba the provincial cadres claim not to have taken sides in what was happening at the national level, though the two provincial leaders were Youssefists. The cadres did not attend the Kairouan congress, but some farmers from the area who happened to be in Kairouan were brought before the congress and designated as regional officers of UNAT. At Souk El Arba they installed themselves in the UGAT office, politely vacated with records left intact by the UGAT regional committee. Four or five members of the latter were subsequently included in the UNAT committee; two of them becoming president and general secretary of the regional union, respectively.

in power, at issue also was the role of the trade union. For Ben Salah the UGTT was to continue after independence to have a political role. Working in coöperation with, or possibly even fusing with the Neo-Destour, it was to provide the government with a coherent social and economic doctrine that would determine policies. Whatever the structural links that might be devised between party and trade union, Ben Salah had engaged the UGTT in national politics, as the political instrument of social revolution.

Habib Achour's position, limiting the trade union to the apolitical pursuit of specific workers' interests, triumphed at the unity congress of 1957 with the prearranged support of UGTT as well as UTT leadership. It was decided that ministers and high government administrators had to give up their trade-union responsibilities. Henceforth one no longer spoke of "UGTT ministers," only of trade-unionists "on vacation." After the congress elections only three former Ben Salah supporters (Ben Azzeddine, Galaoui, Khiari) remained on the UGTT Executive Committee, and one of them had to resign soon thereafter when he entered Bourguiba's cabinet.

The ostensible issues resolved by the UGTT and the UTT, however, were less important than the political impact of the scission. The substitution of Ben Salah by Tlili and the coöption of Habib Achour to the Political Bureau assured close coordination between the latter and the reunified UGTT. In practice the UGTT, like the other national organizations, continued to take general political stands on issues of national policy, as well as to defend workers' specific interests. The only difference was that under Tlili the political positions coincided with those of the Political Bureau and the government. Ben Salah and Tlili as trade-unionists both identified themselves with national rather than class interests.

Bourguiba proudly addressed the 1960 congress of UGTT: "It is because the leaders of the national organizations, just as those of the state, are aware of this order of priority [of national over class interest], which must be respected, that all difficulties have been solved and that social peace has reigned since independence over all Tunisia. This peace was not imposed either by repression or fear, but resulted from the approval, enthusiasm, and loyalty felt for the government's policy."[4]

The activities report presented by the UGTT Executive Bureau to the 1960 congress faithfully echoed Bourguiba's statement. The report, adopted by the congress, defined UGTT, "the continuation of national Tunisian trade-unionism founded in 1924," as "an essentially trade-unionist movement, in theory apolitical, . . . working for an increased

[4]Speech, April 1, 1960.

living standard for the Tunisian proletariat. . . ." It added that the UGTT nevertheless still played a political role, as in the struggle for independence, because "independence, to be effective, must be completely and definitively freed of all sequels of political or economic servitude and permit the evolution of national institutions toward a maximum of democracy.

That is why our trade-union Central, organically affiliated to no political party though the majority of its members belong to the Neo-Destour party for its socialistic action and programs, continues, however, to associate itself with the activities of the National Front, within which it occupies second place after the party and which serves to coördinate various national political, economic, and cultural organizations in everything concerning their common objectives.[5]

The political role of UTAC and UNAT after independence was comparable to that of the UGTT, though the latter had greater prestige and power as a well-organized mass movement. Indeed, at least in public, the role of the national organizations as pressure groups for professional interests seemed submerged by their political role as organizations supporting the government. If UNAT's official aims were "to defend the interests of its adherents and work for economic prosperity," its constitution stated that "it is the tie between the government and the farmers that is to achieve these aims."[6] In the case of UTAC, one could not be sure whose interests were to be defended; after independence the organization changed its name to Union Tunisienne des Industriels et Commerçants (UTIC), thus promoting artisans to the ranks of industrialists, but in 1963 a compromise was reached: the name was changed to Union Tunisienne des Industriels, Commerçants, et Artisans (UTICA), possibly in recognition of ubiquitous obstacles to industrialization. UTICA's objectives were clearly those of the party and the government: the general secretary once excused a two-year postponing of its national congress by the "exigencies of national mobilization" after the Sakiet incident.[7]

The three organizations participated in the National Front for the National Assembly elections of 1956 and 1959. This entailed supporting lists drawn up by the Political Bureau, which selected a few leaders of the national organizations on the basis of their party record. By 1957 three of the leaders of UGTT and UTICA were members of the Political Bureau. UNFT also supported the National Front in 1959, and its president was elected to the National Assembly. The national

[5]UGTT, *Activities Report,* Eighth National Congress, April, 1960, pp. 7-8.

[6]Article 3, Basic Statutes passed by Second Congress, April 16, 1959.

[7]Ferdjani Bel Hadj Ammar's opening speech, Fifth Congress, October 28, 1960.

organizations participated, too, in the municipal council elections. Many of their local leaders, including twenty women in 1960, were elected on the social development lists of the Neo-Destour. Even the incumbent general secretary of UGET, the student organization, became a Tunis city councilor in 1960.

In times of national crisis the national organizations made joint resolutions and communiqués with the Neo-Destour. After such events as the kidnaping of Ben Bella, the bombardment of Sakiet, or the Battle of Bizerte, the Tunisian people were "mobilized" by the UGTT, UTICA, UNAT, UNFT, and UGET, as well as the Neo-Destour. When Bourguiba wished to make an important pronouncement, he sometimes addressed the "cadres of the nation," which included the regional leaders of the national organizations as well as the party. In political "campaigns," too, the national organizations were called upon to assist the party and the government. The UGTT and UTICA were especially useful in fund-raising drives.[8]

The structure and mechanisms for assuring political conformity varied with the nature of each organization's membership and history. UTICA and UNAT were unwieldy groupings, with relatively little contact between the leadership and a disparate mass of traditional, transitional, and modern businessmen and farmers, large and small. That their history was hardly distinguishable from that of the party tended to facilitate party control. The UNFT was also a relatively ineffective paper organization, recently created, and easily controlled because its leaders were relatives or admirers of Bourguiba or wives of his lieutenants. The UGTT, in contrast, was a solid organization of relatively homogeneous workers, many of whom were veteran trade-unionists steeped in the mystique of Mohammed Ali and Farhat Hached. UGET was a special case; despite the weakness of an organization having an automatic turnover of leaders and members, student nonconformity presented the party with problems that were perhaps insoluble.

UTICA, UNAT, and the UNFT had the trappings of democratic mass organization and claimed, respectively, 20,000, 150,000, and 40,000 members in 1960. UTICA and UNAT, at least, grouped a respectable 25-30 per cent of all Tunisians engaged in crafts, business, and farming. The secretary general admitted, however, that UTICA's membership had dropped by half since 1948. By 1960 the UNFT, after a slow start,

[8]The National Loan in 1957 was the occasion of an outright donation by UGTT and appeals to its membership by UTAC. The UGTT could also "consent" to the government's special 1 per cent tax on the low salaries of government employees for the expansion of the Tunisian Army.

had created 116 local sections and implanted itself in all major towns throughout the country.[9]

UTICA's and UNAT's primary units were *syndicats* respectively elected in every town or sheikhat. At the level of the governorate, regional assemblies of *syndicats* elected an executive regional committee, and at triennial national congresses delegates from the *syndicats* respectively elected 30 and 21-man administrative commissions. The latter in turn elected the executive bureaus. To meet the diverse specialized problems of their members, UNAT and UTICA instituted professional federations operating from their central offices. UTICA in 1962, like the party in 1958, replaced the elected regional committees with appointed economic committees in each governorate;[10] those opposed to economic planning or price controls were weeded out of the organization. Presumably the consultative governorate councils, created in 1964 and composed of representatives designated by the national organizations as well as party and municipal officials, would further serve to maintain discipline within UTICA and UNAT.

Party control seemed to be exercised at all levels. Even the local leader of UNAT or UTICA was almost invariably a veteran party member, subject to party discipline, if not actually a party branch officer. When the president of UNAT became exasperated with a local UNAT leader, he checked with an influential branch president before ridding UNAT of the troublemaker.[11] It was, after all, exclusively the responsibility of the party and the regional administration to maintain the political balance between local personalities. At the regional level, UNAT and UTICA committees seemed totally integrated in 1962 with the commissioner's social development committee. Even when the UNAT or UTICA leader was not a member of the party's coördinating committee, he cleared his regional activities with the commissioner.

In the provinces the party's main problem was not so much to control UTICA and UNAT as to activate them. The UNFT, too, seemed utterly dependent upon the commissioner's services and advice. In Gabes, when the local UNFT leader married and took the UNFT office keys with her to Tunis, the UNFT committee simply disbanded, until the commissioner recovered the keys and trained another young woman to take her place. Outside Tunis, UTICA and UNAT also seemed inactive, though the regional officers could present local grievances to the governor. However, in the important cities—Tunis,

[9]*Rapport Moral*, Second Congress, August 13-16, 1960.
[10]*La Presse*, February 24, 1962.
[11]After previous troubles, the man had been reinstated in UNAT at the request of the party.

Sousse, and Sfax— UTIC leaders were also prominent members of the chambers of commerce and occasionally influenced important decisions. Playing on the sympathy of a number of Sahel ministers, for instance, the commercial leaders of Sousse persuaded the government in 1961 to channel more exports through the city's inactive port and thereby stimulate business. But in the intensively cultivated Sahel, where farmers' strength might be expected, there were few signs of UNAT's existence.

As participants in the National Front, the two organizations at the national level depended upon the Neo-Destour for seats in the National Assembly and in various consultative bodies. Five of the twelve national officers of UTICA elected in 1960 were deputies in the National Assembly; three of UNAT's top collaborators were also deputies. Although UNAT's president was not a member of the Political Bureau— probably because UNAT was not considered sufficently important—he was the reliable Bourguiba supporter who had divided UGAT in 1955. Even at the national level the party's main concern was not so much to curb UNAT and UTICA as to encourage them to think up productive ideas and train their adherents to be modern entrepreneurs. Thus the party and its leaders in UTICA encouraged the election of new leadership in 1960. Less than half of the new administrative commission was carried over from the previous elections in 1955.

The Case of the Workers

The party controlled the UGTT with great care and some embarrassment. Until he lost the secretaryship in 1963, Ahmed Tlili privately advocated a formal fusion of the UGTT and the party to clarify an "equivocal position." The myth of an autonomous, militant labor movement persisted, but constant compromises with the regime had seriously weakened the UGTT. The compromises were profitable, however: at the expense of the organization's vitality, most of its classic objectives became those of the government. Through its policy of close cooperation with the Neo-Destour regime, the UGTT could list as major "victories" the government's option for a planned economy, its ambitious policy of mass education, advanced social legislation, workers' cooperatives and management committees, an advanced statute for agricultural workers, and the creation of consultative bodies on which the UGTT had an important voice. But by supporting the government, the UGTT lost much of its liberty of action and mass appeal. The right to strike, which Bourguiba considered "sacred" in 1956 because he had to respect trade-union power, was nowhere guaranteed in

Tunisian legislation and rarely practiced.[12] Take-home pay after 1956 remained constant or decreased, while the cost of living increased.

Reliable membership statistics were impossible to obtain. Trade-union officials in 1961 claimed 100,000-150,000 adherents, as compared with 182,000 in 1956. Active dues-paying membership, however, was probably far lower. On the basis of official graphs giving the proportional number of adherents in each federation, the UGTT seemed to have less than 65,000 members in 1959.[13] Less reliably, the number of delegates attending the 1960 congress indicated a total membership of 80,000.[14] In any event, it would seem that UGTT membership had greatly declined after the scission.

Since the reunification of 1957 the UGTT had tightened and centralized its organization. Local *syndicats* had to group at least a hundred workers to send a delegate to the triennial congress. Regional unions, the centers of political agitation before independence, were overshadowed by the new professional federations.[15] In 1960 the regional union of Tunis, an especially militant organization in 1955 and 1956, was virtually abolished; its democratically elected officers were replaced by appointees of the central office.

Three of the ten federation leaders in 1962 were also members of the nine-man Excutive Bureau. Regional and federal congresses were biennial, and the congress was triennial. These bodies, respectively, elected the regional executive committees, the federal executives, and

[12]Note the respecitve statistics in Tunisia and Morocco regarding the number of labor disputes, the number of workers involved, and the number of man-days lost, 1956-1958.

	Disputes		Workers		Man-days	
	Tunisia/Morocco		Tunisia/Morocco		Tunisia/Morocco	
1956	252	1,987	14,923	76,486	74,798	404,410
1957	63	118	5,405	22,818	25,160	112,436
1958	45	220	1,412	131,840	1,886	256,992

Source: ILO, *Labor Survey of North Africa* (1960), p. 171.

[13]*Activities Report*, Eighth Congress, p. 90. A second graph gives the proportions of members in each regional union. Assuming that these graphs indicate membership as well as proportions, UGTT might be construed as having a membership of 63,050.

[14]There were 412 delegates, and one delegate was to represent 200 members.

[15]The regions lost financial autonomy; instead of directly receiving half of the dues of the local *syndicats,* the central office in Tunis paid and limited their expenses. The regions were henceforth to be centers of political and trade-union education and coördinate the activities of the *syndicats,* while the federations were to look after concrete interests of their adherents. In each governorate there was to be one regional *syndicat* for each relevant federation, in addition to the regional union.

the central's Executive Bureau. Between congresses supervision was theoretically exercised by a 132-man National Council, and an enlarged administrative commission grouping general secretaries of the regions and the federations. But these organs did not meet as frequently under Tlili as the UGTT statutes required.

Until 1963 Tlili was the party's main instrument of control over the UGTT.[16] The centralization of the UGTT in Tlili's hands assured overall harmony between UGTT, party, and government. In the interests of national production, strikes were not tolerated unless they had an affective or tactical political significance. On anniversaries of the Algerian Revolution, the UGTT called "general strikes" within the context of the Neo-Destour's National Front. Against French-owned companies the regime permitted strikes in the context of decolonization. But when strikes were not politically opportune, they abruptly ceased or were not publicized. Once in the absence of the governor of Gafsa, Habib Achour rejected the arbitration of the governor's delegate and called for a strike against the Sfax-Gafsa Company, which was then under French management. The delegate immediately reported to Mehiri, who ordered Habib Achour to leave Gafsa. In the pinch Tlili went along with Mehiri, and Habib Achour as a member of the Political Bureau had to desist.

Tlili and other trade-union leaders maintained that at least 90 per cent of the UGTT members were also party members. Impossible to verify, such a claim, even if true, did not preclude the need for other control devices. There was, as with UTICA and UNAT, a great overlapping of membership among the UGTT cadres. In 1962, six of the nine Executive members were committed to the National Front as deputies in the National Assembly,[17] while four regional union and federation heads were also deputies. More ominously—especially in Tunis, where one-third of the UGTT membership was concentrated—the Neo-Destour operated professional branches within key *syndicats.*

Even Tlili, who preferred to underline the harmony between the party and the UGTT, once declared at a conference of party and trade-union cadres that better coöperation was needed between the profes-

[16]Other than Tlili and Habib Achour, no one of national stature remained on the Executive Bureau. Of the personalities on the Bureau before the scission, Ahmed Ben Salah, Abdallah Farhat, Mustapha Filali, Mahmoud Khiari, and Amor Riahi (a high civil servant) all departed, though only one member of the 1960 Bureau was not on the Administrative Council in 1956.

[17]The other three Executive Bureau members had been deputies and strong supporters of Ben Salah in 1956; they were not renominated to the National Assembly in 1959. At the ninth congress of the UGTT (March 28-31, 1963), one of the deputies failed to be reëlected to the Executive Bureau, but another deputy (Nouri Boudali, a former Bureau member) took his place.

sional branches and the *syndicats*. He pointed to the confusion that arose when the branch took the role of the *syndicat* by giving factory managers lists of workers (presumably deserving Neo-Destour youth, an organization Tlili privately criticized) to hire. He explained that the branches had been formed with the UGTT's approval in 1949 and 1950, when the party, preparing for political strikes, had needed to inject activists into the trade unions. (Possibly Tlili's explanation was incomplete: according to a reliable party official, professional branches were multiplied in 1956 as a warning to Ben Salah.) The implication was that professional party branches were no longer needed.

Instead, in 1962, the party multiplied them as it stepped up its propaganda for economic planning and austerity. The National Council of the UGTT, meeting in September, asserted that the branches were unnecessary and were creating confusion in the workers' minds." The Political Bureau publicly assured the UGTT that the branches would not meddle in trade-union matters, and Tlili called on local UGTT officials to join the branches and capture leading positions. Other trade-union leaders, however, were more disturbed by the party's organizational efforts. Bourguiba finally commented: "I am sure that the professional branches that the party has created will . . . facilitate an efficient symbiosis between cadres and militants of the Neo-Destour and the UGTT. . . " for furthering the "socialist" objectives of the Plan.[18]

Actually, the new professional branches, at least in Tunis, seemed to perform trade-union functions. One of them after obtaining a $120,000 loan for a workers' building coöperative, partially satisfied a workers' demand for more production bonuses. At its assembly in 1961 the president was not convincing when he insisted to a local UGTT leader that the branch could not make professional demands through the Neo-Destour commissioner. The commissioner in question was none other than Abdelaziz Bouraoui, a member of the UGTT Executive Bureau.

In Sfax, Habib Achour's trade-union stronghold, six professional party branches were established in early 1962. The head of the regional union denied that they were an embarrassment to the UGTT, but one of his subordinates indicated that outlying rural party branches, headed by large cultivators and grouping agricultural workers, sometimes hurt UGTT efforts to organize the latter. The Neo-Destour-dominated city council, too, competed with the UGTT's local economic enterprises. After the trade union in 1958 organized a transportation coöperative, the city council set up its own transportation company. When the

[18]Interview in *Jeune-Afrique,* December 24, 1962.

UGTT refused to enter the new company, the city council gave the coöperative a concession for only a small fraction of the city's bus routes and thus blocked any expansion of the UGTT coöperative.

In Gafsa, Tlili's stronghold and the third most important center of the UGTT, relations between the party and the UGTT were generally good. Before independence Tlili had headed both the Neo-Destour federation and the UGTT's regional union. From 1958 to 1960 the Neo-Destour commissioner was Abdelaziz Bouraoui, the trade-unionist. In individual mining centers, however, tensions sometimes developed between the party and the UGTT. Metlaoui was a case in point. Here trade-unionism had a longer history than the Neo-Destour, though in 1961 the eighteen elected local officers of the UGTT were all members of the party and the general secretary had been a local party leader since 1949. At the *syndicat's* elections in 1961 a member of the party's Gafsa coördinating commission put himself forward as a candidate. The general secretary and other members of the outgoing bureau threatened to resign if the party man were elected. The head of the regional union frantically telephoned Tlili for advice, while the former's brother, a member of the coördinating commission, influenced the commissioner and the governor not to intervene. The mere fact that these prominent officials took an interest in the affair suggested that it concerned relations between the party and the UGTT as well as conflicting local personalities. Despite his party record, the general secretary of the local *syndicat* was a trade-unionist foremost.

The party apparatus at all levels usually served to moderate the professional demands and grievances of the workers. In answer to dissatisfaction at the 1960 congress, Tlili is reported bluntly to have asserted that the party was stronger than the UGTT. That the UGTT could hold even 7,000 out of the roughly 25,000 Tunisian *fonctionnaires* was probably due to the government's automatic deduction of union dues from employees' salaries.[19] Among unskilled workers, membership was often a necessary condition for employment, Tunisia being an employer's market.

The schoolteachers vociferously criticized the government's education policy, the secretary of education, and working conditions. In a press conference at the beginning of the 1960-61 school year, Messadi blamed the schoolteachers for any shortcomings: "The weakness of certain results was a direct function purely of the inadequacy of certain masters to adapt themselves to the new [pedagogical] methods and

[19]In theory, trade-union membership is voluntary, but voluntary subscriptions were renewed year after year without the members' consent, and they could disaffiliate only by a complicated administrative procedure.

not of the programs themselves."[20] At their union congress the high-school teachers answered in a resolution demanding "that their relations with their direct and indirect superiors be based on mutual respect . . . that these same superiors stop hurting the dignity of the professor by questioning his pedagogic aptitude when they try to find reasons for the decrease in educational standards . . . that their trade-union delegates be respected as such. . . ." The resolution criticized administrative procedures of the Ministry that "tend to camouflage the patent weaknesses of the Education Reform. . . ." The teachers concluded "that the only way to get out of this critical situation is to re-think the programs of the Education Reform and to consult, to this end, the teachers and their trade-union representatives."[21]

Although a former president of the UGTT Federation of School-teachers, Messadi did not make a point of consulting the trade union on general policy matters. Morale inside the primary-school teachers' union was not raised when Tlili in 1960 dismissed three elected members of the executive for Communist leanings.[22] The pro-Communist *Tribune du Progrès* reported that in March, 1962, the high-school teachers' *syndicat* discussed "the smothering of trade-union liberties with the accord of the leaders of the UGTT, who use all means to keep the rank and file of *syndicats* from making their claims heard."[23] More than one hundred teachers attended the meeting.[24]

The federation of post-office employees was silenced after Rachid Driss replaced Mahmoud Khiari, a trade-unionist (who had supported Ben Salah), as secretary of communications. In the absence of Tlili, the UGTT ceremony on December 9, 1957, commemorating the assassination of Farhat Hached, was the scene of an attack upon the government. The UGTT accused it of using a (August 3) 1956 decree—designed to accelerate Tunisification of government administrations by facilitating dismissal procedures—to dismiss nationalist trade-unionists. The head of the Tunis regional union, subsequently promoted out of the UGTT explained: "We know that a certain number of people don't like the working class and try to make propaganda to the effect that the actual leaders of the UGTT have been weakened. . . ."[25] Four years later the UGTT was not making any protests. The *Tribune du*

[20]*Le Petit Matin,* October 4, 1960.
[21]*Ibid.,* December 31, 1960.
[22]With the votes of Zitouna-trained teachers who had been admitted into the reformed system, Tlili arranged safe candidates for new elections.
[23]*Tribune du Progrès,* No. 16-17 (March-April, 1962).
[24]In 1960-61 there were, not including Zitouna teachers, 466 Tunisian secondary school teachers.
[25]*Le Petit Matin,* December 10, 1957.

Progrès protested that in the postal administration technical personnel had not sufficiently benefited from the July 10, 1961, decree establishing higher salary bases for all government technical services.[26] The UGTT maintained silence during the dispute. As the newspaper reported, "It is painful to observe, throughout this affair, the offhandedness of the leaders of the National Federation of the UGTT. Never has a leader of this organization deigned to join the numerous delegations sent by the interested group to the minister, to support them."[27] The poorly paid, unrecognized employees were urged to "democratize" their *syndicat,* "in sclerosis after years of lethargy."[28] Albeit for international political reasons, the *Tribune* was the only newspaper in Tunisia that dared, in the face of UGTT silence, to publicize specific grievances of the little *fonctionnaire.*

After the scission the UGTT was further weakened when its former general secretary became minister of social affairs. Ben Salah supporters remained inside the UGTT, but internal union politics were complicated by personal rivalry between Tlili and Ben Salah. The latter as minister was put in the uncomfortable position by Bourguiba of pressing unpopular measures upon the UGTT. On July 6, 1960, Ben Salah had to defend in the National Assembly the tightening of social legislation that Bourguiba had called for in March against the wishes of the UGTT.[29] Ben Salah also fathered a law defining the status of professional associations; the law omitted any mention of a right to strike. When social security legislation was revised, Ben Salah and Tlili had a bitter argument as to whether family allowances should be awarded for more than four children; the government man, Ben Salah, took the less generous view.

As secretary of plan and finances, accomplishing UGTT's cherished objective of economic planning, Ben Salah tried to regain contact with his old organization. Tlili naturally stood in his way, and in Sfax on August 5, 1961, delivered a blistering anti-Communist speech. When

[26]*Tribune du Progrès,* Nos. 9, 12-13, 18-19 (August, November-December, 1961, May-June, 1962).
[27]*Ibid.,* November-December, 1961.
[28]*Ibid.,* May-June.
[29]The law on work relations allowed managers much greater flexibility to dismiss workers: "Dismissals for a serious fault, professional inadequacy, or insufficient production due to evident bad will do not give right to any reparation" (*Le Petit Matin,* July 7, 1960). At the same session, the three-man arbitration boards for labor disputes were modified to give UGTT and UTICA representatives only consultative status. This modification was against the UGTT interest because the trade-union representatives in the past had often boycotted the boards when arbitration was not working in their favor.

Tlili commented about economic planning, he gave the Neo-Destour full credit for its inspiration, without even mentioning Ben Salah.[30]

At a congress of coöperators in 1962, Habib Achour came into conflict with Mustapha Filali. The latter, an old ally of Ben Salah, was director of the state's new Coöperative Bank and president of the congress. He favored centralized credit facilities, whereas Achour, father of the UGTT's coöperatives, favored diversified credit (including private investment) and liberal competition among coöperatives.[31] As Ben Salah's structural reforms of the Tunisian economy took hold, UGTT autonomy was being threatened economically as well as politically.

On the eve of its ninth congress the UGTT seemed moribund and riddled with internal dissension. Even a modest UGTT school, launched in 1961 to train cadres, failed to get off the ground.[32] Memories of the 1956 scission lingered on,[33] for it had seriously divided and confused the rank and file. On the Executive Bureau, former Ben Salah supporters, discontented with Tlili's personal style of leadership, hoped to have Bourguiba's permission to remove him.[34] Some trade-unionists complained that Tlili, as treasurer of the Neo-Destour, vice-president of the National Assembly, and active supporter of the pro-Western ICFTU on the Pan-African labor scene, did not devote sufficient time to domestic trade-union problems. The discontented elements realized that they required the party's support to effect any important changes within the UGTT; they hoped that Ben Salah's rise to power might have repercussions within the UGTT.

What happened at the ninth congress, held in Tunis, March 28-31, 1963, did not necessarily strengthen the Ben Salah forces. Tlili, ap-

[30]See his El 'Amal article, June 1, 1961. Although a member of the Political Bureau, he did not take part in its activities for the Week of the Plan in June, 1961. His Activities Report to the UGTT Congress in 1960 had emphasized the need for economic planning, but on a "simple" scale, with "modest and precise projects, rapid and careful execution" (p. 24).

[31]Tribune du Progrès, No. 18-19 (May-June, 1962).

[32]In its classes trade-unionists were punished when they asked embarrassing questions. Lecturers were difficult to find because of the poor relations existing between the central office and schoolteachers' union rank and file.

[33]The regional union leader in Sousse, a Ben Salah supporter, claimed in 1961 that he stayed clear of trade-union politics in Sfax, a former UTT stronghold, although his government job as labor inspector took him there often.

[34]In early 1962 they prevailed upon Tlili's one loyal supporter to resign from the Executive Bureau. But when in July, 1962, the Neo-Destour Political Bureau decided that it was time to dismiss Tlili from the UGTT and give him an ambassadorship, the issue became that of the UGTT's autonomy. The labor leaders insisted to Bourguiba that the party had no right to interfere with the UTT's choice of officers. Scandal within the UGTT was avoided when Bourguiba annulled the Political Bureau's decision.

parently with Bourguiba's permission, was removed from the office of general secretary, but the man who took his place was Habib Achour, the veteran trade-unionist from Sfax who had led the UTT opposition to Ben Salah in 1956. Although a member of the Political Bureau, Achour's loyalties, both by temperament and by virtue of his close ties with Ferhat Hached, seemed to lie more with the UGTT than with the party. Independent and outspoken, Achour seemed the leader most capable of maintaining an autonomous UGTT image in the face of tightened party control and a planned economy. It was not clear what his relationship would be to the Ben Salah forces inside the UGTT, which since 1961 had quietly supported his ambitions to succeed Tlili. Evidently Bourguiba had decided that the risks of working with Achour were less than the risk of pushing the election of a less popular trade-unionist who would be more amenable to the party.[35] Although defeated as general secretary in a prearranged vote, Tlili successfully ran for reëlection to the Executive Committee, which was little changed.[36]

The early momentum of the UGTT under Ben Salah waned in the years following independence. The union was compelled by political circumstances to operate within the context of a single-party system rather than to develop as a competitive political force, as in Morocco. The party, however, achieved political control over the UGTT, as over the other national organizations, primarily by democratic means. Though a part of the regime, the UGTT retained its organizational identity and a democratic structure through which grievances were channeled from below and government policies explained from above. If the UGTT no longer presented a militant revolutionary appearance, its social and economic ideas of 1956 were implemented by the government in succeeding years. Like the other national organizations, the UGTT also participated in shaping the governmental legislation,

[35]Earlier, the heir apparent seemed to be Abdelaziz Bouraoui, a trade-unionist from Sfax who had accompanied Achour in the UTT and subsequently became a Neo-Destour commissioner as well as a member of the UGTT Executive Bureau. Bouraoui was closer to the party apparatus, though Achour as a member of the Political Bureau was nominally the senior party man. In trade-unionist circles Achour had the standing and seniority; to have had Bouraoui elected over Achour would therefore have reflected undue party interference in the affairs of the UGTT.
[36]The new Executive Committee consisted of Habib Achour, Mohammed Ben Azzedine, Abdelaziz Bouraoui, Ahmed Tlili, Salah Galaoui, Hassouna Ben Tahar, Nouri Boudali, Rabah Mahfoudh, and Amor Djamali. The last three were newcomers since the eighth congress, replacing Mohammed Erray, Habib Tliba, and Ali Hafaiedh. Nouri Boudali had briefly headed the UGTT in 1953, after Hached's assassination, and like Bouraoui had subsequently served as a Neo-Destour commissioner.

through its seats in the National Assembly and other consultative bodies.

The Case of the Students

UGET, the students' organization, was the most non-conformist of the national organizations. Imitating its French counterpart, it considered its members to be "intellectual workers" whose interests were to be defended like those of trade-unionists. UGET representatives had a voice on the Department of Education's scholarship commission,[37] and successfully urged the government to provide inexpensive student board and lodging. UGET until 1963 also considered itself to have a political role as the representative of Tunisia's future elite. As its student charter read, "In his role as an intellectual, the student considers it his duty to look for truth, to propagate and to defend it . . . and to apprehend the sense of history." Perhaps this was too much to expect of any national organization in a single-party regime. At the eleventh congress of UGET, held August 15-19, 1963, the charter was replaced by a new one expressing the duty of UGET to serve the nation—and hence the Neo-Destour Party.

Politicized before independence as an instrument of the Neo-Destour's independence campaign, UGET continued after independence to take political positions on a wide range of issues, including foreign policy as well as social and economic policy. Professing to be a radical and progressive force in Tunisian politics, it advocated the recognition of Communist China, rigorous economic planning, the limitation of private property, agricultural producer coöperatives in place of private holdings, nationalization of key industries, and rapid economic decolonization, Most of UGET's resolutions had been implemented by January 10, 1964, the day Bourguiba and Chou En-lai established diplomatic relations.

UGET's leftist orientation was natural in the context of Parisian student politics. The influence, too, of *progressiste* French instructors in Tunisia was out of proportion to their small number. The students perhaps needed simple doctrinaire answers to complex social problems.[38] There was no university community, in the sense of a close-

[37]In 1961-62, 505 out of 519 new students received grants; of the old students whose demands were rejected (25 per cent), most were academic failures. *L'Etudiant Tunisien*, March, 1962.
[38]Most students were on scholarship, and of the 201 new students receiving scholarships in 1959-60, 41 per cent came from families with annual incomes of less than $750.

knit campus with a variety of activities and organizations, in either Tunis or Paris.[39]

The party easily controlled UGET until 1959. The students coöperated with the party and provided the leadership and most of the membership of the Neo-Destour Federation of France. Partly in memory of their student days in Paris, the leaders of the Neo-Destour, including Bourguiba, treated the Federation with flattering consideration. It actively participated in the congresses of Sfax and Sousse, and its cadres returned to high positions in the new Tunisian administration. The Federation supported UGET, the leadership of the two being virtually identical. In the summer of 1956 the general secretary of UGET was appointed director of the Neo-Destour. UGET, it appeared, was the party's youthful, progressive, Westward-oriented face. In the struggle and then in the honeymoon of independence, few Tunisian students came under the influence of Communist ideas.

The downfall of Ben Salah sparked the first internal crisis in UGET. The new general secretary of UGET supported Ben Salah and, in early 1957, issued a communiqué to that effect. Before UGET's annual summer congress, he was removed from office by party loyalists. The general secretary elected at the congress, a close associate of the party director, maintained control of the organization by overweighting the representation of students in Tunis (of the 21-man Administrative Council, 14 had to be students in Tunis, 5 in France, and 2 in the Middle East), and by absorbing the Zitouna students' organization into UGET. At the 1959 congress, when he retired from UGET, latent tensions within the UGET erupted. The congress elected a majority of nonparty students to the new Administrative Council, and the student who received the most votes was reputed to be a Communist. Opposition to party control and affirmation of UGET's "autonomy" seemed as widespread among students of Tunis as those of France. Most of the Neo-Destour Federation of France leaders did not run for election, presumably for fear of being defeated. Fortunately for the party, it was the Administrative Council rather than the congress which elected the Executive Bureau. The autonomists decided to elect a Federation man as general secretary. They thought that they could effect com-

[39]In 1952-53, when UGET was founded, there were 212 Tunisian Muslim students at the Institut d'Hautes Etudes in Tunis, 660 in the higher studies programs of Zitouna, and 300 in French universities. By 1960-61 the balance had greatly shifted: 1,860 were studying in Tunis, but of these only 254 were at Zitouna. Between 1,500 and 2,000 students were abroad, mostly in France; and Paris remained the intellectual pole of attraction. In contrast, after independence UGET's political center of gravity shifted from Paris to Tunis. These statistics were cited by Michel Lelong in *IBLÁ*, No. 93, (1960, 1st trim.), 77-85.

promises with him in office, and they feared that the Neo-Destour would otherwise provoke a scission or abolish UGET.

The new general secretary lost prestige among the students when he accepted a Neo-Destour nomination as one of Tunis' city councilors. The reputed Communist, however, was persuaded secretly to join and work for the Neo-Destour. Popular and capable, Mohammed Sayah was easily elected general secretary of UGET in 1960. With the rise of Ben Salah in January, 1961, it appeared that UGET, without forsaking its progressive principles, might be a loyal and active national organization.

Student views, however, were not quite those of the regime. An article in UGET's monthly newspaper quoted Lenin on the union of practice and theory and advocated national work camps "like those in Cuba or in other countries making forward leaps."[40] Another article asked why the Neo-Destour had not carried out agrarian reform and coöperative farming as proposed at the Sfax congress. "It is because the option for agrarian reform was simply temporary and tactical on the part of the Neo-Destour. . . . The Tunisian bourgeoisie which was largely represented in the government did not want agrarian reform or collectivization." While affirming its support for Bourguiba, UGET "consider[ed] that the role of the UN [in the Congo] should have been to safeguard the integrity of the territory and to aid the legitimate [Lumumba's] government. . . ." (Tunisia had loyally supported the UN, not Lumumba.) Meanwhile the autonomists had seen through the general secretary's disguise. As a reliable correspondent hinted about UGET: "The illness . . . is serious. Since independence many congresses have more or less publicly disavowed their retiring executive committees, but the new leaders were not able to transform 'the nature of things'."[41] Furthermore, the students were not happy over Ben Salah's silence about agrarian reform, though he expressed the desire to consult them on his Plan.

On February 21, eight days after the assassination of Lumumba, UGET celebrated international student anticolonialism day with its Algerian counterpart, UGEMA, and, under party pressure, with the Neo-Destour Youth and the Neo-Destour students' coördinating committee. The authorities had forbidden UGET to organize a demonstration in front of the Belgian Embassy, but permitted a public meeting in a large auditorium. Most of the participants were nonstudents brought along by the Neo-Destour Youth; public order was kept by its youth squads.

[40] L'Etudiant Tunisien, January, 1961.
[41] Afrique-Action, January 23, 1961.

Soon after the meeting began, a group of students shouting "Vive Bourguiba! Tschombé assassin!" arrived at the auditorium, but the Neo-Destour Youth squad would not let them in. An autonomist member of the UGET Executive Bureau, who tried with other UGET leaders to get the students into the hall, was slapped by a Neo-Destour Youth official and, with two other students, taken away by the police for an identity check. Allowed into the hall, the students vociferously protested the arrest of the Executive member. After UGET's general secretary vainly appealed for silence, the youth official vilified the students as "petit bourgeois and spoiled youth," and compared them to "the real youth" in his organization that "died on the frontier" for the nation. Under his threat to call the police, the protesting students left the meeting. Soon thereafter some members of the Executive Bureau, the Tunis federation, and local sections passed a resolution—over the general secretary's veto—condemning the violence of "civilians animated by manifest hostility against students," and their "brutal methods . . . contradictory to the democratic spirit of our constitution." Mohammed Sayah temporarily resigned as general secretary.[42]

The Neo-Destour promptly regained control of UGET from within. At a difficult meeting in Paris of UGET's Federation of France at which the party and the automomists mobilized all their forces, the Neo-Destour narrowly prevailed. A resolution was passed expressing regret for the incidents but attacking neither the general secretary of UGET nor the Neo-Destour Youth. An emergency session of the Administrative Council, held in Tunis, March 4-7, with a Neo-Destour majority, reaffirmed confidence in their leader, Sayah, but published a full account of the February 21 incident. The three autonomists on the nine-man Executive Bureau resigned, but were reinstated; two other vacancies were filled by reliable party elements.

The following summer the Bizerte crisis provided the occasion for a more complete housecleaning at UGET's annual congress. No autonomists were elected even to the Administrative Council. UGET's federations were abolished. Reporting on the struggle between the autonomists and the Neo-Destour majority, *Afrique-Action* commented

[42]See *L'Etudiant Tunisien*, February-March, 1961; *Afrique-Action*, March 6. 1961; and *Tribune du Progrès*, No. 4, March, 1961. Compare these reliable accounts of what happened at the meeting with the version by the general secretary of the Neo-Destour Youth in *Afrique-Action*, March 13, 1961. He claimed merely that the group of late arrivals obstructed the meeting by shouting and provoked "a brush between some youths." The police then supposedly arrested one student and one Neo-Destour youth leader, and the latecomers, invited to sit down, continued to obstruct the meeting. The daily press made no reference to violence or police arrests. *El 'Amal* claimed that thirty Communist students had tried vainly to disrupt the meeting.

that "it is the first time in the history of UGET that one thus throws into the 'opposition' militants who do not hold all the opinions of the majority."[43] At a press conference the general secretary disclaimed the existence of a majority and a minority at the congress.[44]

A polemic ensued between *Tribune du Progrès,* which took up the cause of the autonomists, and the UGET officers. The former attacked the latter's use of procedural devices to smother discussion at the congress and said that UGET: "had not escaped this [general] evolution [in Tunisia of the 'satellization' of the national organizations about the Neo-Destour], and, indeed, it has found militants to aid and favor such a phenomenon."[45]

UGET answered "the systematic smear campaigns of a partisan press" by arguing that its congress had been democratic. Real autonomy signified "not isolation [but] . . . collaboration with the national organizations tending to achieve common objectives and serving the national cause."[46]

Though controlled by neither Communists nor fellow travelers, UGET in 1962 was clearly more "autonomous" than the other national organizations. It advocated "authoritarian" economic planning and roundly criticized Ben Salah for not limiting private property holdings and nationalizing foreign trade. It criticized the government's decision in late 1961 to rent out state lands to private farmers rather than exploit them as state farms. In international student affairs it adhered to a neutralist policy of participating both in the non-Communist International Student Conference and in the pro-Communist International Union of Students. UGET's voice was heard, along with that of the other national organizations, in the elaboration of Tunisia's ten-year planning perspectives. The open polemic of 1961-62 on the issue of UGET's autonomy seemed a healthy contrast to the atmosphere of conformity in Tunisian political life. The party's control of UGET was exercised diplomatically, by more or less democratic means.

In the spring of 1963 UGET was beset with a more serious crisis. The autonomists of the Paris section, of whom a number were Communist members or sympathizers, defeated the Neo-Destour candidates at the annual elections.[47] The UGET Executive Bureau retaliated by

[43]*Afrique-Action,* September 2, 1961.
[44]*La Presse,* September 6, 1961.
[45]*Tribune du Progrès,* No. 12-13 (November-December, 1961).
[46]*L'Etudiant Tunisien,* January, 1962.
[47]*Jeune-Afrique,* May 13-19, 1963. The Neo-Destour list received 121 votes to the opposition's 141, or 153 (depending on whose count). The Paris section totaled 480 members, out of a Paris student population of 1,200. Among the politicized students, however, trouble had long been brewing. In the autumn the autonomists had

annulling the elections.[48] Students in the Neo-Destour's parallel student organization struck a further blow against the autonomists when on August 9 they called upon the government to pass a law "requiring the collective participation of youth and students in serving the state, each according to his professional training and educational background."[49] The following week UGET held its eleventh congress in an isolated town, Le Kef, where the party could control the proceedings more easily than in Tunis, the usual meeting place. In changing UGET's charter, the congress ratified the party's decision, intimated months earlier by a resolution of the National Council, to transform UGET into an official instrument of the party. The newly elected general secretary, a loyal Destourian, promised to accept "leftist opposition" within UGET, as long as it agreed to the "conditions of the majority." But he subsequently dissolved the rebellious Paris section and promised that "every student exhibiting a systematic destructive inclination would be expelled."

Many Tunisian students displayed little interest in UGET, which had the reputation of being the springboard of a few student politicians to high government careers. The autonomists capitalized on apathy among the rank and file of students and were perhaps themselves a symptom of more general disaffection for the regime among the educated youth. By the early 1960's spectacular leaps from the university into high government jobs had become the exception, and most students without friends in high places faced the prospect of tedious jobs in a bureaucracy headed by men not much older than themselves. In politics there was little feeling of participation because the party's small ruling clique dominated political life. Students, too, were generally not attracted to the party, which appeared to them as a bureaucracy to mobilize the uneducated masses rather than to foster discussion at a respectable intellectual level.

Afrique-Action's characterization of UGET seemed just:

After 1957 UGET ceased to be a "movement" to become an "institution." In losing the spontaneity of the early years, it acquired a more comfortable

---

defeated the Neo-Destour candidate for the Tunisian place on the excutive committee of the Muslim North African Student Association (AEMNA). The Paris section of UGET had also protested in February against the outlawing of the Tunisian Communist Party. As a result, the Paris section's executive committee was dissolved by the UGET Executive Bureau in Tunis on the ground that it was "politically partisan, using syndical organs for political ends." For other details of student unrest see Douglas E. Ashford, *Second and Third Generation Elites in the Maghreb* (U. S. Department of State, Bureau of Intelligence and Research, 1964), p. 29.

[48]*Jeune-Afrique,* June 3-9, 1963, correspondence column.
[49]For this and subsequent quotations see *Maghreb Labor Digest,* October, 1963.

efficiency; 85 per cent of the students presently receive appreciable state aid.

Activism is no longer a mass phenomenon. But colloquiums, seminars, meetings with leaders and visits to recent economic achievements prepare students to a certain extent for their future roles as cadres. For the activism of the heroic period has been substituted the slow "civic" training of future leaders in the Tunisian administration and economy.[50]

UGET's progressive political orientation, challenged by the slightly more radical orientation of the autonomists, seemed faithfully to reflect the attitudes, if not of all students, at least of a rising generation of potential leaders. It had been to the credit of both the party and UGET that nonconformist attitudes could be articulated up to a point, challenging those in power and therefore helping to bridge the gulf between them and those who one day would seek power. After the dialogue was interrupted in 1963, however, it seemed that the gulf was deepening.

[50]*Afrique-Action*, July 17, 1961.

VII   THE CONSULTATIVE PROCESS

IMPORTANT DECISIONS in Tunisia were taken by one man. There were no clear checks upon his power. Bourguiba controlled the party, and the party controlled the national organizations. Various channels of consultation, however, served to mitigate the rigors of a monopoly of power. In the absence of a systematic Neo-Destour ideology, differences of opinion existed, especially on social and economic domestic issues, and were tolerated within the system. Important decisions in domestic affairs sometimes reflected compromises achieved between conflicting ideas and interests. For the sake of national solidarity, conflict was veiled or hidden, but the party and the national organizations nevertheless had forums for resolving genuine differences.

The National Assembly

The most prominent of these forums was the National Assembly. For a number of reasons, despite Tunisia's constitutional separation of powers, the legislative branch could not be considered as a balance to the executive branch of government. At the inaugural session of the National Assembly, Bourguiba lectured the deputies about their role under the new constitution.

It is really pointless to compare the respective powers of the President and the Assembly. . . . What is important is loyal and harmonious coöperation [between the two]. . . . If one wanted to concentrate on foreseeing all possible cases of disagreement, one would never see the end of it. . . . The balance of powers . . . really means that two antagonistic forces neutralize themselves. The result is paralysis for both. . . . It is more normal that the man invested with the confidence of the nation act and report his action to the National Assembly[1]

Bourguiba's meaning seemed clear: he was not to be challenged by the Assembly; rather, the latter would coöperate with him on his terms. Constitutionally the powers of the Assembly were sharply limited,[2] and the internal organization of the Assembly ensured discipline and

[1]Speech, November 20, 1959.
[2]It was permitted to be in session for a maximum of six months of the year; additional meetings could be held only at the request of the President of the Republic or a majority of the deputies (Art. 29). Deputies might propose legislation, but

subservience to the government. The nine-man bureau of the Assembly[3] effectively directed the work of the Assembly. It was elected annually, by acclamation, on the basis of a list drawn up by the Political Bureau.[4]

Even when in session, the Assembly met rarely in plenary—roughly fifteen times a year to ratify legislation discussed in commission. The President of the Republic was supposed to keep the Assembly informed on general policy, which he "shall draw up . . . and control its execution," either in person or by message.[5] Bourguiba in fact spoke before the Assembly only twice a year. He used it as a formal platform, especially for announcing internationally important policies to foreign diplomats invited for the occasion. In the presence of the National Assembly, he delivered an ultimatum to France two days before the Battle of Bizerte. The Assembly never debated his policy speeches, though in accord with the Bureau it could pass general resolutions on such matters as nuclear testing or repression in Algeria. Outside the commissions, an individual deputy could ask questions of the government only in writing through the President of the Assembly, and the answer was not to be made public unless the minister decided to announce it in plenary.[6]

"the proposals of the President of the Republic take precedence" (Art. 28). During its first three years the Assembly discussed only presidential proposals. Moreover, legislation was taken by presidential decree when the Assembly was not in session. Though decree laws were always subsequently put before the Assembly for ratification, in accordance with the constitution (Art. 1), the routine tended further to limit the legislative significance of the Assembly. Constitutionally the Assembly had the power to overrule a presidential veto, on a second reading with a two-thirds majority, but such a situation did not arise and seemed politically inconceivable.

[3]It consisted of a president, two vice-presidents, and the presidents and rapporteurs of the three permanent commissions of the Assembly. It decided the Assembly's agenda in the presence of a representative of the government. In plenary the agenda was voted upon by the deputies without discussion (Standing Orders, National Assembly, Art. 12), and only by absolute majority could they add an item to it. The item must already have been discussed in commission, and only the representative of the government, the President and rapporteur of the relevant commission, the deputy requesting the item, and a deputy against its inclusion were entitled to speak in the agenda debate. No legislative project could reach plenary unless it had already been studied by the permanent commission(s) (Art. 39). Commission meetings were convened only at the request of the President of the Assembly (Art. 28). If the government deemed a legislative project to be urgent, the commission(s) had to submit its (their) report within a week to the President of the Assembly (Art. 35).

[4]Rebelling against the party's control of elections, Mahmoud Materi, former president of the Neo-Destour Party, abstained in 1960 and protested that the voting should be secret. Le Petit Matin, October 7, 1960.

[5]Constitution, Art. 43.

[6]Standing Orders, Art. 12.

Most of the legislative work was carried on in permanent commissions. Not even an amendment could be discussed in plenary without a preliminary report from the relevant commission.[7] There were three permanent commissions: for political affairs, for legislative affairs, and for financial, economic, and social affairs. Elected annually, they together comprised a majority of the deputies.[8]

Commissions could call upon a minister to explain legislation under study. But all commission meetings were secret, attended only by deputies and representatives of the government.[9] Commissions might modify as well as accept or reject legislation presented by the government, but their scope was limited: "The Commissions examine amendments presented them and accept or reject them without twisting the proposals or presenting additional irrelevant material in their reports."[10]

The Assembly was well disciplined. Its agenda was controlled by the Bureau. Legislation was channeled through the commissions, whose work was also controlled by the Bureau. Discussion in plenary, indeed, was almost nonexistent. The rapporteur of the relevant commission read his report and after brief comments the legislation was usually adopted unanimously. Cabinet members might also attend the plenary, but any debate focused upon specific legislation rather than on general policy. Usually full discussion in the privacy of the commissions would already have produced agreement in favor of the legislation.

The procedure for passing the government's budget—an opportunity for lengthy discussion and debate in most legislative assemblies—illustrated the exceptionally efficient nature of the Tunisian legislative process.[11] On December 11, 1960, the National Assembly was still discussing whether to reorganize its permanent commissions, rather than studying the 1961 budget in commission. The budget was ratified in four plenary sessions at the end of the month; in one day the budgets of seven ministries were approved. The 1962 budget was submitted to

[7]Ibid., Arts. 39, 42.

[8]The first two had ten members each, and the latter had thirty members; no deputy might belong to more than one commission (Art. 27).

[9]Article 24.

[10]Article 38.

[11]The constitution stated merely that the Assembly "shall decide the final figures of the national budget" (Art. 35), with procedure to be defined in an organic law (Art. 34). The latter stipulated that the annual budget must be submitted to the Assembly by November 15 of the preceding year, in order to be passed no later than December 31. The government was to provide all documents "necessary for the information of the National Assembly." In practice, although information was not lacking, the deputies had less time to study the budget.

the Assembly only on December 7, 1961, and had to be passed within three weeks. Though normal budget expenditures were voted chapter by chapter, development expenditures and budget receipts were voted on as a whole. Neither amendments nor additional articles could be presented unless they tended to reduce expenditure or increase rceipts.

The National Assembly was not an arena that might publicly display divergencies within the single-party system. Political debate, normal to most legislative assemblies, was kept to a minimum, and most of the work took place unnoticed by the public in the permanent commissions. For *Afrique-Action,* and for most educated Tunisians who followed politics, the National Assembly was a fair target for ridicule.

What do our deputies do [for their wages]? . . . [They] find their personal work disturbed by their parliamentary obligations and their wives irritated by their long stays at the Bardo Palace. You didn't know that? . . . They are among the most serious deputies in the world. Rare are those whose absence must be noted at the plenary sessions. It's a fact: they are there. After the public meetings, work in secret in sorts of seminars that are called commissions. . . . Tired [in plenary], the deputies vote. Contrary to what one often thinks, they are not always unanimous votes. Some vote against. Others abstain. . . .[12]

Composition of the Assembly

In its composition, however, the National Assembly was fairly representative of the forces within the single-party system. In consultation with the national organizations, the Political Bureau selected the candidates for the victorious lists of the National Front.[13] With the exception of Bourguiba, Tunisia's top leaders were included among the Assembly's ninety deputies. There were twelve members of the Poli-

[12]*Afrique-Action,* December 19, 1960.
[13]Only 43 of the Constituent Assembly's 98 members were renominated by the party. Of the 12 independents on the National Front lists of 1956, only Mahmoud Materi, Albert Bessis, and Mahmoud Zerzeri survived. The others were Tahar Ben Ammar, Mohammed Badra, Azzeddine Abassi, Chadly Rhaiem, Fathi Zouhir, Mohammed Chenik, Aziz Djellouli, Mahmoud Khiari, and Cherif Mrad. Many former deputies were not eligible for the National Assembly because of jobs in the administration or in public enterprises. But some were not renominated because they had been critical of the government. Vociferous Ben Salah supporters in UGTT were eliminated (Mahmoud Ben Azzeddine, Salah Galaoui, Mohammed Erray— all of the UGTT Executive Bureau; Sliman Zouari, former head of the Tunis Regional Union; and Mahmoud Khiari, a former member of the Executive Bureau). They were replaced in 1959 by other trade-unionists who presumably supported Tlili and Achour (Hassouna Ben Tahar, Nouri Boudali, Abdelaziz Bouraoui, Hamdi Youssef, Rachid Djebari, Amor Djemali, Ali Hafaiedh, Rabah Mahfoudh, Salah M'Barek).

tical Bureau,[14] nine ministers,[15] and the director of Bourguiba's cabinet. Eight former ministers[16] and four former governors[17] were also deputies, along with four political commissioners,[18] three former commissioners,[19] and the secretary general until 1961 of the Neo-Destour Youth.[20] Thus more than a third of the ninety deputies since independence had held high positions in the party-government apparatus. Some of the national and regional leaders of the national organizations were deputies;[21] so professional politicians comprised more than half of the Assembly. Roughly thirteen of the deputies in 1962 were politicians, like Masmoudi, who were in voluntary or forced retirement, but at least forty had important political positions outside the National Assembly.

Whatever the formal powers of the Assembly, its members seemed on the whole to be more politically experienced and influential as individuals than the members of any other elected body in Tunisia.[22] The deputies' education was also impressive in the Tunisian context. Thirty-one had completed their studies at French universities, and an additional twenty-five had a good modern secondary school education, supplemented in at least seven cases by further specialized studies. Thus fifty-six deputies, a majority of the Assembly, had had a thorough modern French education and could be expected to typify Tunisia's Westernized elite. Thirteen deputies had a secondary diploma from

[14]Only Hedi Nouira, ineligible, and Taieb Slim, an ambassador, were not included.
[15]Only Monthar Ben Ammar and Chedly Klibi, appointed in 1961, were not included. Conversely, Azzeddine Abassi and Abdesselam Knani, the only two ministers in 1959 not included in the Assembly, subsequently lost their ministerial positions.
[16]Ahmed Mestiri, Lamine Chabbi, Azouz Rebai, Ferdjani Bel Hadj Ammar, Mohammed Chakroun, Mohammed Masmoudi, Mahmoud Materi, and Mustapha Filali.
[17]Bechir Achoura, Salah Ayache, Mohammed Makni, and Mustapha Khabthani.
[18]Ahmed Drira, Taieb Tekeya, Abdelaziz Bouraoui, and Abdelmajid Razgallah.
[19]Ahmed Ben Abdelkrim, Sadok Guermazi, Mohammed Ganouni.
[20]Mahmoud Maamouri.
[21]For the UGTT see above, n. 14. Tlili, Habib Achour, Achmed Ben Hamida, Amor Riahi, and Habib Tliba were deputies in both the Constituent and the National Assembly. UTICA was represented by Ferdjani Bel Hadj Ammar, Hadj Mohammed Ben Abdelkader, Abdesselam Achour, Hedi Bouslema, Mahmoud Zerzeri, and Ali Sellami. UNAT was represented by Sadok Khalfallah, Tahar Azaiz, Abdelhamid Bergaoui, and Abderrahmane Toukabri. The only woman deputy, Radhia Haddad, was president of the UNFT. Students were not represented, because the minimum age for a deputy was thirty—a constitutional provision originally designed in part to limit the Tunisian Communist Party's choice of candidates.
[22]The only comparable group of individuals might have been the Neo-Destour's National Council of 1955-1957. Of the 32 elected members of the latter, seventeen were deputies in 1956 or 1959. Most of the 65 delegates elected to the National Council in 1962, except for 13 deputies and the delegates from Tunis, were provincial cadres without national reputation or experience.

Zitouna, and of these six had completed their traditional university studies. Eight deputies had a mediocre education in grade schools and secondary schools; twelve had a little education of the Zitouna type, hardly beyond that of their village *kouttab*. One was illiterate.

Most of the deputies were of Tunisia's professional middle classes. There were fifteen lawyers, seven doctors, twelve professors (including secondary school *professeurs* and four Zitouna professors), five high civil servants, six schoolteachers, one pharmacist, one journalist, and one agricultural expert. Fifteen deputies had modern or traditional business background, twelve were farmers, and fourteen were manual or clerical workers. The ninetieth was the Assembly's only woman deputy, a professional leader related to the well-known Ben Ammar family.

The geographic origins of the deputies suggested the political preponderance of Tunis and the Sahel. According to the constitution, "Every deputy in the National Assembly is considered as representing the whole country" (Art. 25). Efforts were made to nominate deputies having personal roots in their respective constituencies, but this was not always possible.[23] In Beja, Kasserine, Le Kef, and Bizerte, those who headed the electoral lists had no personal ties with the region.[24] Many candidates on the provincial lists had spent most of their lives in Tunis but had family ties in their native region.

In the Tunisian context of intermeshed affiliations, it was difficult to determine the deputies' ties with the national organizations. Of the ninety deputies, fifty seem never to have participated in a national organization. Three were Independents, including Materi and Guiga; the others were veteran members of the party. Of the forty remaining deputies, twenty-one had at some time been associated with the UGTT, nine with UTICA, nine with UNAT, and one with UNFT. However, the twenty-one UGTT deputies included people like Abdallah Farhat, who, though a member of the UGTT Executive Bureau in 1956, was better known for activities in Bourguiba's entourage. In-

[23]Seven natives of Tunis, four of the Sousse area, and two of Sfax were placed in other constituencies: four in Beja, two in Le Kef, Kasserine, and Souk El Arba, and one in Kairouan, Cap Bon, Bizerte, and Mednine.
[24]Except perhaps for Habib Achour in Beja. His UTT in 1956 had great strength among the workers of Beja. That Chaker rather than Achour headed the list in Sfax seemed a curious reflection of party-trade-union rivalries in that city. Chaker was the younger brother of the Neo-Destour martyr, Hedi Chaker, and Habib Achour was the famed right-hand man of that other martyr from Sfax, Farhat Hached.

deed, by 1962 seven of the twenty-one were veteran leaders no longer active in the UGTT after having assumed government positions.[25]

Patterns of "Debate"

Within the National Assembly, unity and solidarity precluded specific affiliations with groups. All deputies had been elected as members of the National Front. In plenary no voting alignments were visible, and most votes were virtually unanimous. In the rare instances of close balloting, any blocs were obscured by procedure; votes on laws were by show of hands and not individually recorded. In the one close public vote personally observed, Tlili of the UGTT strongly identified himself with the issue, but a member of the Executive Bureau, Bouraoui, abstained and at least one other UGTT deputy voted against Tlili's position.

Privately, however, leaders of the UGTT, UTICA, and UNAT all indicated that they tried through deputies of their organizations to defend the economic and social interests of their respective constituents. These interests were defended primarily in commission. Blocs based on the national organizations might therefore be expected to appear in the financial, economic, and social affairs commission.

Of the thirty members of this commission, twenty-three had current or past ties with one of the national organizations. Eleven were from the UGTT, seven from UTICA, four from UNAT, and one from the UNFT. The seven affiliated exclusively to the party included a doctor, a lawyer, four businessmen, and a farmer; so it would appear that businessmen had a clear majority on the commission. The UGTT leaders claimed to have privately discussed pending legislation and, with the support of the UNFT deputy and the lawyer, to have had great success in getting their point of view adopted by the commission. Practical compromises between Tunisia's interest groups evidently occurred in this well-balanced commission.

Neo-Destour control seemed to be exercised only sparingly, on important issues. Possibly the unpopular national solidarity tax, passed with little discussion in June, 1962, reflected party discipline like the annual Assembly Bureau elections. But on many occasions, in plenary discussions of secondary issues, members of the Political Bureau took opposite sides. There were indications that the Assembly was trying to increase its power in relation to the government and to disprove the public's belief that it was merely a rubber stamp.

Before the Bizerte crisis the deputies on two occasions displayed a measure of independence. By a vote of 25 to 21, with 13 abstentions,

[25]Farhat, Ben Salah, Chabbi, Amor Riahi, Messadi, Filali, Boudali.

they voted to send back to commission a government decree law, actively defended in plenary by Ladgham and the secretary of agriculture, dissolving the (agricultural development) office of Sidi Bou Zid.[26] Tlili, a deputy from this region as well as a member of the Political Bureau, launched the attack against the government project with support of UNAT and most of the UGTT deputies. He demanded that the government clarify its agricultural policy and noted its inconsistency, for the agriculture office had been established only the previous year. He implicitly supported the technician who had headed the office against the politically minded governor of Gafsa who had caused it to be dissolved. Ladgham's promise that the credits accorded the office would still be used for developing the area did not forestall the government's first clear-cut defeat in the Assembly. Subsequently the government had to reactivate the office, although the governor rather than a technician was appointed to direct it.

Three weeks later the deputies successfully rebelled against the President of the Assembly. In a brief and stormy session, they rejected the latter's bidding to vote one law to ratify ten government decree laws, and insisted upon voting separately on each decree law, and the President in the end accepted this procedure.[27]

After the Bizerte crisis and the controversy about personal power, the Neo-Destour decided to demonstrate how democratic the regime was by organizing meetings throughout the country of the deputies with their constituents. After the meetings the deputies held a plenary session to discuss their visits. In place of a series of oral reports, however, they decided to form a commission to draw up a written report, which might then be used in the discussion of the budget. It seemed that such a report might be an effective parliamentary device for challenging government policies. In the end, however, the report was not published. It was simply presented to the government and remained a state secret.

The passage of the 1962 budget was the occasion for discussions livelier than in the past. For five full days the deputies confronted the ministers with questions and comments about their respective departments. However, there was no real debate. After the presentation of a commission report, the floor would be open to a variety of interventions by the deputies. The cabinet member concerned would then answer the questions raised, and the deputies would unanimously ratify his budget. No amendments were presented on which a real

[26]*La Presse,* May 21, 1961.
[27]National Assembly Debates, June 15, 1961, No. 14.

debate might be focused.[28] If the original government budget had undergone any modifications, these were minor and had occurred secretly in commission with the consent of the government.

Despite the slight increase in parliamentary activity in 1961, the National Assembly remained politically subordinated to the government. In Tunisia's presidential regime it could serve only as a consultative mechanism and as a distinguished audience to applaud Bourguiba's speeches. Possibly it reflected the general will by exhibiting the President's popularity.

Only rarely did Assembly debates arouse public interest, when they concerned social values rather than legislation as such. Curiously, in light of the deputies' impressive educational attainments, such debates reflected a traditionalist bias that contrasted with Bourguiba's modernist orientation. The issue of birth control was raised in December, 1961, when Ben Salah as secretary of health and social affairs presented a law permitting the sale of contraceptives in Tunisia. It aroused so much controversy that it was sent back to commission before finally being passed. Some of the minority had religious grounds, citing an ambiguous passage of the Quran. Others cited the disastrous effect upon family morality that the new freedom forebode. A former minister suggested that to be strong and prosperous the nation needed a young and numerous population. He also spoke of the "ennobling" virtues of maternal sacrifice.[29]

In the nationalist climate after the Bizerte crisis the conservatives in the Assembly had more success. The Assembly with virtual unanimity passed a law prohibiting the sale of alcoholic beverages to Muslims. Even Masmoudi argued that "social, medical, and other considerations must be subordinated" to the religious issue.[30] In sponsoring the legislation, the government had intended to suppress a trend toward alcoholism among the poorer classes, and the police were given orders to apply the law selectively to this end. But in the December budget debate, a Neo-Destour political commissioner criticized the government for its loose application of the law. Another deputy claimed that strict enforcement was "necessary for conserving our prestige as legislators."[31] It seemed doubtful, however, that many deputies were themselves total abstainers.

In the shelter of its commissions, the Assembly performed the useful service of reconciling conflicting economic and social interests. The

[28]*Le Petit Matin,* December 26-30, 1961.
[29]*Afrique-Action,* January 9, 1961.
[30]*La Presse,* November 15, 1961.
[31]*Le Petit Matin,* December 27, 1961.

financial, economic, and social affairs commission was its most important instrument, although ironically the commission was almost abolished for the sake of efficiency.[32] The commission did not seem to have made great changes in government legislation. But the deputies were able to effect minor ones, usually agreed to by a large majority of the commission and the government. The 1961 budget showed a million-dollar deficit which the finance secretary tried to cover by increasing the taxes on tea, coffee, sugar, and spices. The measure would have hurt both the UGTT consumer and the small UTICA shopkeeper. Cooperating closely in commission, the two organizations succeeded in convincing the government to look elsewhere for the needed revenue.[33]. The national organizations could be expected in commission to use their collective voice to influence legislation when their interests coincided.

The Drafting of a Law

The national organizations had various means of influence inside and outside the commission. The nature of the social security legislation of 1960 and the process of its elaboration and passage suggested their importance in consultation on specific legislation.[34]

Toward the end of 1957 the Social Affairs Department was attempting, with the aid of ILO experts, to draft legislation to rationalize the diverse social security systems operating in different industrial sectors. Social security provided only for family allowances, and covered most

[32]In the thirty-man body it had sometimes been difficult to achieve the necessary two-thirds quorum, and pending legislation had been delayed. The president of the Assembly proposed either that it be split into three ten-man commissions for financial, economic, and social affairs, respectively, or that ten alternate members be added to the commission. After an inconclusive debate in December, 1960, the former proposal was neither adopted nor rejected (*La Dépêche Tunisienne*, December 7, 1960). Four days later the plenary was again convened to discuss the proposals of a six-man ad hoc commission, which could not agree on any one proposal. Ahmed Tlili, Ferdjani Bel Hadj Ammar, and Chaker, the director of the party, intervened in favor of maintaining the existing commission. Chaker commented that "the fact of missing 2 out of 87 sessions is not as serious as certain people have remarked" (*Le Petit Matin*, December 11, 1960). He proposed that absentee commission members resign and be replaced. At Ladgham's suggestion the deputies agreed to suspend the plenary session and to call upon members of the commission to meet with members of the government to effect a compromise. The problem was not again discussed in plenary, and the commission was not changed. The whole episode had perhaps been intended as a warning to the commission to dispose of government legislation more rapidly and promptly.

[33]Interview with Ferdjani Bel Hadj Ammar, January 20, 1961.

[34]The following story, in the absence of newspaper accounts or other documentation, is based upon the author's interviews with Bourguiba, Ben Salah, M'Hammed Snoussi (the President's legal adviser), Balma (a civil servant in charge of administering social security), a number of UGTT and UTICA officials, and a personal friend.

categories of workers in industry and commerce but not in agriculture. It had functioned since 1944 through three private funds. In 1957 a law was drafted which dealt only with family allowances in these sectors. In late 1958 the three funds were centralized in an organism which included business and labor representatives on its board of directors.

In May, 1958, Ahmed Ben Salah took charge of Social Affairs and combined it with his Public Health Department. He wished to extend social security to cover maternity, health, and life insurance benefits, and to include other wage workers, notably in agriculture. The UGTT had long urged these reforms, and the Neo-Destour Sfax congress had made a resolution in this direction. Helped by ILO studies, Ben Salah in early 1959 presented draft proposals to the government. His idea, revolutionary for a country accustomed to French social legislation, was to limit family allowances to cover no more than four children. A Cabinet Council meeting presided over by Bourguiba and including the UGTT and UTICA leaders discussed Ben Salah's proposals, but tentatively shelved them for further study. In the absence of necessary statistics, Bourguiba rejected the inclusion of pensions and invalids' benefits in the scheme.

After two months of technical drafting sessions at the presidency, the legislative draft was forwarded to the UGTT, UTICA, the chambers of commerce, European business directors, and doctors. Then for more than a year the legislation was stalled. Privately Ben Salah blamed Tlili for the delay and asserted that he had exercised pressure upon Bourguiba to delay Ben Salah's bill. A friend of Tlili suggested that he was angry with Ben Salah for rejecting a social security scheme, devised by a Tlili associate, that would have given more benefits to the workers. Whatever the personal rivalries between Ben Salah and Tlili, the UGTT reactions to the draft bill were to assert worker demands rather than to make "observations" requested by the presidency. The UGTT wanted to include a generalized pension scheme and continued family allowances for more than four children.

Two more Cabinet Council meetings were held. Tlili received the guarantee that existing benefits would be maintained for families already having more than four children. At the Cabinet Council of October 24, 1960, the draft law was formally approved by the government and submitted to the National Assembly for ratification. A separate law set up a commission of government officials, employers, and workers' representatives to study the problem of pensions and invalids' benefits, and Tlili hoped that within a year a pension scheme could be included in the social security system.[35]

[35]Interview in *La Presse*, October 26, 1960.

Before the social security law reached the Assembly, UGTT representatives and an expert from Ben Salah's ministry agreed at informal meetings to a number of minor changes. Benefits of the families of ill and deceased workers were slightly increased. Ben Salah approved of the modifications after consultation with Bourguiba.

The Bureau of the National Assembly submitted the bill to the Financial, Economic, and Social Affairs Commission, where the points of view of UGTT and UTICA were again presented through their deputies. Discussion centered on details rather than on the principle of the legislation, which UTICA was politically compelled to accept. The UGTT won increases in the number of days of wages awarded to the family of a deceased worker and in the number of days allowed for sick leave. But the commission rejected the UGTT's attempt to extend family allowances to cover student sons up to the age of 21 rather than 20. The bill was approved with the minor UGTT amendments. It was discussed again in plenary on December 6, but was quickly ratified by a single vote on all 131 articles.

In a sense the passage of the law was a triumph for the UGTT over UTICA, for the latter had argued that Tunisia could not afford the luxury of extensive social legislation, while the former had long advocated a generalized social security system. UTICA was concerned about the small shopkeepers and artisans who could hardly afford to apply modern social legislation to their employees. The Djerban shopkeeper's apprentice was normally trained by a patron who expected him to work, eat, and sleep with him in the store until enough money was saved to permit the patron to set him up in business. The patron could not afford to have him work only eight hours a day with paid vacations. Within the Djerban community traditional behavior was incompatible with the legislation; UTICA was put in the embarrassing position of trying to persuade its adherents to obey the law and thus losing their support.

The final bill, however, represented a compromise that UTICA was generally willing to accept, for its terms were favorable to important business interests. The law provided for an across-the-board salary raise of 5 per cent for all workers and employees. This would automatically be contributed to the social security fund, and business firms would contribute an additional 15 per cent of their workers' salaries to the fund. In the past, however, the mining industry had paid out roughly 27 per cent of the salaries to its social security fund, while the building industry paid 22.5 per cent. Ben Salah estimated that the law would save these two key industries, respectively, $600,000 to 700,000 and $500,000 annually. Other industries less important to Tunisian economic growth were harder hit, but the total business contribution was estimated at $700,000 less than under the previous system.[36] Certain categories of small shopkeepers and artisans were exempted from the legislation. In over-all benefits most workers made significant gains, while the rise in wages, not going into the workers' pockets, did not threaten inflation and, as *Tribune du Progrès* cynically pointed out,[37] could be used as an argument against further wage increases.

The framing and passing of the social security legislation typified the process of consultation and compromise that characterized Bourguiba's rule. Most of the discussion was not public. The newspapers reported only what happened in the National Assembly plenary, where the prearranged decision was ratified. The decisive push for the law came from Bourguiba, as he claimed,[38] after initial hesitation. His numerous personal contacts, especially with Ben Salah and Tlili, were probably more significant than the official channels discussed above. The UGTT must have made it amply clear to Bourguiba that the workers, with salaries blocked since 1954, were in need of some major "victory" like the social security bill. In June, 1960, UTICA had secured its "victory"—the passage of a law facilitating the dismissal of incompetent workers. Bourguiba thus seems to have carefully balanced the demands of workers and employees. When once he had decided upon the general principles of the new legislation, the national organizations were allowed to participate in its elaboration.

The Birth of the Plan

The elaboration of Ben Salah's plan further illustrated the process of consultation and compromise involved in important decision-making; it also exemplified Bourguiba's crucial role and the very modest one assigned to the National Assembly.

As for the social security legislation, it was Bourguiba who provided the decisive impetus for economic planning. In an interview with the author he corroborated the rumor that he had decided as early as the autumn of 1959 to embark upon this course. While touring northwestern Tunisia at that time, he had been shocked by the abysmal poverty of some of the Khroumir tribesmen, and had determined to introduce drastic economic and political measures to accelerate Tunisian development.

In the early years of independence, Tunisia lacked a coherent set of economic objectives and priorities, apart from "economic decoloniza-

[36]*Ibid.*
[37]*Tribune du Progrès,* No. 1 (December, 1960).
[38]Interview, November 11, 1961.

tion," or the taking over of national economic decision-making—a process determined by political tactics in the context of Franco-Tunisian relations rather than by any theory of economic development.[39] The government's budget expanded considerably, but there was little economic growth. Capital flights to France, estimated at roughly $70,000,000, were halted only in late 1958. After rising about 21 per cent in 1951, the ratio of investment to gross national product fell below 10 per cent in 1957 and remained stagnant at this level until 1962, though gross investment increased slightly after reaching its lowest point in 1957. Good harvests in 1957, 1958, and 1959, and guaranteed export markets for wheat and wine in France, served to maintain a favorable Tunisian trade balance. United States aid, which had reached $50,000,000 in 1961, made up for growing trade deficits in 1961 and 1962. Economic growth, however, barely kept pace with the population increase.[40]

Until 1962 the government's economic policy had one constant aim: to maintain the stability of its currency and avoid inflation by conserving its foreign exchange reserves and a balanced budget. It was hoped that orthodox financial policies would encourage foreign investment, despite the Algerian war, and that Tunisian entrepreneurs would reveal themselves. But foreign investment, perhaps because of the unsettled situation in Algeria, did not materialize in significant quantities; French firms, too, unsure of the government's aim, pursued cautious policies. Bourguiba's growing exasperation with Tunisian businessmen was reflected in a speech in late 1957: "the national organizations, UTAC and UNAT, are not up to their job, which should be to educate minds and to elicit initiative. No effort is made to look for the most profitable areas for investment."

In early 1958 Bourguiba established a National Planning Council that included representatives of the national organizations and interested government departments. Despite great fanfare, the Council met rarely and accomplished little, but it perhaps served, in Bourguiba's words, as a "psychological shock" to stimulate greater awareness of Tunisia's economic problems. A year later, after the nation's attention had been diverted to the problems of Sakiet Sidi Youssef and the evacuation of French troops, the battle of the dinar against the French devaluation served again to focus attention upon economic

[39] As one Tunisian economist put it, "For five years independent Tunisia evolved by groping. In itself pragmatism is not bad . . . but it becomes dangerous when it is developed into a system of economic policy." See Moncef Guen, *La Tunisie Indépendante Face à Son Economie* (Tunis, 1961), p. 272.

[40] For a concise account of the evolution of the Tunisian economy until 1960, see *La Situation Economique à la fin de 1959* (Tunis: Service des Statistiques, 1960).

problems. Then the Neo-Destour congress in Sousse, March 2-5, 1959, defined the party's new mission: "To mobilize all the conscious popular forces and resources for economic growth and prosperity," and called for clearing up the "sterile and anarchical factors of the economy by the rule of a national Plan."[41] The new "struggle against under-development" became the nation's propaganda theme.

The decisive "psychological shock" came, however, in January, 1961, when, after months of rumors, Bourguiba officially appointed Ben Salah to head a new planning ministry. Even so, many businessmen, landowners, and politicians who distrusted Ben Salah's economic doc-trines expected to be able to undermine his reforms. They privately argued that Bourguiba was showing himself to be progressive by using Ben Salah, but would then discredit and discard him, as in 1956. In response, Bourguiba publicly expressed his confidence in Ben Salah and articulated with increasing vigor a conception of planning and "Neo-Destour socialism."

At first he simply defined planning, in Bourguibist fashion, as "an application of reason to action," to succeed "without recourse to con-straint."

First, we should make an exact survey of our situation. Next we should create the tools, the driving gear, the steering wheel. . . . The people must follow every touch on the steering wheel, every change of direction, every instruction. Our goals should be clarified. Thus, what is required is a prop-erly functioning machine which lights up our field of action with its head-lights. . . . It will still be necessary to ensure that the people sincerely and freely give their agreement and back up their leaders.[42]

In June he introduced the idea of "Neo-Destour socialism," defined as "the use of reason in the general interest." "If by bad management the farmer jeopardizes his own affairs and the yield of his land, he will not be the sole loser. The whole nation will lose with him. We are all bound together. Thus the concept of socialism takes on its full mean-ing." But Bourguiba added a note of rigor to the new idea by castigat-ing wholesalers who were dodging Ben Salah's price controls: "We will not hesitate to send these criminals to the gallows."[43]

Bourguiba tried to give his brand of socialism a religious coating by describing the Companions of the Prophet as "socialists before the in-

[41]Neo-Destour Covenant, passed at the 1959 congress.
[42]Speech of February 6, 1961.
[43]Speech of June 11, 1961.

vention of the word."[44] It was also to have social connotations, being "a method . . . of solidarity and association as members of one family united in all circumstances.[45] Put simply, national cohesion under Bourguiba was now to apply to economic as well as political matters.

The Tunisian reaction was mixed. Price controls on basic food items —the first tangible impact of economic planning before the Plan was officially adopted—aroused much opposition. Wholesalers and shop-keepers often refused to sell commodities in scarce supply. During Ramadan (February-March), 1962, there was a severe shortage of eggs, normally consumed in quantities during this month of evening feasts. The poor suffered because shopkeepers said they could no longer afford to extend the customary credit.

By 1962, however, Bourguiba had dashed the hopes of those who opposed Ben Salah by committing his own prestige to the latter's efforts. In March he declared: "I personally claim responsibility for the Plan and control its application. Nothing in this field is done without my consent."[46]

In fact, however, even as Bourguiba tried to convince the people of the merits of his basic political decisions, he left open for discussion and consultation the practical reforms and economic decisions that the option for planning entailed. It was Ben Salah's task to draw up concrete proposals that everyone, including skeptical businessmen and landowners, could be persuaded to accept.

[44]For possible connections between Islam and Neo-Destour socialism, see Michel Lelong, "Valeurs traditionelles et idéologies nouvelles dans les perspectives tunisiennes de développment," *IBLA*, No. 94 (1961), 149-166. Some modernist Tunisian intellectuals have tried to draw connections, while others have argued that the modern socialist's tie to Islam is sentimental at best. Solidarity and equality are values common to both ideologies, and each might be reinterpreted in the intellectual context of Tunisia. As yet, however, "Islamic socialism" is not an articulated ideology. Perhaps it summarizes aspirations that remain confused.

[45] Speech of June 24, 1961.

[46]Speech of March 12, 1962. Bourguiba implied another reason behind his option for "socialism"—the experience of Egypt before the 1952 military coup: "With our rapidly growing population, the rising generations are exerting pressure on us. If we are not careful now, in ten or twenty years time there will be a marked disproportion between the national income and the number of people we have to feed. A race against the clock is going on between our economic development and the demographic increase. Unless we take, as of today, the necessary measures, the country in a few decades will experience serious convulsions. The disinherited will find leaders to express their grudges. Their children, brought up in hatred, will infiltrate the ranks of the army. Then one day at dawn, they will try to seize power and arrest the Head of State, Sovereign or President of the Republic with his ministers. They will want to put an end to corruption. The national resources will have become too small for a vastly increased population. The new masters, once faced with the difficulties of power, will look for diversions. The whole thing will become nothing but an adventure."

Ben Salah's first move was to publish an article[47] promising the widest possible consultation for drawing up the Plan and setting aside a full year for the double task of elaborating it and mobilizing popular support for it. In late February,[48] 1961, he inaugurated a suggestions committee through which the students of UGET could present their ideas to the planners. In Tunis he also set up a suggestions committee of leading private businessmen, bankers, and directors of mixed and state corporations. Meanwhile he toured the provinces to consult committees set up by the governors and the political commissioners. Continuous consultation with the Tunis business leaders was especially important not only for their practical suggestions but for establishing a climate of confidence.

In August Ben Salah published a first draft of the Ten-Year Perspectives and distributed it to other government departments, the governorates, the party, and the national organizations. In each governorate the party established study commissions, composed of members of the national organizations, civil servants, schoolteachers, shopkeepers, and important landowners, to examine and report upon the Perspectives. In Souk El Arba, a small province with a very small educated elite, the governor distributed a thousand abridged copies of the Perspectives to the general public. On the basis of the commission reports, the party sent provincial leaders to propagate the Perspectives to every local branch, organizing as many as sixteen mass meetings a day in late September. The reports were sent to the Political Bureau. The governors also sent technical reports and an analysis of public opinion to Ben Salah and Mehiri.

Independently of the party, the national organizations also studied the Perspectives. The UGTT set up a commission consisting of its Executive Bureau members, its delegates on the Economic and Social Council, two additional National Assembly deputies, and various "technicians" including a young American-trained economist who was in private business. Its criticisms of the Perspectives were explicit and detailed but were not published.[49] One UGTT Executive Bureau mem-

[47]*Afrique-Action,* January 16, 1961.
[48]*La Presse,* February 23, 1961.
[49]A member of the Executive Committee listed the nine most important ones: (1) employment targets were too optimistic; (2) the assumption of a declining birth rate was questionable; (3) a four-to-one investment coefficient seemed too optimistic; (4) the target of a 26 per cent savings rate was unrealistic; (5) the projected investment for ports and airdromes was superfluous; (6) in light of world markets, too many olive trees were planned and greater diversification was needed; (7) more direct rather than indirect (colonialist) taxation was needed; (8) the UGTT wanted more agricultural production coöperatives than were planned; (9) the UGTT wanted full nationalization of foreign trade rather than the proposed strengthening of government supervision.

ber subsequently commented privately that the Perspectives were more in the nature of a political manifesto than a realistic program for development.

In October the Perspectives were fully discussed in four technical commissions including planners, other government officials from relevant ministries, the party, the national organizations (with UGET), and qualified individuals. The commissions were divided into subcommissions which examined plans in each economic sector at a series of about a hundred meetings. From the minutes of these sessions reported in the local press,[50] it was clear that the national organizations had the opportunity of presenting their points of view. In some commissions there were sharp disagreements between the organizations. On the issue of the disposition of former colon lands, the UGTT, UGET, and the Ministry of Agriculture favored the creation of production coöperatives after a preliminary period of state management. UTICA and UNAT, on the other hand, advocated private ownership, to be encouraged by renting or selling the state lands. UNAT specifically advocated 99-year leases in some cases, while suggesting coöperatives on a limited experimental basis.[51] Ben Salah's proposed structural reforms in the commercial sector provided another field for controversy. UGET, the UGTT, and the party favored the nationalization of commerce, with the profits to be invested in industry, while UTICA and UNAT advocated free competition between state, coöperative, and private enterprise.[52]

As discussions continued in the technical commissions, the Neo-Destour completed its examination of the Perspectives. While the reports from the political commissioners arrived at headquarters, national commissions were appointed by the director of the party to analyze and write reports upon the respective sectors of the Perspectives. At the end of October the director remarked "certain reservations" that had reached him,[53] presumably through the commissions. On November 18, however, he announced Ben Salah's coöption to the Political Bureau.

This decision of the Political Bureau implies that the Party is determined from now on to assume responsibility more directly for the elaboration and

---

[50]*Le Petit Matin,* October and November, 1961.

[51]*Ibid.,* October 20, 1961. Bourguiba decided in Cabinet Council on October 23 to rent state lands for four-year periods. Mehiri explained the necessity of this stop-gap measure to the National Assembly on November 28, when it unanimously ratified the decree law establishing the State Domains Office.

[52]*Ibid.,* November 26, 1961.

[53]*La Presse,* October 31, 1961, Chaker communiqué on meeting of October 30, 1961.

application of the plan . . . and to reënforce the links between the organs of the party and [the planners].

By this organic collaboration, the plan will be neither the work of a person nor of a group of experts, but of the Party. . . .[54]

The director announced that the National Council would be convened in February (actually it met in March) to examine the Three-Year Plan (1962-64) that was being elaborated on the basis of the Perspectives.

On November 20 the High Committee of the Plan, presided over by Ladgham and including ministers and representatives of the party and national organizations, met to conclude the series of meetings of the technical commissions. It decided that the controversial production coöperatives would be instituted on an experimental basis only.[55] Also accepted were a number of technical revisions in the Ten-Year Perspectives, although the broad objectives and projected growth rates were unchanged. The most important change was to reduce ten-year investment in housing by $130,000,000 (as the party seems already to have decided in early September).[56] Projected investments for youth and sports—of particular concern to the party in 1961—were increased. Investment in education over the ten-year period was also increased appreciably when miscalculations were discovered in the initial Perspectives. The discussions in the technical commissions helped to calm the business community, worried about Ben Salah's structural reforms for modernizing commerce. The businessmen were persuaded to accept the idea of centralizing the sale of imported goods in privately run regional shops. As the discussions ended, Mahmoud Zerzeri was praising the Plans in the *Bulletin* of his chamber of commerce:

If one might have feared here and there that planning would reflect only the dogmatic views of a minority where authoritarian technocrats would give free rein to their demons, one must recognize that the preparatory work was achieved in seriousness, objectivity, and the desire to obtain the broadest and most precise information. . . . A chance was given for everyone to make himself heard and present his arguments.

Ben Salah's old foe went on to praise the "sympathetic atmosphere" and "climate of understanding and mutual confidence" that Ben Salah's method of consultation had produced.[57]

[54]*Ibid.*, November 18, 1961.
[55]Communiqué of High Committee, *ibid.*, November 21, 1961.
[56]Baccouche, September 30, 1961, said that 70,000 popular lodgings would be cut. In the revised Ten Year-Perspectives published in May, 1962, these were indeed cut from 200,000 to 130,000.
[57]*Le Petit Matin*, December 9, 1961.

In the meantime the Three-Year Plan was being drafted on the basis of the consultations. On March 17 the Cabinet Council approved the Plan and submitted it to the Neo-Destour National Council on March 20. After four days of discussion, mostly in commission, the sixty-five delegates gave the Plan the seal of party approval. Modifications, if any, were minor, but the Plan was then sent to another consultative body before being submitted to the National Assembly.

The Economic and Social Council, mentioned in the constitution (Article 58), was established in early 1961 but had remained inactive (despite the January 16, 1961, decree law stating that it should meet at least once a month) until it was consulted about the Plan. Of its thirty members, only five were politicians in the party or national organizations, and the rest were experts.[58] After meeting daily for a month, the Council submitted its report to the National Assembly, divided on April 25 into five *ad hoc* commissions to study the Plan.[59]

In these commissions the deputies made a number of recommendations for minor modifications of the Plan. They suggested, for instance, that investments providing for an Olympic sports stadium might be better used elsewhere, or should be spread over a ten-year rather than a three-year period. But their recommendations were in no way binding. The report of the Economic and Social Council, said to include comparable recommendations, was to be published in the *Journal Officiel*. Bourguiba and Ben Salah, however, were free to follow or reject all recommendations.

On May 30, more than a year after Ben Salah undertook his first consultations, the Three-Year Plan reached plenary. Bourguiba's entire cabinet attended what amounted to a formal ceremony. The commission reports were read, and only one deputy made an intervention, asking Ben Salah a question about credit facilities. The Plan's three-year investment funds were unanimously voted.[60]

The executive branch clearly overshadowed the legislative branch of government. As the discussions about the social security bill and the Plan indicated, direct consultation between the government administration and the national organizations was more important than discussion inside the Assembly. Despite its distinguished membership,

[58] Appointed by Bourguiba, they consisted of five "persons qualified in economic, social, scientific, and cultural domains," ten "representatives of workers, employees, civil servants, technicians, and cadres," two "representatives of national industrial enterprises," three "representatives of private industrial enterprises, two representatives of public commercial and three of private commercial enterprises, and five representatives of the farmers." *La Presse*, January 31, 1961, decree of January 30.

[59] *Le Petit Matin*, April 26, 1962.

[60] *La Presse*, May 31, 1962.

the latter as an institution had little influence or prestige. Its role seemed limited to effecting minor modifications in legislation, the broad lines of which were not a subject of controversy by the time Bourguiba approved and submitted it to the Assembly.

Within the context of Bourguiba's dominant authority, however, a high degree of consultation was possible. At all levels the party, the national organizations and the administration discussed policies, although Bourguiba had the final word. Decision-making reflected the interests informally articulated by these bodies. Bourguiba tried, at least in domestic affairs, to take account of their interests in his decisions. He considered it important to have everyone's backing for the basic policies of economic planning.

Diverse points of view could perhaps be more effectively expressed outside the National Assembly, away from the public eye, than in formal representative institutions. The informality of the Tunisian process of consultation allowed for the articulation of interests without engendering a demagogic opposition. Interestingly, the debates in the National Assembly were most lively when they concerned religious matters, whereas nascent economic interests were aired in more confidential settings. A more powerful parliament, in which all issues were openly discussed, might have played to the religious feelings of the people rather than resolving conflicts between modern interest groups.

The informality of the pattern allowed more effective participation of Tunisians who were not professional Neo-Destour politicians. Any educated Tunisian with an economic interest could express his point of view in at least one of the innumerable vehicles of consultation on economic planning. In the Tunisian context all the vehicles had roughly equal importance; the National Assembly had little special prestige or political preeminence. In a more formally "democratic" setting the educated and interested Tunisian would have had little opportunity for expression unless he were a veteran party activist or leader of a national organization. In the absence of a rich associational life, informal consultation probably helped to keep the political system open to new men and ideas.

CONCLUSION

Tunisia is one of the few emergent nations today practicing a successful politics of modernization. Since 1956 the Neo-Destour has provided an adequate framework for rapid and effective decision-making. With the support of the party, Bourguiba was able to tackle the essential problems confronting his society, despite the country's weakness and vulnerability during the Franco-Algerian conflict. With a brilliant sense of timing, he consolidated the new state and launched key social reforms, while awaiting the strategic moment to embark upon a policy of full economic decolonization, planning, and "socialism." The emergent political system also successfully pursued the task of national integration by maintaining the cohesion of the educated elite and by structuring the society at all levels with an effective chain of command. The party was able, at the same time, to pursue its task of political education and even to give the people some opportunity to rule themselves at the local level.

There were special conditions, however, that made permissive single-party rule possible in Tunisia. The natural homogeneity of the society and the timing and full play of the colonial dialectic have few equivalents, if any, in Africa. The Neo-Destour did not manufacture a modernist consensus out of shapeless material; rather, many of the ingredients were already present as early as 1934. With this very important qualification, however, some generalization about the dynamics of mass party rule in newly independent countries are possible.

Representation and political recruitment were complex and difficult problems for the permissive mass party regime to resolve. By 1959 the party's formal representative structures had fallen into disuse, and the cult of personality seemed to pervade political life, possibly undermining the commitment of the educated elite to democratic values. The cost of the subordination of party to state was apathy at the grass roots that was increasingly apparent by 1961. Some disaffection, too, among students and civil servants indicated that the party was not succeeding in recruiting the young intelligentisia or in maintaining the earlier rhythm of political enthusiasm.

On the positive side, however, the regime provided channels for the expression of public opinion and modern economic interests. The party allowed local leaders to express their grievances, although there were no clear-cut procedures committing higher party officials to following the will or the rank and file. Bourguiba's style of leadership, the multitude of informal patterns of consultation, and the sensitivity of party leaders to opinions from below, rather than any formal institutional devices, ensured that the leaders' decisions usually took account of public opinion and economic interests. The drafting of social security legislation and the elaboration of the Tunisian Plan illustrated the process.

Tunisia's informal patterns of representation are possibly more effective than the channels of rigorously organized parties in comparable mass party regimes. Representation in Tunisia seemed more in accord with the structure of a transitional society than the "democratic centralism" of neo-Leninist parties. Policy in Tunisia was not dictated by the oligarchy of a tightly disciplined party purporting to embody the general will. Rather, Bourguiba considered the opinions of both those who manipulated the party apparatus and outsiders who could "represent" the interests and ideas of the modern economic sectors and the educated elite. Furthermore, in the absence of a rigid ideology and a cult of party supremacy, the regime was able to recruit individuals who would be unable to advance in the party hierarchy. Other channels —the government and various informal consultative bodies—gave talented individuals the chance to express themselves and exert political influence. Through Bourguiba, the regime remained open to new ideas, and on occasion he would give a young innovator the chance to implement his ideas.

Nevertheless, the signs of discontent since 1961 ought not to be dismissed as reflecting only a natural letdown after the high expectations of independence. They could also be construed as pointing to an inherent paradox in the "permissive" type of mass party regime. Besides the favorable historical and social factors that foster consensus, a leader is needed as the fulcrum of this type of system, to protect it against the abuses of party politicians in power. The leader more than any other single factor guarantees the permissiveness of the system. He is the substitute for a rigidly disciplined hierarchical structure; his claim to leadership offsets that of the party, giving rise to a cult of personality rather than a cult of party supremacy, and thereby mitigating the rigors of single-party rule. But herein lies the paradox of the permissive regime: no institution may develop while the leader, to maintain his supremacy, fragments any countervailing centers of power. Such fragmentation keeps the system open by permitting the leader to be accessible to diverse groups and individuals, but it inhibits the rise of stable factions that might have a stake in developing democratic procedures for resolving their conflicts within the system. To survive, the leader appeals to new generations, balances them against the older generations, and disdains institutional restraints. Thus he inhibits the development of institutions that might help to keep the system open after his departure.

The cumulative impact of the events of 1961—the Kairouan riots of January 17, the Bizerte disaster of July, and the public debate in the autumn about the virtues of personal power—was to bring into question the underlying premise of the permissive mass party regime: Bourguiba's political infallibility. Throughout this period, too, events in North Africa clearly showed up Tunisia's loss of prestige among her neighbors. Tunisia was no longer the *état pilote* that would show the Maghreb how best to modernize; rather, its image became that of a little country weakened by economic difficulties and overly eager to conform to De Gaulle's "neo-colonialist" designs—an image that, at least for the Algerians then negotiating with France, made Bourguiba's intransigence over Bizerte seem an all the more pitiful effort to keep in step with the triumphant forces of revolution and emancipation.

With the solid support of the party, however, Bourguiba weathered the Bizerte crisis and launched the Plan in an atmosphere of relative consensus. The party acquired a new rallying cry and the makings of a flexible ideology in the new Neo-Destour socialism. In place of the enthusiasm of earlier years, when the struggle against the vestiges of colonialism provided a focus for national mobilization, a calm realization of the gigantic tasks of economic development was filtering down even to the party branches of outlying villages. Significantly, the meetings of the Political Bureau were given greater prominence after the Bizerte crisis. With the inclusion of Ahmed Ben Salah in November, 1961, and the return to Tunisia of Mongi Slim (appointed foreign secretary in August, 1962), the Bureau had more weight.

Recent trends in Tunisia suggest that the regime, as if in recognition of its inherent paradox, is attempting to incorporate some of the virtues of neo-Leninist mass party regimes into its permissive pattern. On the one hand, in coping with the problem of political apathy, Bourguiba since the Bizerte crisis seems to have upgraded the role of the party apparatus in decision-making. The reforms in party structure initiated since the National Council meeting of March, 1963, may serve to resurrect the party's deliberative organs and provide a greater measure of internal party democracy. On the other hand, since the launching of the Plan, the regime's policies have increasingly emphasized radical reform. With the land nationalization decrees of independent Algeria as an example, Bourguiba proceeded, on May 12, 1964, to complete his policies of economic decolonization by taking over the remaining million acres of land belonging to foreign individuals and corporations and to domestic corporations.[1] It seemed merely a matter of time before he would limit the landholdings of Tunisia's few indigenous large landowners. Ben Salah's apparent success in creating a new coöperative sector of agriculture was preparing the way. At the same time, by recruiting Neo-Destour youths to man many of the new coöperatives, the regime was finding a new means of revivifying this crucial sector of the party.

In short, Bourguiba was attempting decisive measures to halt the corrosive influence of power upon the party structure he had so assiduously built up over a thirty-year period. Pressured by events and possibly, too, by the party leaders who had supported him in the aftermath of the Bizerte crisis, Bourguiba was reaffirming a revolutionary stance and giving the party a vanguard role.

It is too early to make a definitive assessment of Tunisia's pattern of modernization, or to predict how successful it will eventually be in meeting the revolutionary challenges that the society will continue to face. The Tunisian experience until now, however, does suggest that the permissive mass party model remains among the most promising for tackling the staggering problems of development.

Tunisia's regime has proved especially adaptable. While retaining its permissive quality under Bourguiba, it seems to be absorbing some of the virtues of the neo-Leninist model. One of the risks inherent in the permissive pattern was that the party, divested of effective responsibility, might wither away, becoming a relatively unresponsive bureaucracy incapable of eliciting the enthusiasm and nationalist fervor needed for development. A related danger was that policy might be too rational and technocratic to capture widespread support. A measure of revolutionary *élan*, orchestrated by a durable and energetic party, would seem to be an essential antidote to political stagnation. Since

---

[1] Of the 400,000 hectares affected, it was estimated that 150,000 belonged to French individuals, 45,000 to Italians, 15,000 to Maltese, 120,000 to French corporations, and 27,000 to unincorporated French companies. About 100 Tunisian holdings were affected. Previously—the most recent agreement having been signed in March, 1963—Tunisia had bought 300,000 ha. of French settler land with the assistance of the French Government. However, one reason for Bourguiba's decision of outright expropriation of the remainder may have been financial. As explained by a Tunisian journalist, Tunisia still owed indemnities of $5,000,000 for previous land purchases, and recovering the remainder with French governmental assistance would cost many additional millions. France retaliated by suspending foreign aid to Tunisia that would have totaled $20,000,000 (plus $22,000,000 in backing for private loans to Tunisia) in 1964.

the Bizerte crisis, Tunisia appears to be regaining some of the revolutionary momentum that is associated with neo-Leninist regimes.

Possibly such adaptability is peculiar to the permissive type of mass party regime, although there is no *a priori* reason why neo-Leninist regimes might not become more flexible by tempering party supremacy with greater freedom of governmental initiative. In this writer's opinion, successful modernization under any mass party regime hinges on the regime's ability to maintain a separation of power between party and government bureaucracy, such that neither dominates the other either in theory or in practice. Under these conditions, as the Tunisian experience suggests, it is possible to avoid the extremes of "revolutionary" ideological party rule and technical bureaucratic rule. Without a balance between party and bureaucratic rule, it would seem that the underpinning of these regimes, the mass party, must inevitably be transformed into an agent of government, either supreme as in the Soviet case or subservient as in nominal single-party case.

Balance within the political system means that neither party politicians nor government technicians may always have their way. Within a neo-Leninist regime it would mean that the political ideologues of the party might have their grandiose revolutionary aspirations curtailed by professionals more attuned to existing realities. But balance does not necessarily mean that policies be pale compromises that fail to come to grips with the social revolution unleashed by the mass party. Indeed, there is an opposite danger that, when aspirations are not tailored to realities, the revolutionary symbol may be mistaken for the deed.

Balanced political life under Bourguiba seems to date to have resulted in relatively flexible policies more suited to coming to grips in systematic fashion with Tunisia's vast problems. Of course Tunisian policies aimed at modernization have been largely the design of one man rather than the product of a system. Nevertheless, Bourguiba has worked in the context of a system that permitted a more careful approach to economic planning than has been possible in countries where revolutionary politicians were not induced to adapt their objectives to social and diplomatic realities.

The future of Tunisia's mass party regime, however, remains as open to question as that of any of its African counterparts. The abortive plot of December 24, 1962, upon Bourguiba's life underlined the precarious basis upon which this regime rests. The one great problem that it has not yet had to face is that of the succession. No African mass party regime has had to select a successor to its heroic leader (though before independence Modibo Keita replaced the late Mamadou Konaté as head of Mali's mass party). Yet, as one contemporary Western theorist suggests, the prime function of any political party may be that of ensuring the succession—whether in the context of constitutional democracies, totalitarian dictatorships, or regimes of the Tunisian variety.[2] Of all the one-party states to date, only Mexico has resolved this problem effectively, by institutionalizing the succession at regular (six-year) intervals. In Mexico no president may succeed himself, but the factions and diverse interests within the party have been sufficiently agreed over the past three decades to ensure orderly transfers of power.[3]

The dynamics of Tunisia's permissive pattern will become clearer once a succession crisis has been weathered. The departure of Bourguiba will entail the emergence of a new political pattern, since there is no living Tunisian able to take Bourguiba's place as the heroic leader balancing political forces by virtue of his personal prestige. What, then, might happen?

One possibility is that the presidential monarchy may be institutionalized. Were Bourguiba to retire from office—in 1969 and in 1974 he will have completed five-year terms—he might be able to choose his own successor. It may be significant that he had his son elected in his place as mayor of Monastir in May, 1963. It may be even more significant that he appointed him, as of January 1, 1964, to the newly created top-level post of General Secretary of the Tunisian Government and then in November made him foreign minister (replacing Mongi Slim) and assistant general secretary of the party. But since the deposition of the Bey in 1957, no one in the Neo-Destour has ever suggested that Tunisia ought to be a monarchy.

A second possibility is that the mass party regime become a dominant party type that admits one or more opposition parties. The formal constitutional organs of government might then play a greater role in selecting top leadership.[4] However, it does not seem likely that the Neo-Destour will permit the existence in the foreseeable future of any opposition party that had a chance of winning elections. On the two occasions when an effective opposition existed—Taalbi's in 1937 and Ben Youssef's in 1955—the political competition resulted in violence intensified by perennial local rivalries. Moreover, the Neo-Destour is the symbol, by virtue of its thirty-year history, of Tunisia's national

[2]Carl J. Friedrich, *Man and His Government* (1963), pp. 502 ff.
[3]For a discussion of nomination procedures within the Mexican PRI, see Robert E. Scott, *Mexican Government in Transition* (1959), pp. 197-223.
[4]Under the constitution (Art. 51), if the President of the Republic cannot fulfill his term of office, the National Assembly is to elect a sucessor during the fifth week after the vacancy occurs. However, the party controls the Assembly.

identity. As long as those who fought its nationalist struggle remain in power, there is no reason to expect that they will voluntarily relinquish their monopoly. Those within the party who rejected its discipline would in all likelihood be politically suppressed.

If, then, as seems most likely, party rule outlasts that of its founder, the permissive mass party pattern could develop in any of three directions: (1) toward nominal single-party rule, (2) toward neo-Leninist and possibly totalitarian rule, or (3) toward a greater degree of pluralism institutionalized in the context of mass party rule.

Under the first alternative, which remains possible despite Tunisia's steady rhythm to date of revolution and consolidation, the Neo-Destour would retain power but dissipate its momentum; party structure would wither away amid the apathy that affects not only some of its erstwhile militants but also the rising generation of students disillusioned with opportunists and court politics. Though the Plan guarantees jobs to the new generation of students commensurate with their education,[5] dissatisfaction and frustration may increase unless the regime devises adequate channels to give them a sense of political participation. The large size of this group, in contrast to that of past student generations, suggests that harmony may be increasingly difficult to maintain among the educated elite.[6] If the party were to wither away, the basis of political participation would narrow until, perhaps, the regime were overthrown by the younger generation.[7]

Political stagnation might be avoided, alternatively, if the Neo-Destour developed increasingly neo-Leninist and, perhaps eventually, totalitarian structures. But even in a Neo-Destour no longer headed by Bourguiba, such a course does not seem likely. The party's ideology has been too thoroughly impregnated with the Bourguibist distrust of

[5]For a projection until 1971 of the number of student graduates contrasted with the number of jobs available to them, see *Perspectives Décennales de Développement, 1962-71*, p. 311. The Tunisians estimate that by 1971 the number of jobs will exceed the number of sufficiently trained Tunisian cadres by 2,670.

[6]Even in the year of independence, 1955-56, after substantial postwar investment in education at all levels, there were only 862 Tunisian university students; in 1961 there were 3,360. In October, 1961, 8,532 children were entering secondary schools, and under its development program the Ministry of Education expected roughly 41,700 in October, 1971. The growth of Tunisia's educated elite would sharply accelerate.

[7]If the regime were to harden, groups on the periphery of the party—young graduates, disgruntled civil servants, and those who resented the regime's religious and economic reforms—might try to use the army as an instrument to attain power. As yet, however, there is no sign of politicization in the army; in Tunisia, unlike other Arab countries with a weak party structure, there is no political vacuum that a military officer might feel a calling to fill. On March 2, 1963, however, Bourguiba called upon the army as well as the party to develop cadres of higher quality. See *Jeune-Afrique*, March 11-17, 1963.

doctrinal rigidity; the new "socialism" is hardly a rigorously articulated ideology that might justify totalitarian means for implementing its goals.

For the third alternative to be a real possibility, a more systematic use of the party's deliberative organs would seem necessary, to allow and encourage the expression of the various points of view of the political and professional elites. Within the party, the cliques and factions, constantly shifting under Bourguiba's style of leadership, probably anticipate the battle over the succession. These were tentatively identified as follows: (1) the Mehiri clique, composed of a number of members of the Political Bureau, especially from Tunis, that stands for party supremacy; (2) a group under Ben Salah that stands for socialism and economic planning and has retained some influence in the UGTT; (3) Masmoudi and his associates, who stand for democratic competition, a free press, and flexible economic planning that would not compromise the interests of members involved in modern business enterprises originally subsidized by the government. The two latter groups were able at times to enlist the sympathies of the "outsiders" of the system—the students and the modern nonpolitical elite—but they were not strong in the professional political circles of the Neo-Destour.

Were more internal democracy practiced, the "outsiders" might be more readily attracted into the fold. Democratic procedures, too, might become more of a habit. While the party is successfully developing local self-government, the party bureaucrats, at least until 1963, were discouraging more regular participation in national politics. Cadre conferences were not a real substitute for congresses where issues could be debated and resolutions passed. With his power effectively consolidated, however, Bourguiba could well afford to encourage the party to develop more democratic procedures.

If the party reorganization of 1963-64 genuinely encourages greater deliberation within the party, the eventual succession may allow a relatively smooth transition. Under a compromise candidate acceptable to all the groups vaguely discernible within the party, it is conceivable that the party could remain open to the new social forces that the Plan, especially educational reform, is generating. The play of factions might then strengthen institutions for articulating and reconciling divergent views and interests inside the party, even without an arbiter having Bourguiba's great prestige.

It would be unwise to make rash predictions about Tunisian political development. The permissive mass party regime has no rigorous internal logic determining its evolution. Bourguiba's leadership is fundamentally unpredictable because he continues to improvise and to innovate. Conceivably, as the regime settles down to the tasks of economic development and social change, he may devise new channels of representation and help to institutionalize those that already exist within the party's well-articulated framework. Over the past thirty years, at least, Bourguiba's Neo-Destour has evolved a broad consensus and a political system illuminating Tunisia's path into the modern world.

APPENDIX

Tunisian Elections

SINCE INDEPENDENCE Tunisia has experienced three national elections, one for the Constituent Assembly on March 25, 1956, and two for the presidency and National Assembly on November 8, 1959, and November 9, 1964. By-elections for the Constituent Assembly were held on August 26, 1956. In addition, municipal elections were organized in 1957, 1960, and 1963.

Even when, until 1960, opposition lists contested those of the Neo-Destour, their impact was minimal. The only national opposition was the Tunisian Communist Party, which managed in 1956, running in twelve of the eighteen constituencies, to garner 7,890 out of 597,907 votes. Subsequently, with the voluntary dissolution of the USTT, the Communist-dominated trade union, Communist influence outside Tunis virtually disappeared. In the 1959 elections this party polled only 242 votes in Gafsa, after winning 903 votes in 1956. In Beja, another relative Communist "stronghold" in 1956 (1,877 votes out of 25,615), it did not contest the 1959 elections. But in the city of Tunis, the Communists steadily gained, from 1,487 votes in 1956, to 2,762 in the 1957 municipal elections, and 3,229 in 1959, though their percentage of the vote remained negligible. Independent lists were a significant factor only in the 1957 municipal elections, where they reflected local rather than national political differences.

Tunisian electoral returns are of interest mainly so far as they give an indication of mass political participation—or at least, more realistically, of the Neo-Destour's effectiveness in turning out the vote. This may in theory be measured by the proportion of registered voters who actually vote.[1] The results of the 1956 national election in terms of the 1959 and 1964 constituencies are given in table A-1.

[1] This is at best a rough approximation, because Tunisian electoral data are unreliable and inadequate. Often the results published by the newspapers after an election do not agree, and even those tabulated by the Ministry of the Interior contain careless errors. Whether the ballots are occasionally stuffed, as was alleged of the 1963 municipal elections in Tunis, is an unanswerable question. The data are inadequate because one cannot precisely infer from the fluctuating registration figures who is eligible to vote. Since 1957, women have been eligible, but registration is not automatic as it is for men. The rise in registration since 1956 is due in part to women, but in part also to an influx of new voters and also (as is apparent when one compares registration in the 1956 national elections with that of the 1956 by-elections, when women were still not eligible) to deficient voter registration in the 1956 election. One way of checking registration data might be to compare the number of registered voters in a given constituency with the population figures in the 1956 census. One could assume that half the population is of vot-

TABLE A-1

Voting Participation in National Elections

Constituency (governorate)	1956 elections			1959 elections			1964 elections		
	Registered voters	Voting	Per cent voting	Registered voters	Voting	Per cent voting	Registered voters	Voting	Per cent voting
Beja and Le Kef	99,774	89,754	90.0	144,494	136,694	95.0	172,945	166,776	96.5
Bizerte[a]	43,336	36,118	82.3	59,475	55,919	94.0	69,166	68,667	99.1
Cap Bon	47,235	43,090	91.3	84,427	77,946	92.3	93,236	92,256	99.0
Gabes	26,092	23,308	89.3	62,307	58,413	93.7	72,061	69,986	97.2
Gafsa	50,444	43,314	86.0	66,196	64,695	97.8	84,672	81,363	96.1
Kairouan	41,864	38,548	91.8	59,379	58,238	98.0	72,490	71,610	98.8
Kasserine	30,041	27,195	90.6	43,280	40,831	94.2	61,604	60,563	98.2
Mednine	62,403	37,735	60.4	67,207	65,607	97.7	70,516	68,467	97.2
Sfax	63,567	55,049	86.6	91,653	85,785	93.6	96,675	93,458	96.7
Souk el Arba	37,286	33,212	89.1	58,921	58,178	98.7	85,453	84,905	99.3
Sousse	92,925	79,181	85.3	133,944	118,740	85.0	148,778	146,590	98.3
Tunis	128,184	92,728	72.3	228,294	186,913	82.0	274,113	253,303	92.3
National totals	723,151	599,232	82.8	1,099,577	1,007,959	91.6	1,301,709	1,257,944[b]	96.8

[a] The 1956 national election figures for Bizerte are probably incorrect, although the ones given above are official. *Le Petit Matin* provided what appear to be more accurate statistics: 48,518 registered voters, 43,948 voting; these would bring the national average participation up to 83.4 per cent. On their face, the Gabes 1956 figures would seem low, but this may be explained by the existence in the area at that time of dissident Youssefist tribesmen.

[b] The official totals of 1,257,947 voting out of a registered population of 1,301,543 did not quite correspond to the sum of the official figures given by province in *L'Action,* November 9, 1964.

---

ing age and that this segment of the population is annually increasing by about 1 per cent. But one would also need to know either how many women were registered or whether all men of voting age were actually registered—data not available to the writer.

In tables A-1 and A-2, I have used the official returns of the Ministry of the Interior for the elections of 1956, 1959, and 1960, supplemented by the returns published in the daily press for other elections and for the breakdowns of the 1956 election into units that by addition could be compared with those of the 1956 returns. I wish to thank Susan Alliston Moore for her painstaking cross-checking of the variable newspaper reports.

Political participation steadily expanded. Registration, including women on a voluntary basis, increased by more than one-third in 1959, while actual voting increased by more than two-thirds. The increased participation in Mednine was especially striking because it included Djerba, a former Youssefist stronghold where only 28.7 per cent had voted in 1956. The city of Tunis, too, had been a weak spot for the Bourguibists in 1956, with an abstention rate of 41.3 per cent (the constituency of Tunis in Table A-1 includes the suburbs and outlying rural areas). Surprisingly, the provinces of greatest political sophistication and party strength, Tunis and Sousse, showed the highest abstention rates. Was this because some voters, living in the cities, were less amenable to party pressure, because they were politically disaffected, or because they were satisfied but saw no sense in voting for a preordained outcome?

For the mass of Tunisians, the absence of an opposition apparently had little negative impact upon voting behavior. Participation in the municipal elections of 1957, which were contested in sixteen of the 94 towns, was somewhat lower than in 1960 and 1963, when there was no opposition in any of the 116 towns concerned.

Table A-2 gives the returns in all three elections for the sixteen towns that experienced an opposition in 1957, along with those of other major modern cities and the totals in selected governorates and in the country as a whole. Of the sixteen towns in question, only four had lower participation in 1960; in others registration sometimes fell because women who had not voted (as in Djemmal[3]) were not inscribed on the rolls in 1960. Political competition evidently did not stimulate political participation as much as other factors—notably Neo-Destour activity at the local level. Party activity undoubtedly varied according to local leadership ability and the amount of pressure these leaders were willing to exert upon the electorate. In 24 of the 94 towns holding elections in both 1957 and 1960, the absolute number of voters was smaller in 1960; they were disproportionately located in the three southern governorates (Sfax, Mednine, Gabes) which had especially weak branches and/or party commissioners in 1960. In 1963 participation declined in Beja and the Sahel, while increases in parts of the South reflected party efforts in this area. Significantly, Tunisia's three largest and most modern cities of Tunisia, Sfax, and Sousse remained well below the national average.

Thus Tunisian elections reflect an extraordinarily high and generally increasing rate of political participation under the supervision of the ruling party. Before 1964, participation in politically advanced areas tended to remain significantly below the national norm, thereby suggesting that overall participation might decline as the masses became politically more mature. But the landslide of November 8, 1964, when the percentage of voters exceeded 91% even in the city of Tunis, suggested an opposite conclusion. Whatever their meaning to the people, elections in Tunisia had become a national ritual under the monolithic control of a party that would not permit participation to decline.

[3] See note 31 to Chap. V.

TABLE A-2

Voting Participation in Municipal Elections

Township	1957 elections			1960 elections			1963 elections		
	Registered voters	*Voting*	*Per cent voting*	*Registered voters*	*Voting*	*Per cent voting*	*Registered voters*	*Voting*	*Per cent voting*
Beja	6,857	5,698	83.2	8,464	7,630	91.8	8,980	7,002	77.8
Bou Arada[a] ..	496	412	83.1	613	521	84.9	721	701	97.3
Djemmal[a]	4,654	2,600	56.0	3,659	3,101	84.8	3,911	3,119	79.8
Feriana	1,915	1,245	65.2	1,272	1,160	91.4	1,306	1,210	92.7
Gafour	731	626	85.7	1,130	1,106	97.8	1,241	859	69.2
Ghardimaou	509	428	84.2	585	587	100.3	1,562	1,528	98.0
Hammam-Lif	4,782	3,861	80.8	7,602	6,662	87.7	8,723	6,179	70.9
Hammam-Sousse[a]	5,783	3,309	57.2	3,343	2,362	70.7	3,592	2,346	65.2
Monastir[a]	3,428	3,351	97.8	6,203	6,165	99.4	5,429	4,983	92.0
Nabeul[a]	6.135	4,449	72.7	5,404	4,786	88.7	8,642	6,823	79.0
Souk el Arba[a]	2,257	1,636	72.6	4,039	3,938	97.5	5,150	5,096	99.0
Souk el Khemis	1,059	922	86.9	903	864	95.7	997	977	98.1
Teboursouk ..	1,846	1,435	77.7	1,725	1,279	73.7	1,517	1,226	81.0
Thala	1,074	850	79.4	1,604	1,450	90.5	1,847	1,697	91.9
Tunis	86,378	72,563	83.2	112,898	85,307	75.5	146,794	120,977	82.3
Zeramdine	2,513	1,178	47.0	1,943	1,502	77.3	2,510	2,415	96.3
Sfax	14,254	10,480	73.7	16,553	10,900	66.1	16,139	12,445	77.1
Sousse	11,036	7,168	65.1	12,235	9,764	79.9	13,205	9,868	74.7
Selected governorates:									
Beja	10,873	9,080	83.2	14,872	13,191	88.6	15,911	12,390	78.0
Gabes	19,483	16,606	85.2	19,114	16,732	87.4	19,594	16,948	86.4
Mednine	12,397	10,094	81.4	11,932	10,552	89.0	13,000	10,655	81.5
Sfax	20,029	14,029	70.1	21,310	14,366	67.7	21,920	17,110	77.2
Sousse	74,461	48,088	64.6	73,566	64,305	87.3	79,727	66,584	83.6
National totals	358,253	278,078	77.6	433,484	364,701	84.3	514,203	436,102	84.8

[a] Towns where the opposition captured municipal council seats in 1957.

BIBLIOGRAPHICAL ESSAY

EVEN THE study of mass political parties in Africa is a relatively recent enterprise. The pioneering works are those of David E. Apter, *Ghana in Transition* (rev. ed., 1963), James S. Coleman, *Nigeria: Background to Nationalism* (1958), Thomas Hodgkin, *Nationalism in Colonial Africa* (1956) and *African Political Parties* (1961), and Robert Rézette, *Les Partis Politiques Marocains* (1955). The latter two writers have been strongly influenced by the concepts of Maurice Duverger, *Political Parties* (English ed., 1954), although in this connection the concluding essay of Sigmund Neumann in *Modern Political Parties* (1956) ought also to be mentioned.

Inevitably, the literature on a regime based upon the mass party is sparse. Rupert Emerson, in *Political Modernization: The Single-Party System* (1964), has concisely summarized the arguments of the defenders and prosecutors of these regimes. Apart from Apter's concluding chapter in the above-cited work, the only directly relevant published monograph is that of Aristide R. Zolberg, *One-Party Government in the Ivory Coast* (1964), which covers very little of the post-independence period. The excellent study by Richard Skhlar, *Nigerian Political Parties* (1963), has some relevance, so far as Nigeria's regions may be considered autonomous units. A useful compendium of information is provided in Gwendolyn Carter, ed., *African One-Party States* (1962), despite this work's disappointing lack of generalization. More theoretically oriented is Immanuel Wallerstein's *Africa: The Politics of Independence* (1961), which, along with his article on African parties to appear in Joseph LaPalombara and Myron Weiner, eds., *Political Parties and Political Development,* places him in the forefront of theorists of the African mass party regime, along with Ruth Schachter (Morgenthau), whose doctoral dissertation is summarized in "Single-Party Systems in West Africa," *American Political Science Review,* June, 1961, pp. 294-307. In the same issue should be noted Robert C. Tucker's controversial analysis of single-party regimes, "Toward a Comparative Politics of Movement-Regimes," pp. 281-293. As an antidote to misleading comparisons between mass party and totalitarian regimes, the work by Carl J. Friedrich and Zbigniew K. Brzezinski, *Totalitarian Dictatorship and Autocracy* (1956), remains useful despite the changing face of some hitherto totalitarian countries. One ought also to listen carefully to the African leaders' own analyses of their single-party regimes, in the extremely useful compilation of Paul E. Sigmund, Jr., *The Ideologies of the Developing Nations* (1963), pp. 136-250. In light of the widespread importance of personal leadership, W. G. Runciman's excellent article, "Charismatic Legitimacy and One-Party Rule in Ghana," *Archives Européennes de Sociologie,* IV (1963), 148-165, should be mentioned, as should Martin Kilson's "Authoritarianism and Single-Party Tendencies in Africa," *World Politics*, January, 1963, pp. 262-294.

The best introduction to North Africa in any language is by Charles F. Gallagher, *The United States and North Africa* (1964), a brilliant and sensitive survey of an area he knows well. His reports since 1957 for the American University Field Service are also first-rate, as is his contribution on Tunisia to the above-cited Gwendolyn Carter volume. Though already out of date, the Royal Institute of International Affairs volume edited by Nevill Barbour, *A Survey of North West Africa* (1959), remains a useful reference. More specifically focused upon Tunisia, *Tunisia: The Politics of Modernization* (1964), by Charles A. Micaud, Leon Carl Brown, and the present writer, provides a general analysis of the Tunisian path of development.

André Raymond, *La Tunisie* (1961), offers a concise survey of Tunisia that may be supplemented by A. Basset, L. Berger, R. Brunschvig *et al.*, *Initiation à la Tunisie* (1950). Jean Despois, *La Tunisie: Ses Régions* (1961), is a short but excellent geographical survey that complements his longer, classic work on the Sahel, *La Tunisie Orientale: Sahel et Basse Steppe* (rev. ed., 1955). For the history of the area until 1830, the best work is by Charles-André Julien, *Histoire de l'Afrique du Nord*, 2 vols. (1951); his *L'Afrique du Nord en Marche* (1952), unfortunately out of print, is the *sine qua non* for all North African political studies. Although (justifiably, in this writer's view) polemical in places, it provides the most reliable account of the rise of nationalism and French responses, until 1952. The more scholarly work by Jean Ganiage, *Les Origines du Protectorat Francais en Tunisie, 1861-1881* (1959), is also very useful, giving insight into Tunisia's traditional society, as is Arthur Girault, *Principes de Colonisation et de Législation Coloniale* V (1928), for its description of the legal framework of French rule. Despite its Marxist slant and blatant exaggeration of the role of the Tunisian Communist Party in the nationalist movement, Paul Sebag, *La Tunisie* (1951), offers many reliable items of information about the colonial period. But the most brilliant interpretation of the contradictions upon which the colonial regimes of North Africa rested is to be found in Jacques Berque, *Le Maghreb entre Deux Guerres* (1962), a work which transcends political polemics to arrive at insights combining sociological research and artistic vision. This book is not easy reading, even for a Frenchman, because Berque is attempting to objectify his own concrete categories of experience; but it is well worth the effort to the reader who is already familiar with North Africa. With a great deal of common sense, Leon Carl Brown, "Tunisia under the French Protectorate: A Study of Ideological Change" (unpublished doctoral dissertation, Harvard, 1962), grasps the essence of those historical developments that helped to make Tunisia uniquely modern among its neighbors. Nicola A. Ziadeh, *Origins of Nationalism in Tunisia* (1962), covers some of the same ground.

The indispensable work of analyzing Tunisia's political evolution over the past four decades is Roger Le Tourneau's *Evolution Politique de l'Afrique du Nord Musulmane 1920-1961* (1962), a study, admirable for its careful precision and objectivity, which brings Julien's work up to date. Though Le Tourneau had access to confidential French sources, Moncef Dellagi, a Tunisian writing a doctoral dissertation that is primarily a history of the Neo-Destour, should be able to add useful information on the Tunisian side.

In English, Benjamin Rivlin, "The Tunisian Nationalist Movement: Four Decades of Evolution," *Middle East Journal*, Spring, 1952, pp. 167-193, provides a useful summary; for more details, the *Survey of International Affairs*, published since 1937 by the Royal Institute for International Affairs, originally under Arnold Toynbee, is a good source.

For the decade following the First World War, one should consult Rodd Balek (Charles Monchicourt), *La Tunisie après la Guerre 1919-1921* (1922), and Cavé, *Sur les Traces de Rodd Balek: Les Problèmes Tunisiens après 1921* (1929). Charles Monchicourt, *La Région du Haut Tell en Tunisie* (1913), provides insights into tribal politics.

On the Tunisian side, Chadly Khairallah, *Le Mouvement Jeune-Tunisien* (Tunis, 1957), offers an interesting collection of documents concerning the generation of nationalists before World War I. Abdelaziz Taalbi's *La Tunisie Martyre* (1920) is, of course, the prime document of the subsequent generation. The account of Tunisian politics by Allal El Fassi, *The Independence Movements in Arab North Africa* (1954), is worth consulting.

William S. Lee, "The Transfer of Power in Tunisia 1950-1956" (unpublished doctoral dissertation, Oxford, 1963), provides the most careful account of political forces in Tunisia just prior to independence. For this period Jean Rous, *Tunisie . . . Attention!* (1952), and Pierre Boyer de Latour, *Verités sur l'Afrique du Nord* (1956), provide useful documentation, as do the many articles on legal matters by Victor Silvera, who has continued since independence to publish numerous articles, especially in the *Revue Juridique et Politique d'Outre-Mer*.

Supplementing legal with political analysis, Charles Debbasch, *La République Tunisienne* (1962), offers the best general, if superficial, introduction to contemporary Tunisian politics. His articles in the above-cited *Revue*, 1959, pp. 32-54, 415-431, are an astute contribution to an understanding of parliamentary politics under the Neo-Destour. Abdallah's article, "Le Neo-Destour depuis l'Indépendance," *op. cit.*, 1963, pp. 573-657, deserves mention. In the same vein, Keith Callard, "The Republic of Bourguiba," *International Journal*, 1961, pp. 17-36, captures the drift of Tunisian politics in the late 'fifties. Marc Heurgon, "Tunisie, un an d'indépendance," *Esprit*, June, 1957, pp. 953-968, ought also to be cited, along with the chapter on Tunisia in I. William Zartman, *Government and Politics in Northern Africa* (1963), pp. 66-84. For close-up personal glimpses of Bourguiba, Jean Lacourture, *Cinq Hommes et la France* (1961), pp. 109-180, is excellent journalism: the interviews recorded by Roger Stéphane, *La Tunisie de Bourguiba* (1958), shed further light on the man. Félix Garas, *Bourguiba et la Naissance d'une Nation* (1956), views him through rosier though less accurate lenses.

For understanding the over-all process of modernization that is transforming Tunisian society, Henri de Montety offers, along with Berque and Gallagher, the most reasoned and sympathetic observations—for which, having been a French civil servant in Tunisia for many years, he is eminently qualified. His article, "Vieilles familles et nouvelle elite en Tunisie," written in 1940 for a confidential publication, is the essential source for understanding changing patterns of social stratification in Tunisia. His other more recent publications include *Femmes de Tunisie* (1958), a somewhat optimistic account of female emancipation; "Révolution moderniste à l'Universite Ez-Zitouna," *L'Afrique et l'Asie*, 1951, pp. 24-35; "Lé Developpement des classes moyennes en Tunisie," in *Développement d'une Classe Moyenne dans les Pays Tropicaux et Sub-Tropicaux* (Brussels: INCIDI, 1956); and a contribution to the generally useful issue, *Visages de la Tunisie, 1960, Cahiers Nord-Africains*, No. 77 (Paris: Etudes Sociales Nord-Africaines, 1960).

The best introduction to the Tunisian economy is by René Gallissot, *L'Economie de l'Afrique du Nord* (1961). A more detailed monograph is by Moncef Guen, *La Tunisie Indépendante face à son économie* (Tunis, 1961), which may be supplemented by the more general survey by Salah-Eddine Tlatli, *Tunisie Nouvelle: Problèmes et Perspectives* (1957). The Tunisian Government's *Perspectives Décennales de Développement, 1962-71* (Secrétariat d'Etat au Plan et aux Finances), or Ten-Year Perspectives, provides a detailed picture of the Tunisian economy. Gabriel Ardant, in *La Tunisie d'Aujourd'hui et de Demain* (1961), gives a more digestible analysis of Tunisian economic development which also reflected official Tunisian thinking.

The most colorful as well as useful primary sources on Tunisian politics are Bourguiba's speeches, published since June 16, 1956, by the Tunisian Information Department. Many of Bourguiba's statements and writings before independence were collected in his *La Tunisie et la France* (1954) and *Le Destour et la France* (1937). Of greater philosophic import is the posthumously published diary of one of Bourguiba's early colleagues, Tahar Sfar, *Journal d'un Exilé* (1960), which helps to make Bourguiba's militantly modernizing tone comprehensible. Another of Bourguiba's colleagues, Hedi Nouira, wrote an exceedingly useful article about the party, "Le Néo-Destour," in *Politique Etrangère*, June-July, 1954, pp. 317-334. The best subsequent sources are published party documents, *National Congress of Sfax* (1956; available only in Arabic), *The Covenant of the Neo-Destour Party and the Internal Statutes* (1959, available only in Arabic), and *Les Congrès du Néo-Destour* (Tunisian Secretariat of State for Information, 1959, published in a French and in a slightly more detailed Arabic version). For the Neo-Destour Youth and other youth groups, see *Youth Movements in Tunisia* (Tunisian Secretariat of State for Information, 1960, available only in Arabic). The other national organizations, especially the UGTT, have published a number of official congress reports and brochures that unfortunately are not always easy to obtain.

The Tunisian press is a prime source of information, although a tacit self-censorship makes it less of a gold mine than, say, the virulently partisan Moroccan press. The most useful daily papers are the two official party organs, *L'Action* and *El 'Amal*. The former, which was launched in late 1962, should not be confused with another far more daring independent newspaper, the weekly *L'Action*, which had the quasi-official support of the party from its founding in April, 1955, until September, 1958, when it ceased publication, only to be resuscitated in October, 1960, under a new name, *Afrique-Action*, which was changed in November, 1961, to its present name of *Jeune-Afrique*. It is the best and most experienced Tunisian newspaper. Other organs associated with Bourguiba in the past include *La Voix du Tunisien* (1930-1932), *L'Action Tunisienne* (1932-1938), and *Mission* (1948-1952). The UGTT has its own paper, *Ech-Chaab*, which appears irregularly; UGET's monthly, *L'Etudiant Tunisien*, has occasionally criticized the regime, though not as sharply as *Tribune du Progrès*, a Communist-inspired monthly (1960-1962). The Neo-Destour publishes a monthly youth magazine, *Esh-Shebab*, as well as publications directed at students and at the cadres of particular regions.

Slightly outside the official family of newspapers, the Arabic daily *Es-Sabah*, which used to be Youssefist, sometimes publishes Neo-Destour activities in greater detail than *El 'Amal*. The French daily, *Le Petit Matin*, used to be an invaluable source of information to the non-Arabic reader, but today *L'Action* has greater resources. *Le Monde*, of course, provides the best coverage of any foreign newspaper.

To judge from the first volume, covering 1962, the *Annuaire de l'Afrique du Nord* (Paris: Centre National de la Recherche Scientifique, 1964) promises to be an indispensable reference work for all future research in North Africa. Assembled by the new Centre d'Etudes Nord-Africains in Aix-en-Provence, it brings together important documents, scholarly articles, a detailed chronology of political, diplomatic, economic, social, and cultural events in the three countries, and an exhaustive annual bibliography of articles and books on North Africa. The new series *Maghreb* (no. 1; January-February 1964), published six times a year by La *Documentation Francaise*, promises to be a useful chronological summary of political and economic happenings.

The quarterly *IBLA*, published in Tunis by the White Fathers' Institut de Belles Lettres Arabes, often carries useful articles and commentaries about contemporary Tunisian social and economic problems. The *Cahiers de Tunisie*, published by the University of Tunis, is also an important source of scholarly articles. *Aspects et Perspectives de l'Economie Tunisienne* sometimes provides revealing articles about administrative as well as economic problems, because some of Tunisia's top young civil servants write for it. In France the *Revue Juridique et Politique d'Outre-Mer*, *L'Afrique et l'Asie*, *Revue de Défense Nationale*, and *Orient* are especially useful to the student of Tunisian affairs. In America the *Middle East Journal* provides some coverage.

For further bibliographical information, the best source is Maurice Flory, Roger Le Tourneau, Jean-Paul Trystram, "L'Afrique du Nord: Etat des travaux," *Revue Française de Science Politique,* June, 1959, pp. 411-453. The English reader may wish to consult Benjamin Rivlin, "A Selective Survey of the Literature in the Social Sciences and Related Fields on Modern North Africa," *American Political Science Review,* September, 1954, pp. 826-848, and Paul E. A. Romeril, "Tunisian Nationalism—A Bibliographical Outline," *Middle East Journal,* 1960, pp. 206-215. For complete coverage of all work, including important newspaper articles, published since 1961, one should, of course, consult the appropriate volume of the above-cited *Annuaire de l'Afrique du Nord.*

INDEX

Abassi, Azzedine, 83n., 185n., 186n.
'Abduh, Mohammed, 26, 49
Achour, Abdesselam, 186n.
Achour, Habib, 86, 86n., 160, 169, 185n.; and coöperatives, 173; deputy, 186n., 187n.; for apolitical trade union, 87, 162; heads UGTT, 169, 174, 174n., 185n.; in prison, 85-86n.; on Political Bureau, 88, 94n., 118, 124, 168
L'Action, 72, 73, 76, 78, 79, 85n., 86; suppressed, 90-92
L'Action Tunisienne, 30, 32, 42
AEMNA (Association des Etudiants Musulmanes d'Afrique du Nord), 179-180n.
Afrique-Action, 78-79; becomes *Jeune Afrique*, 79n.; criticizes Bourguiba, 99-100, 121; on National Assembly, 185; on UGET, 178-179, 180-181
Agriculture: chamber of, 24; effects of colonization, 19-20, 21-22. *See also* UGAT; UNAT
Akouda (pop., 7,635), 145-146n.
Algeria, 3n., 10, 11, 16, 22, 26, 47, 57, 183, 195, 206
Algerian war, 48, 70, 195
Ali, Mohammed, 37, 159, 164; founds CGTT, 29
Almohads, 10
Amira, Tahar, 64-65n., 65; heads steel company, 97
Ammar, Ferdjani Bel Hadj: deputy, 186n., 191n.; on Political Bureau, 94n., 118, 124; UTAC leader, 94n., 124, 159, 163n., 186n.
Apter, David E., 71n.
Arabic, penetration of, 10
Arab League, 39
Arab Maghreb Liberation Committee, 61
arch (collective tribal lands), 20, 21
Ashford, Douglas E., 3n., 156n., 179-180n.
Assembly. *See* Constituent Assembly; National Assembly
Attia, Mohammed, 90n.
Ayache, Salah, 186n.

Azaiz, Tahar, 186n.

Baccouche, Hedi, 147-148, 200n.
Baccouche, Salah-Eddine, 88n., 89n.
Badra, Mohammed, 185n.
Bahri, Sheikh, 147-148
Baldi (urban mechant class), 13 and n., 15, 24, 27 and n., 73, 73n., 111n. *See also* Elite, traditional
Balek, Rodd. *See* Monchicourt, Charles
Balma, 191n.
Basset, A., 16n.
Beer, Samuel, 71n.
Beja (province; city pop., 22,668), 19; elections in, 74, 187 and n., 213, 214, 216; trade unions in, 85n., 86, 187n.
Bel Cadhi, Mohammed el-Hedi, 52n.
Belhaouane, Ali, 90n.; depreciates West, 39n.; on Political Bureau, 62n., 66n., 94n., 115n.; replaced, 94n., 118, 119
Bell, Cora, 111n.
Bellalouna, Ahmed, 74n.
Ben Abdelaziz, Hassen, 111n., 138n., 142n.
Ben Abdelkader, Hadj Mohammed, 186n.
Ben Abdelkrim, Ahmed, 186n.
Ben Achour, Fadhl, 52n.
Ben Achour, Tahar, 51, 52n., 57
Ben Ali, Mahjoub, 111n.
Ben Amar, Mohammed, 125n., 157
Ben Ammar, Monthar, 95, 186n.
Ben Ammar, Tahar: loses nomination, 185n.; on trial, 90-91; prime minister, 63n., 72, 93n.; resigns, 75
Ben Attiya, Moktar, 67n.
Ben Azzedine, Mohammed, 162, 174n., 185n.
Ben Bella, Ahmed, 63
Ben Brahim, Tawfiq, 92n.
Ben Dhiaf, 22n.
Ben Djaffar, 64-65n.
Ben Hamida, Achmed, 186n.
Ben Mahmoud, Mohammed al-Moktar, 52n.
Ben Salah, Ahmed, 71-72n., 75, 93, 95, 102, 118, 122, 124, 131n., 141, 185n.,

226 INDEX

Friedrich, Carl J., 46n., 208n.

Gabes (province; city pop., 24,420), 9, 29, 65, 111n., 120, 127n., 129, 134, 135, 157, 165; elections in, 214, 215, 216
Gafour, 216
Gafsa (province; city pop., 24,345), 135, 138-139, 168, 170, 189; elections in, 214; fellagha, 62n., 68, 83n., 111n.; phosphate mines, 29, 168
Galaoui, Salah, 162, 174n., 185n.
Ganiage, Jean, 9 n., 14n.
Ganouni, Mohammed, 186n.
Garas, Felix, 9n., 32n.
German occupation, 38
Ghana, 106n.
Ghardimaou (pop., 2,710), 216
Ghoul, Mohammed El, 85n.
Golvin, L., 13n.
Grand Council, 24
Guen, Moncef, 195n.
Guermazi, Sadok, 186n.
Guiga, Bahri, 30, 33, 94n., 96, 187
Guinea, 4, 125

Habous (religious and welfare foundations), 20, 21, 27, 38, 67n.; reformed, 50, 53. *See also* State Domains Office
Hac, Abdel, 32, 32n.
Hached, Farhat, 52n., 63, 85n.-86n., 160, 164, 171, 174, 187n.; founds UGTT, 36; assassinated, 37 and n.
Haddad, Radhia, 186n.
Haddad, Tahar, 31n.
Hafaiedh, Ali, 174n., 185n.
Hafsids, 10, 11
Hamida, Sadok, 138n.
Hammam-Lif (pop., 22,060), 216
Hammam-Sousse (pop., 9,419), 133n., 141n., 154; elections, 144-146, 145-146n., 147, 151-152, 216
Handicrafts, undermined by imports, 22
Hero-leader. *See* Leader-hero
Hodgkin, Thomas, 1n.
Hugo, Victor, 42
Husainids, 10, 11; bey under, 11-12. *See also* Bey

Ibn Khaldun, 10
ICFTU (International Confederation of Free Trade Unions), 36, 85-86n., 173
Ideology: Destour, 30-31; in mass-party regime, 1, 4; Neo-Destour, 106-107,

157, 196-197, 197n., 204; of Ben Salah, 83-84. *See also* Bourguibism; Socialism
India, 2
Institut d'Hautes Etudes (Tunis), 24, 176n.
Institute of Applied Social Science (Tunis), 3n.
Integration, function (task) of, 3, 4, 5, 6, 134. *See also* Consensus
Interest articulation, 159, 202-204. *See also* Representation
International Confederation of Free Trade Unions. *See* ICFTU
International Student Conference, 179
International Union of Students, 179
Islam: and socialism, 196-197; Hanafi rite, 52n.; Maliki rite, 10, 52n.; observance, 46-47; Rahmaniya order, 133; reform, 31, 48-52; Salafiyyah movement, 27; *shari'a law*, 11; state religion, 50; *sufi* orders, 12. *See also* Habous; Ulama; Zawiya
Istiqlal party (Morocco), 62n.
Italians in Tunisia, 11n., 16, 206n.
Ivory Coast, 4

Jeune Afrique, 79n., 158n. *See also* Afrique-Action
Jews: population, 10, 10n.; on Consultative Conference, 18n.
Julien, Charles-Andre, 8-9n., 12n.

Kairouan, (province; city pop., 33,968), 55, 60n., 67n., 129, 137, 137n., 139, 161, 187n., 214; resistance to Ramadan policy, 59-60, 60n., 152, 205
Kalaa Kebira (pop., 16,700), 145-146n.
Kalaa Sghira (pop., 7,872), 145-146n.
Kallady, Chadly, 80-81
Kasserine (province; city pop., 2,705), 187, 187n., 214
Kebili, 73n.
Keita, Modibo, 208
Kemal Attaturk, 39
Khabthani, Mustapha, 186n.
Khairallah, Chadly, 42
Khaireddine, Prime Minister, 23, 26
Khalfallah, Sadok, 186n.
Khefacha, Hedi, 95
Khiari, Mahmoud: communications minister, 83n., 95-96n., 171; on UGTT, 95-96n., 162, 168n., 185n.
Khroumir tribe, 11, 194
Klibi, Chadly, 95, 96, 186
Knani, Abdesselam, 186n.

DATE DUE

GAYLORD			PRINTED IN U.S.A.